MILLER'S

classic
motorcycles

Created and designed by
Miller's Publications
The Cellars, High Street
Tenterden, Kent TN30 6BN
Telephone: 01580 766411
Fax: 01580 766100

General Editor: Mick Walker
Production Co-ordinator: Philip Hannath
Editorial Co-ordinator: Deborah Wanstall
Editorial Assistants: Joanna Hill, Maureen Horner
Designer: Kari Reeves
Advertisement Designer: Simon Cook
Jacket Design: Victoria Bevan
Advertising Executive: Jill Jackson
Advertising Administrator & Co-ordinator: Melinda Williams
Advertising Assistant: Elizabeth Ellender
Production Assistants: Caroline Bugeja, Gillian Charles, Ethne Tragett
Additional Photography: Robin Saker, Mick Walker
US Advertising Representative: Katharine Buckley,
Buckley Pell Associates, 34 East 64th Street, New York, NY 10021
Tel: 212 223 4996 Fax: 212 223 4997 E-mail: buckley@moveworld.com

First published in Great Britain in 2002
by Miller's, a division of Mitchell Beazley,
imprints of Octopus Publishing Group Ltd,
2–4 Heron Quays, London E14 4JP

© 2002 Octopus Publishing Group Ltd

A CIP catalogue record for this book is
available from the British Library

ISBN 1 84000 632 3

Illustrations and film output by CK Litho, Whitstable, Kent
Printed and bound by Toppan Printing Co (HK) Ltd, China

Front cover illustration:

1965 Harley-Davidson Electra Glide
£8,000–10,000 / $11,500–14,500 ⊞ **MW**

classic motorcycles

GENERAL EDITOR
Mick Walker

FOREWORD
Tommy Robb

Contents

Acknowledgments

The publishers would like to acknowledge the great assistance given by our consultants:

Malcolm Barber — Bonhams, Montpelier Street, Knightsbridge, London SW7 1HH Tel: 0207 393 3900

Rob Carrick — 5 Tinkers Lane, Wimbotsham, King's Lynn, Norfolk PE34 3QE Tel: 01366 388801

James Knight — Bonhams, Montpelier Street, Knightsbridge, London SW7 1HH Tel: 0207 393 3900

Michael Jackson — Cheffins, 49/53 Regent Street, Cambridge CB2 1AF Tel: 01264 810875

Brian Verrall — Caffyns Row, High Street, Handcross, Nr Haywards Heath, West Sussex RH17 6BJ Tel: 01444 400678

Rick Walker — R&M Walker, 45 Caves Close, Terrington St Clement, King's Lynn, Norfolk Tel: 01553 829141

We would like to extend our thanks to all auction houses, their press offices, and dealers who have assisted us in the production of this book, along with the organisers and press offices of the following events:

The International Classic Motor Cycle Show

Louis Vuitton Classic

Foreword

For anyone who enjoys keeping good wines it is always nice to savour the moment when one of the precious bottles is taken out of the wine rack, in order to be savoured and enjoyed.

The same principle applies to a good book and I can honestly say that for the motorcycle enthusiast it would be difficult to avoid having this particular motorcycling reference book in your collection. For this reason I am honoured to have been asked to write the foreword for such a prestigious hardback publication as *Miller's Classic Motorcycles Price Guide 2003/4*.

I suppose the fact that I have been around motorcycles and motorcycle racing since the age of two, when my parents used to pack me into their sidecar outfit along with the picnic hamper and set off for a day at a motorcycle race meeting, is the reason that I am still involved today (sixty-six years later).

Little did I realize when I obtained my first bike, a 197cc James, at the age of fifteen in 1951, that the sport of competitive motorcycling would play such a large and important part in my life. From such humble beginnings I managed to participate in grass tracks, trials, moto cross and sand racing, achieving championship status in most of these events, but my innermost craving was always, to be a road racer.

I managed to persuade my loving parents, that at the age of twenty, this was the direction I wanted to take; they were sceptical, as they probably didn't want to see their only child maimed or injured. Eventually they agreed and from then on luck, determination and ability played a big part in a successful career, that was highlighted when I became a member of the all-conquering 'Works Honda' team in 1962–63 and '64. Although I managed to finish in the first six of the World Championship in four solo classes 50, 125, 250, and 350 for Honda in the same year (a virtually impossible feat in today's GP scene), I can honestly say that my second place in the 350cc class, on the Honda Four ahead of my good friend and probably the world's greatest ever rider, Mike Hailwood on his MV, gave me the greatest satisfaction in a long career that spanned over twenty years, before retiring in 1973, just after winning my first TT race on a Yamaha.

I was also honoured that a number of major factories entrusted me with their expensive 'works' bikes, for apart from the great Honda team I was given the honour of riding for Yamaha, MZ, Bultaco and Bridgestone.

As someone who, fifty years after his first competitive event, still gets a thrill out of riding a racing machine at speed in today's parades, does I suppose, qualify me as a classic racer to write this introduction for a superb classic book, which is a true dictionary for the motorcycle fan.

I hope that you, the reader, get as much enjoyment as I do, by using this excellent publication for research and information during those moments when your memory starts to play tricks on you.

There is one thing of which I am sure, and that is that as you look at some of the photographs and prices of the various machines you used to own many years ago, you will think, as I do, 'I knew that I should have held on to that bike'.

Tommy Robb

How to use this book

I t is our aim to make this Guide easy to use. Motorcycle marques are listed alphabetically and then chronologically. Dirt Bikes, Military Bikes, Mopeds, Police Bikes, Racing Bikes, Scooters, Sidecars and Specials are located after the marques, towards the end of the book. In the Memorabilia section objects are grouped by type. If you cannot find what you are looking for, please consult the index which starts on page 174.

Marque Introduction
provides an overview of the marque including factory changes and in some instances the history of a particular model. Introductions change from year to year and not every section will begin with an introduction.

Ariel (British 1902–70)

Ariel was one of the true pioneers of the British cycle and motorcycle industries. However, it could trace its origins as far back as 1847, when the name was used for a wheel, then later in 1871 for a penny-farthing cycle. It appeared on a variety of bicycles over the following quarter of a century, before the Ariel Cycle Company was incorporated during 1897. This company was owned by the Birmingham based Dunlop Rubber Company, and had come into being because of a rift between the tyre manufacturer

and other cycle companies, who objected to the Dunlop name adorning bicycles. One has to remember that in those days Dunlop had a virtual monopoly on the supply of tyres to the cycle trade.

Then, in 1895, another firm that made parts for the industry, Cycle Components, appointed Charles Sangster to their board. Later, his family played a major role in the development of the British motorcycle industry during the first half of the 20th Century.

1930 Ariel LF, 249cc overhead-valve twin-port single, 65 x 75mm bore and stroke.
£2,000–2,500 / $3,000–3,600 ⊞ BLM
For 1930, all three Ariel 250s (LB, LF and LG) shared the same 65 x 75 dimensions and 249cc capacity. The LB had a side-valve engine, while the others employed overhead-valve units. Both of the latter had twin-port leads; the LF was the de luxe model, and the LG the more sporting version, with additional tuning.

1932 Ariel LB32, 249cc side-valve single, 65 x 75mm bore and stroke, hand gear-change, full electric lighting kit.
£800–1,200 / $1,150–1,750 ⏶ Bon
During 1926, a range of nicely designed single-cylinder models was introduced by Ariel. Designed by Val Page and offered in both side-valve and overhead-valve guises, they provided the company with a sound model base during the financially difficult years of the early 1930s.

Caption
provides a brief description of the motorcycle or item, and could include comments on its history, mileage, any restoration work carried out and current condition.

BMW (German 1923–)

1951 BMW R67, 594cc overhead-valve flat-twin, 72 x 73mm bore and stroke, 26hp at 5,500rpm, 4-speed foot-change gearbox, unrestored.
£2,500–3,000 / $3,600–4,400 ⏶ TEN
A total of 1,470 R67s were built, all in 1951.

1975 BMW R90/6, 980cc overhead-valve flat-twin, Bing carburettors, 5-speed gearbox, single disc front brake, fork gaiters, rev-counter, 1 owner and fewer than 6,500 miles from new.
£3,000–3,750 / $4,400–5,400 ⊞ BLM

Price Guide
these are based on actual prices realised shown in £sterling and a US$ conversion. Remember that Miller's is a PRICE GUIDE not a PRICE LIST and prices are affected by many variables such as location, condition, desirability and so on. Don't forget that if you are selling it is quite likely you will be offered less than the price range. Price ranges for items sold at auction include the buyer's premium.

Miller's Motorcycle Milestones

BMW R90S 898cc (German 1973)
Price range: £2,500–3,500 / $3,600–5,000
The press called the R90S Germany's sexiest superbike, which was an apt description of what became probably BMW's best-loved street bike of the post-war era.
The R90S was launched in a blaze of publicity on 2 October, 1973, at the Paris salon. This setting was fortunate, as it was there, 50 years before, that BMW had presented its very first motorcycle, the Max Friz-designed R32.
Paris in 1973 also marked the arrival of the Stroke 6 range, of which the R90S was the glamour model; the machine that hurled BMW to the very top of the Superbike stakes.

The R90S employed an 898cc (90 x 70.6mm) version of the famous flat-twin engine and, as with all the Stroke 6 models, saw a switch from a four- to five-speed gearbox.
Compared to the standard R90, the 'S' variant put out an additional 7bhp (67bhp). Weighing 200kg (441lb) dry, the R90S could top 125mph.
But it was in its styling that the R90S really represented a major milestone in BMW's history, featuring as it did a dual racing-style seat, fairing cowl, twin hydraulically-operated front disc brakes and an exquisite airbrushed custom paint job in smoked silver-grey (later also in orange) for the bodywork, which meant that no two machines were ever absolutely identical.

Source Code
refers to the 'Key to Illustrations' on page 167 that lists the details of where the item was sourced. Advertisers are also indicated on this page.
The ⏶ icon indicates the item was sold at auction. The ⊞ icon indicates the item originated from a dealer or motorcycle club, see Directory of Motorcycle Clubs on page 172.

Bold Footnote
covers relevant additional information about a motorcycle's restoration and/or racing history, designer, riders and special events in which it may have participated.

Miller's Motorcycle Milestones
highlights important historic motorcycle events and the effect they have had on the motorcycle industry.

Brakes

The most important system of any motorcycle is not the "Go" department, as many young bloods think, but the Stopping department; in that it has the ability to retard the motion of your bike to enable you to safely negotiate any hazard which may lay ahead. This capability should be controllable in both normal and emergency conditions.

The above requirement was not always the case, for in the pioneering days these old bikes had very little in the way of brakes. A leather belt pulled into a large diameter pulley, or a rubber block pushed on to the tyre was enough to slow the Vintage machine. With the relaxed road conditions, low speeds and the lack of other vehicles, these methods were deemed to be sufficient. From the Vintage period, through to the Classic period, the internal expanding single leading shoe drum brake became the prime method of stopping even the largest and heaviest motorcycles, and as time progressed these brakes became bigger and stronger. The Vincent twin – billed as the worlds fastest production motorcycle – featured single leading shoe brakes, but in an effort to slow this 125 mph monster it was equipped with double drums on each wheel. Five-inch brake drums gave way to 7-inch and 8-inch drums in an effort to increase the braking forces, with the adoption of twin leading shoe operation on the super sports machines. On the racetrack even larger drums were often seen, with back-to-back brakes that used four leading shoes, each side.

Today it is a different story, with traffic congestion and loony myopic car drivers; an ability to stop (and stop quickly) is a must. To cope with today's traffic conditions the braking system of your classic motorcycle must be in first class order, and to ensure this brake maintenance must be both regular and meticulous.

As the rider, you will know when something is radically wrong with the braking system, but a gradual deterioration in the efficiency will usually go unnoticed, therefore a regular inspection of the brakes is necessary. With a drum brake the wheel should be removed and the brake plate taken out, to inspect the linings. When carrying out this operation, do not use an airline to blow out the brake dust. The linings should be free from oil or water contamination, and be at the very least 1.5 mm thick, the cam spindle must be free to rotate and be lubricated sparingly. Next check the drum to ensure that it is free from cracks and unscored. Cracked or oval drums can usually be felt through the operating lever during its application, kicking back regularly when used, or even locking the wheel when used extra hard. Replace the wheel and before connecting up the operating cable or rod, ensure that the brake wear indicator pointer is at the unworn end of its quadrant. Before tightening the axle nut, connect and apply the brake to check that the pointer remains within

the usable range. On older machines, without the wear indicator, ensure that the angle between the operating lever and the operating cable or rod, is 90 degrees or less, when the brake is applied. With the brake still applied, to centralise the plate within the drum, tighten up the axle nut

Levers, cables and rods should be checked, to ensure freedom of movement and absence of wear at the pivot points. The routing should be checked to ensure that all cables runs do not snag or chafe. Any cables that show signs of strands breaking should be changed. The final items to be checked are the locking devices, to ensure that these critical areas remain firmly fastened. This means that if a nut can be split pinned, it must be split pinned, and that if self-locking nuts are specified then they must be used.

As the use of drum brakes is not so wide spread on modern machinery, the choice of replacement brake shoes is not so varied. Some manufacturers make replacement shoes for modern bikes, but only in road or motocross grades, this being enough to service the needs of most riders. If the brake linings of a classic bike require replacement, then the traditional method of purchasing the linings, drilling them and riveting them to the shoes, can be used. This system was common fifty years ago, but often led to spongy brakes, due to the linings not being riveted hard enough onto the shoes. Today super efficient adhesives ensure that this problem is a thing of the past.

If linings need replacement then the services of a specialist supplier should be sought, with most marque specialists being able to supply replacement shoes off the shelf. If special or racing grade linings are required, again specialist firms can bond linings of 6 mm thickness on to the customers shoes, which are then machined down to the correct diameter. This machining process thus ensures 100% contact of the linings with the drum, and therefore minimal bedding in is required.

With the advent of the large multi cylinder super-bikes the use of disc brakes became the norm, and the faster these machines became the bigger the discs became. Original single discs and hydraulically operated single piston calipers were fitted, but now specifications include enormous double discs, and in some cases six-pot calipers.

Within the classic motorcycle scene we are not going to achieve the same braking efficiency standards as the modern super bikes, so do not take the braking system of your machine for granted. Inspect the brakes regularly, and do not take any short cuts, as one day you may require to use them in anger. On the road today good brakes are a must, they are your lifeline, so if you value your bike and your neck, then adopt a methodical approach to brake system servicing.

Rob Carrick

The Motorcycle Market

Following the adverse effects on the classic motorcycle market in 2001 with the crisis in the countryside caused by foot and mouth disease and then the tragic events of September 11th in the USA, the motorcycle market settled back to prior levels of action and stability during the latter part of 2001 and early 2002.

Palmer Snell held their 41st auction in October at the Bath and West Showground where highlights included a 1914 Rover 3½ hp for £4,400 ($6,400), a 1917 Sunbeam 3½ hp Touring model for £4,300 ($6,300), and a 1921 Royal Ruby for £2,900 ($4,200). In the west country Palmer Snell have consistently held regular sales in October and March and in 2002 their Spring sale saw a 1949 Vincent-HRD series C Rapide realise £9,000 ($13,000), and a 1956 Triumph Tiger 110 £3,000 ($4,400).

Cheffins, based in Cambridge, include motorcycles in their classic car auctions but never in any numbers, yet they achieved £7,875 ($11,400) for a 1966 Velocette Venom Thruxton. The same may be said for Lambert and Foster in Kent, who recently re-entered the early vehicle market, and included a 1914 Wall Autowheel under this heading.

H & H, based in Buxton, included motorcycles with cars in their spring sale and a 1923 Triumph SD 550cc combination sold for £4,300 ($6,300), and a 1913 Triumph 3½ hp Coventry and sidecar £9,137 ($13,200).

Although Sotheby's have ostensibly withdrawn from the car and motorcycle market (whilst maintaining an association with Poulain in France), they held their last prestige sale devoted entirely to motorcycles and associated literature and automobilia in the USA on September 15th. Notwithstanding the events of September 11th they achieved some phenomenal prices in this sale. Although mainly American machines were represented, some European marques were also included, such as a 1914 Sears Dreadnought 9 hp V twin which realised £87,500 ($126,750), followed by a 1915 Indian F Head V-twin at £18,400 ($26,625), and the Ducati 750SS which was placed 2nd at Imola in April 1972 which commanded a price of £83,600 ($121,250).

It has to be said that the European motorcycle auction market is dominated by Bonham's. Motorcycles were offered at Beaulieu in July last year, at the Beaulieu Autojumble in September, at the Classic & Motorcycle Mechanic's Show at Stafford in October (motorcycles and related material only), and at Harrogate in November.

At the Harrogate auction 31 motorcycles were sold, including a 1913 Henderson four cylinder machine which made £31,050 ($45,000), a 1926 Chater-Lea Brooklands racer £8,280 ($12,000), and a very early 1913 Scott open frame model which realised the same price.

Despite the sizes of the sales figures, and somewhat surprisingly, the major auction houses apart from Bonhams appear to eschew motorcycle sales generally, even if they do include the odd machine, and the only exception this time was Coy's who did an unusual collection of unrestored pre- and post-war British bikes found under the floorboards of a terraced house following their owner's decease.

With the foot and mouth crisis over, Bonhams was back at Stafford in the spring for the International Classic Motorcycle Show in association with Morton's Motorcycle Media. Sales at this auction totalled well over £600,000 ($870,000), with nearly 250 machines on offer. Two well known collections included in this auction, from the estates of the late Austin Munks and Anthony Blight, further increased the interest from home and overseas. The 1939 Brough-Superior SS100, estimated at £30,000–35,000 ($43,500–50,750) made £42,200 ($60,000) and a rare 1938 Velocette KTT Mk VII estimated at £6,500 ($9,500) sold at £19,550 ($28,350), while many other machines exceeded their top estimates by comfortable margins. Unlike other markets, the classic motorcycle market is primarily driven by enthusiasm and, quite clearly, the traumatic events of the past twelve months have done little to diminish this.

Admittedly, Americans were less prominent in the bidding following the 11th September, but Sotheby's Chicago event showed that while they may have been unwilling to travel to overseas events, they were still willing to spend large amounts at sales held on their home ground. By the time of the April 2002 Bonhams sale at Stafford, confidence in air travel had largely returned. As a result the International Classic Motorcycle Show was as international as ever, and at the auction foreign bidders made their presence known to the same extent as in previous years, prices remained stable but quality and rarity as usual commanded a premium.

Malcolm Barber

Aermacchi (Italian 1950–78)

Aeronautica Macchi (soon abbreviated to Aermacchi) was founded in 1912 to manufacture seaplanes, which accounts for the factory being sited on the shores of Lake Varese in Italy. The company became quite large during WWI and continued to concentrate on aircraft in the years that followed. During WWII, abandoning seaplanes, Aermacchi built fighters for use by the Italian Air Force.

After hostilities had ended, the company began producing a three-wheeled truck, which was quite unorthodox, but worked well and is still being made. Then, intent on gaining a stake in the anticipated motorcycle boom, Aermacchi hired Lino Tonti, who had been at Benelli and had worked on aircraft engines during the war. Tonti came up with an attractive, lightweight motorcycle. From the first 125cc, two-stroke, open-frame lightweight, the company went on to build a variety of record breaking motorcycles, employing the wind-tunnel and other resources of the factory's aircraft department. In 1960, the prototype 250cc Ala d'Oro made its first appearance,

in the German GP, ridden by Alberto Pagani. It made such a good showing against the cream of the GP racers that Aermacchi decided to build a small batch of similar machines for sale to private owners. The low initial cost, together with its ease of maintenance and ready availability of reasonably-priced spares, made it immediately popular as a privateer racer. It was no mean performer, particularly on short twisty circuits, where its light weight and good acceleration paid off. The international success of this model, plus the achievement of the scrambles version (Lanfranco Angelini was five times Italian champion on an Aermacchi), was probably the reason that Harley-Davidson embarked on a 50/50 commercial arrangement with the Varese factory in 1960. With the lightweight boom developing in the USA, America's largest manufacturer badly needed a good 250 that could be sold in sports, racing and motocross forms. The collaboration created some great small-capacity race bikes, the most famous being the Ala d'Oro series of 250cc GP bikes.

1952 Aermacchi 125U, 123cc horizontal 2-stroke single, 52 x 58mm bore and stroke, 5bhp at 4,500rpm, unit construction, 3-speed foot-change gearbox, 47mph top speed, unrestored.
£1,000–1,200 / $1,500–1,750 ⊞ NLM
Half motorcycle, half scooter, this was Aermacchi's first design, which was introduced in 1950. It was designed by Ing. Lino Tonti. Today, it is very rare.

1971 Aermacchi TV, 344cc overhead-valve horizontal single, twin-leading-shoe front brake, branched exhaust header, twin silencers, alloy rims, humped-back dualseat, clip-on handlebars, matching speedometer and rev-counter.
£2,200–2,800 / $3,200–4,000 ⊞ MW

▶ **1971 Aermacchi 350 Sprint,** 344cc overhead-valve horizontal single, 5-speed gearbox, kickstarter, 12 volt electrics, European model with open frame, branched exhaust, square-slide Dell'Orto carburettor, dualseat, matching speedometer and rev-counter.
£1,500–1,900 / $2,150–2,750 ⊞ MW

c1962 Aermacchi Ala Verde, overhead-valve horizontal single, wet-sump lubrication.
£2,250–2,750 / $3,300–4,000 ⋋ RM
The Ala Verde was the street version of the 250cc Ala d'Oro race bike.

1967 Aermacchi Ala Verde, 246cc overhead-valve horizontal single, alloy head, iron barrel.
£2,300–2,700 / $3,300–3,900 ⋋ RM
As with the racing Ala d'Oro model, the Ala Verde street bike gained a five-speed gearbox and engine improvements in later years.

AJS *(British 1909–66)*

1922 AJS 350, 349cc side-valve single, forward mounted magneto, hand-change gearbox, chain final drive, unrestored.
£3,000–3,500 / $4,400–5,000 ⊞ VER

Cross Reference
See Colour Review (page 50)

▶ **1926 AJS 350,** 349cc side-valve single, iron head and barrel, hand-change gearbox, chain final drive, drum brake, carrier.
£3,500–4,000 / $5,000–5,800 ⊞ VER

◀ **1926 AJS G4,** 349cc side-valve single.
£2,600–3,200 / $3,750–4,650 ✒ Bon
For 1926, there was little alteration to the specification of the Model G range, but on average the prices were reduced by 11 per cent. On the sporting front, AJS continued to do well, gaining a second in the TT Junior race and a lap record in the Senior. All of these factors contributed to a reasonably successful year. The G4 was the side-valve 350cc single-cylinder model of the range and was all-chain driven, having a kickstart gearbox with the hand-change mounted alongside the petrol tank.

▶ **1927 AJS 350,** 349cc single-cylinder engine, good condition.
£3,800–4,200 / $5,500–6,000 ⊞ PM

1927 AJS H6 Big Port, 349cc overhead-valve single.
£3,500–4,200 / $5,000–6,000 ✒ Bon
After victory in the 1920 Junior TT, AJS' new overhead-valve 350 racer scored a memorable double the following year, Tom Sheard winning the Junior race and Howard Davies the Senior – the first time such a feat had been achieved on a 350. The production version appeared in late 1922, delighting clubmen everywhere with its 'racer on the road' performance. Destined to achieve countless successes in the hands of privateers, the overhead-valve 350 AJS – latterly known as the Big Port – changed only in detail before being superseded by a much-revised M6 model for 1929.

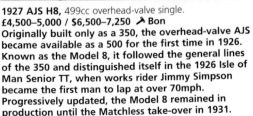

1927 AJS H8, 499cc overhead-valve single.
£4,500–5,000 / $6,500–7,250 ✒ Bon
Originally built only as a 350, the overhead-valve AJS became available as a 500 for the first time in 1926. Known as the Model 8, it followed the general lines of the 350 and distinguished itself in the 1926 Isle of Man Senior TT, when works rider Jimmy Simpson became the first man to lap at over 70mph. Progressively updated, the Model 8 remained in production until the Matchless take-over in 1931.

1936 AJS R10, 495cc overhead-camshaft single, 79 x 101mm bore and stroke, 4-speed gearbox, girder forks, rigid frame, extensively restored, road trim.
£5,000–7,000 / $7,250–10,250 ⊞ **RRN**

1955 AJS Model 18, 498cc overhead-valve single, 82.5 x 93mm bore and stroke, alloy head, iron barrel, 4-speed foot-change gearbox, full-width alloy brake hubs, swinging-arm rear suspension with 'jampot' shocks, AMC Teledraulic forks, all original tinware.
£1,750–2,250 / $2,500–3,300 ⊞ **BLM**

1956 AJS Model 18S, 498cc overhead-valve single, 26bhp at 5,500rpm, 4-speed gearbox, 87mph top speed, unrestored, original specification.
£1,500–1,800 / $2,200–2,600 ⊞ **PM**

1957 AJS Model 16MS, 349cc overhead-valve single, AMC gearbox, full-width alloy brake hubs, dualseat, good condition.
£2,250–2,400 / $3,300–3,500 ⊞ **BLM**
This was the first year of the coil-ignition model.

1957 AJS Model 18S, 498cc overhead-valve single, very original, good condition.
£1,900–2,150 / $2,750–3,000 ⊞ **BB**

Ambassador *(British 1947–65)*

Founded in 1947 by former racing car driver Kaye Don, Ambassador Motor Cycles was based in Ascot, Berkshire. One of the first prototypes built – prior to the opening of the Pontiac Works – had a 494cc, side-valve, vertical-twin JAP engine with coil ignition. Although of rather dated appearance, with girder forks and a substantial rigid frame, it was an attractive machine. In contrast, the first production model built in 1947 employed a Villiers 197cc 5E single-cylinder, two-stroke power unit. By 1949, the 5E engine had been replaced by a 6E type, and the motorcycle was named the Popular. Other models, the Courier and Supreme, appeared, still using the venerable 6E unit.

By 1953, Ambassador had created something of a stir when it introduced a model with an electric starter; there was even a sidecar version of this machine. Later that year, the range experienced a change in engine type from the 6E to the 8E. Next came a model with the larger 224cc 1H engine and a four-speed gearbox.

For 1957, Ambassador announced its first twin, powered by a Villiers 2T unit. In February 1959, ex-Norton engineer Edgar Franks joined the Ascot company as design chief. One of his first moves was to create the Super S, its main claim to fame being an abundance of detachable tinware – no doubt influenced by the Ariel Leader and 'bathtub' Triumphs of the era.

In 1961, the Electra 75 was introduced, pre-dating the Norton 400cc Electra overhead-valve twin by a couple of years. In 1962, Kaye Don retired, and the old Ambassador works at Ascot was closed. Production rights and the brand name were taken over by DMW, and the jigs, tooling, spares and other material transferred to the DMW factory in Dudley; this was completed in February 1963. Production resumed in July 1963, but with the DMW M-type square-tube frame. Production continued until autumn 1965, when the Ambassador name was axed. Today, Ambassadors are much more of a rarity than similar models produced by the likes of James, Francis Barnett and Greeves.

Restored values

The cost of a professional restoration will have an influence on, but no direct relation to, a motorcycle's market value. A restored motorcycle can have a market value lower than the cost of its restoration.

◀ **1960 Ambassador Electra 75,** 249cc Villiers 2T twin-cylinder 2-stroke, electric starter, full-width hubs, whitewall tyres, deeply-valanced front mudguard, comprehensive rear enclosure, concours condition, now very rare.
£2,000–2,500 / $3,000–3,600 ⊞ BTSC

Aprilia *(Italian 1956–)*

▶ **1989 Aprilia Red Rose 125,** 124cc liquid-cooled reed-valve 2-stroke single, 6-speed gearbox, electric starter, disc front brake, original specification.
£800–900 / $1,150–1,300 ⊞ MAY
Although it had been formed in 1956, Aprilia did not begin making motorcycles until the end of the 1960s. However, it wasn't until the 1970s, when it built a range of newly designed off-road bikes, that the company really began to make progress. The early 1980s saw production rise dramatically, thanks to a range of new production roadsters in racing, trail and custom guises.

Ariel *(British 1902–70)*

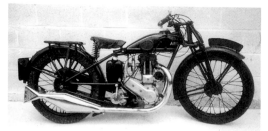

1930 Ariel LF, 249cc overhead-valve twin-port single, 65 x 75mm bore and stroke.
£2,000–2,500 / $3,000–3,600 ⊞ BLM
For 1930, all three Ariel 250s (LB, LF and LG) shared the same 65 x 75mm dimensions and 249cc capacity. The LB had a side-valve engine, while the others employed overhead-valve units. Both of the latter had twin-port leads; the LF was the de luxe model, and the LG the more sporting version, with additional tuning. Although all were known as the Colt, only the overhead-valve models were given this name by Ariel.

1932 Ariel LB32, 249cc side-valve single, 65 x 75mm bore and stroke, hand gear-change, full electric lighting kit.
£800–1,200 / $1,150–1,750 ↗ Bon
During 1926, a range of nicely designed single-cylinder models was introduced by Ariel. Designed by Val Page and offered in both side-valve and overhead-valve guises, they provided the company with a sound model base during the financially difficult years of the early 1930s.

◀ **1938 Ariel 4G Square Four,** 995cc overhead-valve 4-cylinder engine, 2-pipe exhaust, 65 x 75mm bore and stroke, 4-speed foot-change gearbox, girder forks, rigid frame, concours condition.
£5,000–6,000 / $7,250–8,750 ⊞ MW

Dealer prices

Miller's guide prices for dealer motorcycles take into account the value of any guarantees or warranties that may be included in the purchase. Dealers must also observe additional statutory consumer regulations, which do not apply to private sellers. This is factored into our dealer guide prices. Dealer motorcycles are identified by the ⊞ icon; full details of the dealer can be found on page 167.

◀ **1946 Ariel Red Hunter,** 499cc overhead-valve single, 81.8 x 95mm bore and stroke, single-port iron head, iron barrel, girder front forks, rigid frame, single saddle with pillion pad, chrome tank with instrument panel in top, restored.
£3,000–3,500
$4,400–5,000 ⊞ CotC

▶ **1951 Ariel Red Hunter,** 346cc overhead-valve single, iron head and barrel, 4-speed gearbox, sprung saddle and pillion pad, completely restored, one of last telescopics/rigid-framed Red Hunters built.
£2,500–2,900
$3,600–4,250 ⊞ BLM

1956 Ariel 4G Mk II, 995cc overhead-valve 4-cylinder engine, 4-speed foot-change gearbox, full-width alloy front hub, plunger rear suspension, headlamp nacelle, chrome tank panel, dualseat, original, very good condition.
£3,500–4,000 / $5,000–5,800 ⚸ Bon
Designed by Edward Turner, the Square Four was first shown at Olympia in 1930. Originally an overhead-cam 500, the model grew to 601cc before a total redesign saw it emerge as the Model 4G, with 995cc overhead-valve engine, in 1937. Anstey-link plunger rear suspension became an option in 1939, but would not be offered again until 1946, when a telescopic front fork replaced the previous girder type. An exercise in weight shedding saw the cast-iron cylinder head and barrel replaced by alloy components for 1949, the revised model, now capable of 90+mph, being known as the Mark I. Introduced in 1953, the Mark II, with redesigned 'four-pipe' cylinder head, was a genuine 100mph machine.

c1956 Ariel Red Hunter, 346cc overhead-valve single.
£1,500–1,750 / $2,200–2,500 ⊞ BLM
This particular machine has been built using parts from more than one year. The full-width hubs and frame date from 1956, while the iron-head engine and conventional headlamp (as opposed to a nacelle for 1956) are from an earlier machine.

A known continuous history can add value to and enhance the enjoyment of a motorcycle.

1956 Ariel Mk II Square Four, 995cc 4-cylinder engine, 4-pipe exhaust, full-width alloy front hub, headlamp nacelle, dualseat, rear carrier.
£3,500–4,000 / $5,000–5,800 ⚸ CGC
Introduced in 1953, the Mk II version of Ariel's legendary Square Four was acknowledged as a significant improvement over its predecessors. Its all-alloy engine benefited from increased compression, gear pump oiling and four exhaust ports. Telescopic front forks and the pivoted-link rear suspension gave good road-holding, allowing the most to be made of the bike's impressive performance.

▶ **1958 Ariel FH Huntmaster,** 647cc overhead-valve parallel twin, 70 x 84mm bore and stroke, iron head and barrel, 4-speed gearbox, telescopic front forks, swinging-arm frame, headlamp nacelle.
£2,200–2,600
$3,200–3,800 ⊞ BLM
The engine of the Huntmaster was derived from the BSA A10.

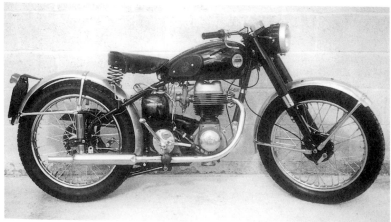

◀ **1959 Ariel LH Colt,** 198cc overhead-valve single, 60 x 70mm bore and stroke, 10bhp at 5,600rpm, plunger rear suspension, non-standard seat and mudguards.
£500–700
$720–1,000 ⊞ BLM
The Colt remained in production from 1954 until late 1959. The engine was based on the BSA 250 C11G, Ariel being part of the BSA group at the time.

1961 Ariel Golden Arrow, 247cc 2-stroke twin, 54 x 54mm bore and stroke, 4-speed gearbox, leading-link front forks, concours condition.
£1,500–1,700 / $2,200–2,450 ⊞ MW
Otherwise known as the Super Sports, the Golden Arrow was the performance model of Ariel's latest and last beam-frame two-stroke. It was distinguished from the lesser models by its gold and white finish, plus chromed engine side casings and fork link covers. This was the first year of production.

1961 Ariel Arrow, 247cc 2-stroke twin, 54 x 54mm bore and stroke, 17.5bhp at 6,400rpm, Avonaire fairing, sports handlebars.
£1,200–1,400 / $1,750–2,000 ⊞ BLM
The Arrow was in production from 1960 to 1964.

1964 Ariel Golden Arrow, 247cc 2-stroke twin.
£1,500–1,700 / $2,175–2,500 ⊞ PS
The Arrow/Leader range was designed by Val Page, arguably Britain's foremost motorcycle designer. This machine was made the year before Ariel closed for good.

Ascot-Pullin *(British 1928–29)*

Introduced in 1928, the Ascot-Pullin was built in Letchworth, Hertfordshire, by the Ascot Motor and Manufacturing Company. Advertised as 'The New Wonder Motorcycle', it was packed with innovations inspired by car industry practice, but failed to appeal to the notoriously conservative motorcycling public. The engine was a horizontally mounted, overhead-valve single that drove the in-unit three-speed gearbox via helical gears. A pressed-steel frame enclosed not only the engine/gearbox unit, but also the fuel and oil tanks, both of which incorporated filler-cap gauges. A pressed-steel dashboard housed the rest of the instrumentation, together with electrical switchgear and ignition/air controls.

However, the Ascot-Pullin's most novel feature was its hydraulic brakes, possibly the first on a motorcycle. Pullin's own design was used at first, but soon was supplanted by a more conventional Lockheed system. Other unusual features conceived with user-friendliness in mind included a telescopic centre stand with alternative 'easy parking' and 'wheel removal' settings, and an exhaust-valve lifter coupled to the kickstart for easy starting. Extras available included an adjustable windscreen with optional wiper, legshields and a rear-view mirror. Although they would be sorted out eventually, the machine's teething problems fatally tarnished its reputation, and production ceased in 1929 after 400–500 had been built.

1930 Ascot-Pullin, 496cc overhead-valve single, 82 x 94mm bore and stroke.
£7,000–8,500 / $10,000–12,500 ➢ Bon
One of only eight or so surviving examples of 1914 TT winner Cyril Pullin's revolutionary design, this machine was restored by ex-VMCC president Walter Green in the 1960s, and has been on museum display in recent years.

Baker *(British 1927–)*

◀ **1928 Baker Model 60,** 247cc Villiers twin-port 2-stroke single, 67 x 70mm bore and stroke.
£500–700 / $720–1,000 ➢ Bon
Frank Baker left Precision to found his own motorcycle company in 1927. His Villiers-engined lightweights ranged from 147cc to 247cc, and their major selling point was a robust straight-tube frame employing only two brazed joints. The twin-port engines were equipped with a Villiers flywheel magneto/generator and incorporated lubrication that worked off crankcase compression.

Benelli *(Italian 1911–)*

1957 Benelli Leonesse, 248cc overhead-valve unit-construction twin, single Dell'Orto carburettor, 4-speed gearbox, alloy drum brakes, telescopic front forks, swinging-arm rear suspension, alloy wheel rims, separate sprung saddle and pillion seat.
£1,200–1,500 / $1,750–2,150 ⊞ NLM
The Leonesse (Lioness) was the star of the 1951 Milan show, being very modern and having an engine of particularly neat design. Although performance was modest, at 65–75mph, it proved a popular bike due to its smoothness and reliability.

▶ **1973 Benelli 650 Tornado S,** 642.8cc overhead-valve unit-construction parallel twin, 84 x 58mm bore and stroke, cylinders inclined forward at 12 degrees, 5-speed gearbox.
£2,500–3,000 / $3,600–4,400 ⊞ NLM
The 650 Tornado entered series production in mid-1971, the S version appearing for 1973. It can be identified by the ribbing on the backplate of the double-sided front drum brake. Another model, the S2, was offered in 1974. This differed by having a small fairing and single seat. Production of all Tornados ceased in mid-1975.

1970 Benelli 125 Sports Special, 123.6cc overhead-valve unit-construction single, horizontal cylinder, 54 x 54mm bore and stroke, 14bhp, Marzocchi front forks, full-width alloy hubs, stainless-steel mudguards, 81mph top speed.
£900–1,000 / $1,300–1,500 ⊞ CotC
Based on the 1950s Motobi designed 175, the Sports Special of 1970 was offered in 125 and 250 (245cc/74 x 57mm) versions; both had five-speed gearboxes.

1974 Benelli 250 2C, 231.4cc piston-port 2-stroke twin, alloy heads, iron barrels, 5-speed gearbox, double-sided Grimeca single-leading-shoe front brake, 18in wheels, very good original condition.
£500–600 / $720–870 ⊞ MAY

▶ **1975 Benelli 750 Sei,** 747.7cc chain-driven single-overhead-camshaft 6-cylinder engine, 56 x 50.6mm bore and stroke, 3 Dell'Orto VHB 24mm carburettors, wet-sump lubrication, ignition by triple contact breakers and coils, 71bhp at 8,500rpm, electric starter, primary drive by combination of inverted-tooth chain and gear, 5-speed gearbox and wet multi-plate clutch, original 6-megaphone exhaust.
£3,500–4,000 / $5,000–5,800 ⋟ NLM
'Sei' means 'six' in Italian.

Miller's Motorcycle Milestones

Benelli 250 Super Sport (Italian 1936)
Price range: £2,500–5,000 / $3,600–7,250
During the mid-1930s, the Italian Benelli concern, based at Pesaro on the Adriatic coast, developed its own form of plunger rear suspension, which was introduced in 1936 on the new 250 Super Sport.

At the Milan show in early 1938, the British magazine *The Motor Cycle* reported that the new Benelli single-cylinder challenger was 'very English in appearance'. This was an accurate statement, even though the 247cc (67 x 70mm) engine featured a single overhead camshaft driven by a train of gears on the offside of the engine. Besides its styling, the little Benelli also closely followed British practice by featuring a twin-port cylinder head, girder forks and separate four-speed gearbox. Nonetheless, the latter assembly was equipped with a very Italian rocking (heel-and-toe) pedal.

The Benelli 250 was usually equipped with hairpin valve springs – soft enough to be changed by hand! On some machines, the exhaust system featured a lever to give 'open road' unbaffled performance. The lubricating oil was contained in a heavily-ribbed extension at the front of the crankcase, while on some bikes, a very neat oil cooler was mounted on top of this sump, set between the twin front downtubes of the frame. With a maximum speed that was a shade over 70mph and 16bhp at 6,500rpm, the Benelli 250 Super Sport was seen by enthusiasts of the day as the ultimate road-legal 250, rivalled only by the Moto Guzzi horizontal single. By comparison, other competitors, such as Bianchi, Gilera and MM, simply did not have the same performance. Benelli also produced a 500 model with a similar engine design, but to many the original 250 was the ultimate sportster from the Pesaro brand in the period leading up to the dark days of WWII.

1981 Benelli 350 Sport Series II, 345.5cc engine, electric starter, 12-spoke gold cast alloy wheels, 'bikini' fairing, triple Brembo hydraulically operated disc brakes, 100mph top speed, standard apart from black 4-into-1 exhaust system.
£1,200–1,400 / $1,750–2,000 ⊞ NLM

Miller's is a price GUIDE not a price LIST

◄ **1976 Benelli 500 Quattro,** 498cc single-overhead-camshaft 4-cylinder engine, chain-driven camshaft, 4-pipe exhaust, 5-speed gearbox, disc front brake, drum rear brake.
£1,000–1,400 / $1,500–2,000 ⋌ Bon
This machine is clearly based on Honda's CB500 four, but with Italian styling.

1981 Benelli 654, 603.94cc single-overhead-camshaft across-the-frame 4-cylinder engine, chain-driven camshaft, 5-speed gearbox, wet multi-plate clutch, duplex frame, triple Brembo brake discs, patented (Moto Guzzi) linked brake control system, 118mph top speed.
£1,500–1,900 / $2,150–2,750 ⊞ NLM
Launched at the Milan show in November 1979, the 654 was derived from the 500 Quattro.

▶ **1981 Benelli 254,** 231cc overhead-camshaft across-the-frame 4-cylinder engine, 44 x 38mm bore and stroke, 4 Dell'Orto 18mm carburettors, 27.8bhp, 5-speed gearbox, 260mm Brembo front disc brake, drum rear brake, 95mph top speed.
£2,200–2,400
$3,200–3,500 ⊞ NLM

BMW *(German 1923–)*

BMW, Bayerische Motoren Werke, can trace its origins back to the late 19th century. During WWI, BMW expanded greatly on the back of high demand from the German government for aero engines, and at its peak, in 1917, BMW employed over 3,500 staff. But after the conflict, BMW's fall from grace was rapid, having been banned from any form of aviation production. The company's first connection with motorcycles occurred in early 1920, when development work began on the 'Flink', which had a 148cc two-stroke engine. Then, in 1921, came the Martin Stolle designed M2B15, a 493cc, horizontally opposed (fore-and-aft), side-valve twin-cylinder engine, which was supplied to companies such as Bison, Heller and Victoria. But it was the Paris Salon of 1923 that was to herald BMW's real entry into the motorcycle arena with Max Friz's creation, the R32. Unlike Stolle's flat-twin, Friz's machine had its cylinder pointing across the frame. The R32 was the beginning of a virtually unbroken line of horizontally opposed 'boxer' twins, and although BMW has used other engine configurations – with one, three and four cylinders – the legendary twin-cylinder models have dominated the German company's two-wheel history. Moreover, it is not just on the street where the BMW flat-twins have carved their own niche in motorcycling's hall of fame, but also in racing, record breaking and off-roading, and with various police and armed forces, both in war and peace. Since 1992, BMWs have had engines with four valves per cylinder, while electronic fuel injection has carried the 'boxer' twin-cylinder concept into the 21st century. Amazingly, of all the BMW twin-cylinder motorcycles built, over half remain in service today – a feat unequalled by any other motorcycle manufacturer.

1927 BMW R47, 494cc overhead-valve flat-twin, 68 x 68mm bore and stroke, 18bhp at 4,000rpm, shaft final drive.
£15,870–19,000 / $23,000–27,500 ⚒ Bon
Following the collapse of its aero engine business after WWI, BMW turned to other areas of manufacture, motorcycles among them. Its first two models, marketed as the Frink and Helios, were failures, but a successful proprietary engine was supplied to other manufacturers, such as Victoria. Designed by chief engineer Max Friz and launched in 1923, the first motorcycle to be sold as a BMW – the R32 – featured a 493cc, twin-cylinder side-valve engine with horizontally opposed cylinders; this 'flat-twin' layout would for ever be associated with the marque. BMW's first sports machine, the R37, appeared in 1924. It boasted an overhead-valve engine producing almost double the R32's power output (good enough for a top speed of more than 70mph), but was built for little more than a year before being replaced by the improved R47, the latter featuring increased power and a driveshaft mounted rear brake in place of the R37's block-and-pulley type. R47 production lasted from 1927 to 1928, during which time 1,720 were built.

Auction prices

Miller's only includes motorcycles declared sold. Our guide prices take into account the buyer's premium, VAT on the premium, and the extent of any published catalogue information relating to condition and provenance. Motorcycles sold at auction are identified by the ⚒ icon; full details of the auction house can be found on page 167.

1929 BMW R63, 735cc overhead-valve flat-twin, 83 x 68mm bore and stroke, side operating kickstart, hand gear-change, shaft final drive, trailing-link front forks with leaf springs, rigid frame, sprung saddle.
£13,000–15,500 / $18,850–22,000 ⚒ Bon
The R63's engine had ultra-short stroke dimensions for its day. A total of 7,500 R63s were built between 1929 and 1934.

1938 BMW R51, 494cc overhead-valve flat-twin, 68 x 68mm bore and stroke, 24bhp at 5,600 rpm.
£6,300–7,500 / $9,250–10,875 ⚒ Bon
During the 1930s, BMW produced a range of 11 motorcycles with capacities between 500cc and 750cc, and among the best were the R5 and R51. This is probably because the flat-twin engine benefited from an overhead-valve configuration combined with the popular capacity of 500cc. The R5, manufactured between 1936 and 1937, became the basis for the company's products for the next 20 years. The 500cc BMWs were intended to compete with the well-established British single-cylinder sporting models of the same capacity, and they were certainly on a par in both performance and road-holding. Manufactured from 1938 to 1940, the R51, although slightly heavier, carried forward all these attributes. Today, even in Germany, it is a rare and desirable machine from a historic period of German motorcycle manufacture.

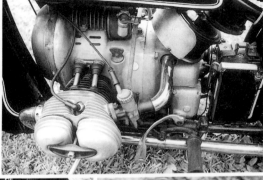

1951 BMW R51/2, 494cc overhead-valve flat-twin, 68 x 68mm bore and stroke, 2 Bing 22mm carburettors, battery/coil ignition, 24bhp at 5,800rpm, 4-speed gearbox, 19in wheels, telescopic front forks, plunger rear suspension, dynamo lighting, 120mph speedometer, Pagusa seating.
£4,000–5,000 / $5,800–7,250 ⊞ MW
The R51/2 was produced in far fewer numbers than the R51 and R51/3.

1951 BMW R67, 594cc overhead-valve flat-twin, 72 x 73mm bore and stroke, 26hp at 5,500rpm, 4-speed foot-change gearbox, unrestored.
£2,500–3,000 / $3,600–4,400 ⚒ TEN
A total of 1,470 R67s were built, all in 1951.

1954 BMW R68, 594cc overhead-valve flat-twin, 72 x 73mm bore and stroke, 35bhp at 7,000rpm, 4-speed foot-change gearbox, side operating kickstarter, telescopic forks, plunger rear suspension, alloy wheel rims.
£4,500–5,000 / $6,500–7,250 ⊞ MW
Built in small numbers between 1952 and 1954, the R68 was BMW's fastest production roadster up to that time, being able to hit 100mph.

1975 BMW R90/6, 980cc overhead-valve flat-twin, Bing carburettors, 5-speed gearbox, single disc front brake, fork gaiters, rev-counter, one owner and fewer than 6,500 miles from new.
£3,000–3,750 / $4,400–5,400 ⊞ BLM

▶ **1976 BMW R60/6,** 599cc overhead-valve flat-twin, 73.5 x 70.6mm bore and stroke, 40bhp at 6,400rpm, fairing, pannier frames.
£1,000–1,200 / $1,500–1,750 ⊞ BLM
In all, 21,070 R60/6 models were built between 1973 and 1976. This particular machine is an ex-police bike, hence the low price.

◄ **1977 BMW R100RS,** 980cc overhead-valve flat-twin, 94 x 70.6mm bore and stroke, 70bhp at 7,250rpm, 5-speed gearbox, original specification, engine completely rebuilt.
£1,800–2,500 / $2,600–3,600 ⚡ Bon
The BMW R100RS marked a major step forward in motorcycle design in one important respect: for the first time on a mass produced machine, the aerodynamics had been developed with both rider comfort and performance in mind. The fairing that resulted from hours in the wind-tunnel has proved to be one of the most enduring and influential designs. The rest of the machine utilized proven BMW technology and was built to the expected high standard. The R100RS was made between 1976 and 1984, production totalling 33,648.

1983 BMW R65, 649cc overhead-valve flat-twin, 82 x 61.5mm bore and stroke, 50bhp at 7,250rpm, cast alloy wheels, pannier frames, front crash bars, standard specification apart from fairing, one owner from new, low mileage.
£1,700–1,900 / $2,450–2,750 ⊞ BLM

1984 BMW K100RS, 987cc inline 4-cylinder engine, 67 x 70mm bore and stroke, fuel injection, 100bhp at 8,000rpm, stainless-steel exhaust, bottom fairing panels, rack and panniers, tank bag tool kit, 68,000 miles from new.
£1,000–1,200 / $1,500–1,750 ⚡ CGC

1986 BMW K100RS, 987cc liquid-cooled double-overhead-camshaft inline 4-cylinder engine, Bosch fuel injection, wet-sump lubrication, 5-speed gearbox, dry clutch, triple disc brakes, 137mph top speed, standard apart from crash bars and colour-coded exhaust shield, 3,000 miles from new.
£1,500–2,000 / $2,200–3,000 ⊞ BLM

► **1988 BMW R100 GS,** 980cc overhead-valve twin, 94 x 70.6mm bore and stroke, 60bhp, shaft final drive, Paralever rear suspension, 180mm-travel front forks, fitted Paris-Dakar kit and panniers, 7 gallon (35 litre) fuel tank.
£2,800–3,200 / $4,000–4,650 ⊞ MW

Brough-Superior
(British 1902–39)

◄ **1924 Brough-Superior SS80,** 998cc side-valve narrow-angle JAP V-twin engine, nickel plated tank, excellent condition.
£28,000–30,000
$40,000–43,000 ⊞ VER

► **1935 Brough-Superior MX80,** 990cc Matchless V-twin engine, siamesed exhaust, foot-change gearbox, sprung saddle and pillion pad.
£11,000–13,000
$16,000–19,000 ⊞ VER

◄ **1936 Brough-Superior SS80,** 990cc Matchless side-valve 50-degree V-twin engine, fishtail silencer.
£10,000–12,000
$14,500–17,500 ⊞ BLM

BSA (British 1906–71, late 70s–)

◄ **1923 BSA 350cc Sports Tourer,** 349cc side-valve single.
£3,800–4,500 / $5,500–6,500 ⋏ Bon
At the beginning of the 1920s, BSA was established as one of the major motorcycle manufacturers in the UK. It had built a good reputation for practical, reliable and cheap motorcycles, and it was able to meet the demands of both the home and colonial markets. Although not specifically producing sports machines during the early years, BSA was careful to ensure that its range of products covered the wide requirements of the market. In the 350cc range, it mostly produced sound side-valve commuter and touring machines, and with a few minor specification changes it was able to include Sports Tourer versions.

► **1924 BSA Model B 2.25hp Round Tank,** 249cc side-valve single-cylinder engine.
£2,250–2,500 / $3,300–3,600 ⊞ PS
The Model B Round Tank's name was derived from the shape of its petrol tank.

1925 BSA, 348cc side-valve single, iron head and barrel, forward mounted magneto, caliper brakes front and rear, chain final drive, girder forks, rigid frame.
£2,850–3,250 / $4,000–4,700 ⊞ CotC

1929 BSA Model S Sloper, 493cc overhead-valve single, inclined cylinder, 80 x 98mm bore and stroke, 90mph top speed, completely restored to original specification.
£2,300–2,700 / $3,350–4,000 ⚒ CGC
The Sloper was introduced for the 1927 season, and with its low seat height and saddle tank it was a true trendsetter. The oil was carried in a sump cast into the crankcases, while the magneto was behind the cylinder. It was supplied without lights, which were a cost option. The Sloper was replaced in 1932 by the Blue Star.

1930 BSA Model E30–14, 771cc side-valve V-twin, 76 x 85mm bore and stroke, hand-change gearbox, chain final drive, drum brakes, girder forks, rigid frame, footboards, unrestored but running.
£6,250–7,000 / $9,000–10,000 ⊞ PMo

1939 BSA B21, 249cc, overhead-valve single, girder forks, rigid frame, in need of cosmetic restoration.
£1,800–2,000 / $2,600–3,000 ⊞ BB
The B21 was produced from 1937 until the outbreak of WWII in 1939, but now it is quite rare.

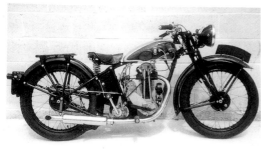

1936 BSA B2, overhead-valve single-port single, 63 x 80mm bore and stroke, iron head and barrel, restored, period specification.
£1,400–1,600 / $2,000–2,300 ⊞ BLM
The B2 lightweight, overhead-valve single, with exposed valve gear and hand-change, was only offered in 1936.

1948 BSA B31, 348cc overhead-valve single, 71 x 88mm bore and stroke, magneto, dynamo, telescopic front forks, rigid frame, 19in wheels.
£1,200–1,500 / $1,750–2,150 ⚒ Bon
Based on the pre-war B29, BSA's rugged B31 was manufactured from 1945 to 1959, its overhead-valve engine providing the basis for the renowned Gold Star. Produced initially with a rigid frame and telescopic front forks, it gained (optional) plunger rear suspension in 1949 and a swinging-arm frame in 1954. A good all-round performer by the standards of its day, the B31 could cruise comfortably all day at 60mph while returning 75+mpg.

1951 BSA A10 Golden Flash, 646cc twin-cylinder engine, 8in front brake, plunger frame, telescopic forks, dualseat, original specification, very good condition.
£2,500–3,000 / $3,600–4,400 ⊞ BLM
The A10 Golden Flash made an excellent solo or sidecar machine.

1954 BSA Bantam D3 Major, 148cc 2-stroke single, 57 x 58mm bore and stroke, piston-port induction, 3-speed foot-change gearbox, undamped telescopic forks, plunger rear suspension, completely rebuilt 2000, new bearings, gaskets, seals, piston and rings, ignition coil, clutch assembly, and primary and rear chains.
£600–750 / $870–1,100 ⊞ PS
The D3 was offered between 1954 and 1957.

1955 BSA Bantam D1, 124cc 2-stroke single, 3-speed foot-change gearbox, standard specification.
£650–750 / $950–1,100 ⊞ BLM
A big-finned head and barrel, tubular silencer and heavier front forks arrived on the D1 for 1954. The 1955 model remained virtually the same, apart from a new rear number plate, toolbox fixing, wider cylinder-stud centres and two extra crankcase screws.

1955 BSA Bantam D3 Major, 148cc piston-port 2-stroke single, 57 x 58mm bore and stroke, 3-speed gearbox.
£500–600 / $720–870 ⤳ Bon
BSA introduced the D3 during 1954 alongside the existing 125cc D1. Displacing 148cc, achieved by a larger bore, it offered a useful increase in performance in comparison to the smaller model, from which it had been derived. Heavier front forks and a larger front brake were fitted to cope with the increase in performance, and the model was offered with plunger rear suspension as standard, although the following season saw the introduction of a pivoted-fork frame as an alternative.

◄ **1955 BSA DB34 Gold Star,** 499cc overhead-valve single, alloy head and barrel, full Clubman's specification with close-ratio gearbox and rev-counter, period accessories including alloy rims and finned tappet inspection cover.
£7,000–8,000 / $10,000–11,500 ⊞ MAY

1956 BSA C12, 248cc overhead-valve pre-unit single, standard apart from rear carrier, concours condition.
£800–900 / $1,150–1,300 ⊞ PM
The C12 was the last of the BSA 250 commuter range, and it benefited from superior handling and more powerful brakes than the earlier models. However, with the introduction of the new C15 unit-construction model for 1958, its time was over.

1956 BSA B33, 499cc overhead-valve pre-unit single, 85 x 88mm bore and stroke, iron head and barrel, 4-speed foot-change gearbox, Ariel-type full-width aluminium brake hubs.
£3,400–3,750 / $4,750–5,500 ⊞ BB
The B33 was one of BSA's best-selling models of the immediate post-war period; production ended in 1960.

1957 BSA B31, 348cc overhead-valve single, 4-speed gearbox, alloy primary chaincase, telescopic forks, swinging-arm frame, Ariel-type full-width aluminium brake hubs, headlamp nacelle, chrome tank sides, original specification.
£1,700–1,900 / $2,500–2,750 ⊞ PM
The B31 used the same cycle parts as its larger-capacity sibling, the 499cc B33, and, consequently did not perform as well. Its main charm was its smooth, very reliable engine.

1958 BSA A10 Road Rocket, 646cc, completely restored, standard specification apart from optional rev-counter and siamesed exhaust system from later Rocket Gold Star.
£3,800–4,250 / $5,500–6,200 ⊞ CotC

1959 BSA Shooting Star, 497cc overhead-valve pre-unit vertical twin, 4-speed foot-change gearbox, full-width brake hubs, painted steel mudguard, original specification.
£2,200–2,500 / $3,200–3,600 ⊞ PS

1961 BSA C15 Star, 247cc overhead-valve unit single, 4-speed foot-change gearbox.
£700–900 / $1,000–1,300 ⊞ BLM
The C15 Series ran from 1957 until 1968. It also sired larger versions in 343cc, 441cc and ultimately 499cc guises.

1962 BSA B40, 343cc overhead-valve unit single, 79 x 70mm bore and stroke, 21bhp at 7,000rpm, 18in wheels.
£1,000–1,300 / $1,500–2,000 ⚞ CGC
The B40 was produced between 1960 and 1965; besides its increased engine size and performance, it had a slightly more substantial appearance compared to the 250 C15, due to certain uprated chassis components.

1962 BSA A50, 499cc overhead-valve twin, 65.5 x 74mm bore and stroke, alloy head, iron barrel, dry-sump lubrication, 4-speed gearbox, full-width hubs, telescopic forks, swinging-arm rear suspension, original specification, concours condition.
£2,200–2,600 / $3,200–3,800 ⊞ MW
This was the first year of production for the new A50 (500) and A65 (650) unit-construction BSA twins.

◄ **1965 BSA Bantam D7 Super,** 172cc piston-port 2-stroke single, 61.5 x 58mm bore and stroke, completely restored, concours condition.
£600–1,000
$870–1,500 ⊞ BLM
The chrome tank distinguishes the Super model from the standard D7.

1966 BSA Lightning Clubman, 654cc overhead-valve unit twin, concours condition.
£4,000–5,000 / $5,800–7,250 ⊞ PMo
In many ways, the Lightning Clubman was the most exotic of the A65 series of unit-construction twins.

1968 BSA B25, 247cc overhead-valve single, 4-speed gearbox, full-width front brake, export model.
£800–900 / $1,150–1,300 ⊞ MAY
The B25 series was developed from the Victor 440 motocrosser, itself derived from the earlier C15/B40 range of BSA's unit singles.

1968 BSA D14C Bushman, 172cc 2-stroke cylinder.
£700–850 / $1,000–1,250 ⚞ PS
The original D10 Bushman arrived for the 1967 season with a high-level exhaust, trail tyres, a single seat, increased ground clearance and lowered gearing. The D14/4C incorporated the same changes as the D14/4S (Supreme) street bike.

1969 BSA Starfire, 247cc overhead-valve unit single, 67 x 70mm bore and stroke, 4-speed gearbox, twin-leading-shoe front brake, fork gaiters, aftermarket megaphone silencer.
£700–900 / $1,000–1,300 ⊞ MAY
This was the first year of the twin-leading-shoe front brake on this model.

1969 BSA A75R Rocket III, 740cc overhead-valve unit triple, 67 x 70mm bore and stroke, 3-into-2 exhaust with 'ray-gun' silencers, original specification.
£3,800–4,000 / $5,500–5,800 ⊞ MW
The Rocket III's engine was a Triumph design, but it was distinct from the Triumph Trident by having its cylinders inclined forward at an angle of 15 degrees. This meant that not only were the cylinders different, but also the crankcase and chaincases. The crankshaft was a BSA product, and it was made by forging it in one plane, then reheating and twisting it to provide 120-degree crank throws. The result was excellent balance and, thus, engine smoothness.

1970 BSA B44 Victor Special, 441cc overhead-valve unit single, 79 x 90mm bore and stroke, 28bhp at 6,500rpm, high-level exhaust, 8in front brake, alloy tank, fork gaiters.
£1,700–2,000 / $2,500–3,000 ⊞ BLM

1970 BSA A65 Thunderbolt, 654cc overhead-valve unit twin, unrestored, original.
£1,800–2,000 / $2,600–3,000 ⚒ Bon
The original A65 twin had been introduced during 1963, and was followed four years later by an expanded and revised range, which included the Thunderbolt tourer, Lightning sports tourer and Spitfire sports bike. The Thunderbolt utilized a single carburettor, unlike the two sporting models, which were fitted with two instruments. When tested by *Motorcycle Mechanics* during 1967, the Thunderbolt recorded over 100mph with handling to match. The brakes, which were regarded as good, were further improved during 1968 with the adoption of the Triumph twin-leading-shoe front unit.

1971 BSA 650cc Lightning, 654cc overhead-valve unit twin, recently restored by John Weedon, concours condition.
£3,500–3,800 / $5,000–5,500 ⚒ Bon
Following Triumph's lead, BSA turned to unit construction for its range of parallel twins as the 1960s dawned, launching the all-new 500cc A50 and 650cc A65 in January 1962. The names Thunderbolt and Lightning were adopted for the single-carburettor and twin-carburettor versions of the 650 respectively, and these continued after the range was given a major makeover for the 1971 season. In this, its final incarnation, BSA's 650 gained a new oil bearing frame, Ceriani-style front forks with exposed stanchions and conical hubs. The lusty, parallel-twin performance remained unimpaired, *Bike* magazine recording figures of 14.09 seconds for the standing quarter mile and a top speed of around 105mph.

1971 BSA A65 Lightning, 654cc overhead-valve unit twin, twin-leading-shoe front brake, conical hubs, export model, standard specification apart from headlamp peak.
£2,500–3,000 / $3,600–4,400 ⊞ BLM
A disadvantage of this oil-in-frame model is the high seat height. The design work was carried out at the infamous Umberslade Hall only months before the BSA group's financial crash.

Cagiva *(Italian 1978–)*

◄ **1986 Cagiva 650 Elefant,** Ducati unit-construction 90-degree V-twin, belt-driven camshaft, desmodromic valve gear, wet-sump lubrication, 5-speed gearbox, Brembo front and rear disc brakes, square-tube swinging-arm frame, leading-axle long-travel front forks, monoshock rear suspension, alloy wheel rims.
£2,000–2,500 / $3,000–3,500 ⊞ NLM

Capriolo *(Italian 1946–64)*

1956 Capriolo 150 Twin, 149cc overhead-valve flat-twin, chain final drive, telescopic front forks, full-width front brake hub, completely restored.
£2,500–3,500 / $3,500–5,000 ⊞ MW
Made by Aero Caproni of Trento, north-east Italy, the Capriolo marque began with a 75cc overhead-valve single with vertical cylinder. Then in 1952, it built its first twin. Known as the Cento 50, it used the same horizontally-opposed twin as fitted to this machine, but had Earles-type front forks and a single-sided front brake.

Ceedos *(British 1919–29)*

◄ **c1921 Ceedos,** 225cc 2-stroke single, oil-pump lubrication, belt final drive, Ruurbaken magneto, aluminium footboards, largely original.
£1,500–1,700 / $2,150–2,450 ⋌ Bon
The Ceedos concern was based in Northampton. Between 1919 and 1929, it produced a range of well-engineered, lightweight two-strokes, followed by Bradshaw and Blackburne powered four-strokes.

Chater-Lea (British 1900–37)

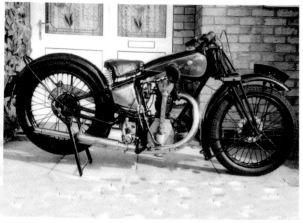

1931 Chater-Lea Camshaft Super Sports, 348cc bevel-driven overhead-camshaft single, 71 x 88mm bore and stroke, hand-change gearbox, chain final drive.
£5,500–6,000 / $8,000–8,700 ✗ Bon

Prior to WWI, Chater-Lea motorcycles accommodated a bewildering range of engines before the firm began offering its own, alongside those of Blackburne and Villiers, in the 1920s. Following the record breaking successes of Dougal Marchant's Blackburne-based, overhead-camshaft Chater-Lea, the company introduced its own design in 1925. This was A. C. Woodman's famous 'face-cam' engine, which used two contoured plates at the top of a vertical, gear-driven shaft to operate the rocker arms. A second oil pump was used to lubricate the valve gear, which was fully enclosed, an unusual feature at the time. Fast and reliable, the cammy Chater-Lea was constructed to the highest of standards and priced accordingly, its £80 / $115 price tag making it the province of only the wealthiest of enthusiasts.

Clément Garrard (British 1902–05)

► 1904 Clément Garrard, 143cc overhead-valve engine with small crankcase and large flywheel, inclined to frame downtube, belt rear drive over jockey pulley.
£4,500–5,000 / $6,500–7,250 ⊞ VER
In 1902, Charles Garrard of Birmingham imported the French Clément clip-on engine unit to fit a standard bicycle. Norton frames were used, and in 1903 a 3hp, narrow-angle V-twin joined the single. But by the end of 1904, the Garrard name had faded away.

Connaught (British 1910–27)

1915 Connaught 2.5hp, 293cc 2-stroke single, completely restored, full running order.
£3,000–3,400 / $4,400–5,000 ⊞ PS
Made by the Bordesley Engineering Company of Birmingham, the Connaught is now a rare machine, only 11 similar two-stroke models being listed in the VMCC's register.

1923 Connaught Popular, 293cc 2-stroke single, largely complete, in need of restoration.
£350–400 / $500–580 ✗ Bon
Connaught production began in 1910 and up to the mid-1920s concentrated upon high-quality two-stroke singles, produced in 293cc and 347cc engine sizes. Post-WWI models featured chain and belt drive with a countershaft gearbox.

Coventry Eagle
(British 1901–40)

1924 Coventry Eagle Flying Eight, 976cc side-valve V-twin, forward-mounted magneto, chain final drive, drum brakes.
£11,000–13,000 / $16,000–19,000 ⚒ Bon

Established in Victorian times as a bicycle manufacturer, Coventry Eagle built a diverse range of motorcycles using proprietary (mainly JAP) engines from 1901 onwards, although machines only began to be produced in significant numbers after WWI. Six Coventry Eagles were offered for 1923, all JAP powered apart from a Blackburne-engined 350, ranging from the formidable Flying Eight to the diminutive S14 Ultra-Lightweight. Most famous of these was the Flying Eight, which, with its 1 litre JAP V-twin engine and muscular good looks, was a worthy rival for the Brough-Superior and a formidable Brooklands racing machine. Introduced in 1923, the Flying Eight was not Coventry Eagle's first V-twin, but it was the first to establish a sporting reputation, thanks to its special 976cc side-valve engine, which guaranteed a top speed of 80mph, an exceptional performance at the time. In 1926, the side-valve version was joined by a new overhead-valve-engined Flying Eight, again JAP powered. Within a few years, however, the onset of the Depression had forced Coventry-Eagle to change tack, the firm concentrating on bread-and-butter lightweights until it ceased motorcycle production in 1939. The last overhead-valve Flying Eight left the factory in 1930, and the final side-valve model the following year.

CZ (Czechoslovakian 1932–)

c1981 CZ 175 Sport, 174cc piston-port 2-stroke single, pump lubrication, 4-speed foot-change gearbox, full-width drum front brake, complete, in need of restoration.
£70–150 / $100–220 ⚒ Bon

CZ, a Czech armaments firm, began motorcycle production during 1932. After WWII, the company became part of the nationalized Czech motorcycle industry, concentrating its efforts on the production of durable lightweights.

1975 CZ 125 Sports, 123cc 2-stroke single, alloy head, iron barrel, 4-speed gearbox, dualseat, aftermarket rear carrier, complete, in need of cosmetic restoration.
£50–100 / $75–145 ⚒ PS

DKW (German 1919–81)

◄ **1960 DKW RT175,** 174cc 2-stroke single, 62 x 58mm bore and stroke, Earles-type front forks, swinging-arm rear suspension, dualseat, complete, in need of cosmetic restoration.
£400–450 / $580–650 ⊞ PS

The RT175 was launched at the Frankfurt motorcycle show in October 1953. During the late 1950s, a large batch of unsold bikes was imported by London dealer Pride & Clarke. Today, it is very rare.

Douglas *(British 1906–57)*

1915 Douglas 2¾hp, 348cc fore-and-aft flat-twin, belt final drive, caliper brakes, flat tank, full lighting equipment, mechanically sound, original specification.
£4,000–4,500 / $5,800–6,500 ⊞ VER

1920 Douglas W20 2¾hp, fore-and-aft flat-twin engine, belt final drive, period accessories including carrier, leather bags, footboards and lighting equipment.
£2,700–3,000 / $4,000–4,400 ⊕ LDM
A feature of the early Douglas flat-twin was its massive 'bacon slicer' external flywheel.

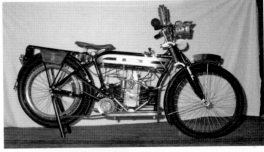

▶ **1923 Douglas 2¾hp,** 348cc overhead-valve flat-twin.
£3,000–3,500 / $4,400–5,000 ⊞ PS
Based in Bristol, Douglas Motors had the distinction of holding a Royal Warrant for supplying motorcycles to Prince Albert and Prince Henry in 1922, the former destined to become King George VI. Easy to start and very reliable, this particular model sold in very large numbers.

1950 Douglas Mk IVS, 348cc overhead-valve flat-twin, 60.8 x 60mm bore and stroke, magneto/dynamo mounted centrally on top of crankcases, 4-speed foot-change gearbox, chain final drive.
£1,800–2,000 / $2,600–3,000 ⊕ LDM
This bike was road tested by *The Motor Cycle* and was reviewed in the magazine of 16 March 1950.

Ducati *(Italian 1946–)*

1951 Ducati 65, 65cc overhead-valve unit-construction single, 2-speed foot-change gearbox, cantilever rear suspension with twin rear shock absorbers, telescopic front forks, single seat, parcel rack, very rare.
£1,000+ / $1,500+ ⊞ **MW**

> **Cross Reference**
> See Colour Review (page 51)

▶ **1954 Ducati 98TL,** 98cc overhead-valve unit single, alloy cylinder head, flywheel magneto ignition, 6bhp at 7,500rpm, 4-speed gearbox, completely restored to concours condition.
£1,800–1,900 / $2,600–2,750 ⊞ **MW**
Built from 1953 until 1958, the 98TL was designed before the famous engineer Fabio Taglioni joined the company. However, by the standards of the day, it was still an impressive design with a lively yet economical engine, and modern suspension with telescopic front forks and a swinging arm at the rear.

◀ **1957 Ducati 98TS,** 98cc overhead-valve unit single, 49 x 52mm bore and stroke, alloy cylinder head, 4-speed foot-change gearbox, full-width alloy brake hubs, full-cradle duplex frame, 2-tone dualseat, valanced mudguards.
£1,600–1,800
$2,300–2,600 ⊶ **IMOC**

▶ **1962 Ducati 250 Daytona,** 248cc bevel-driven overhead-camshaft unit single, 74 x 57.8mm bore and stroke, 20bhp, 4-speed gearbox, heel-and-toe gear-change, 84mph top speed, standard specification apart from alloy rims.
£2,600–2,800
$3,800–4,000 ⊞ **MW**
The Daytona (known as the Diana outside the UK) ran from 1961 until mid-1964.

◀ **c1964 Ducati Mach 1,** 248cc overhead-camshaft single, forged 3-ring piston, 10:1 compression ratio, large valves, 29mm Dell'Orto SS1 carburettor, 5-speed gearbox, clip-ons, rear-sets, racing-style seat, very original.
£5,000–6,000
$7,250–8,750 ⊞ **AtMC**
Introduced in the summer of 1964, the Mach 1 had a specification more akin to a racing bike than a roadster. This particular machine is fitted with the optional large Veglia racing tachometer and alloy wheel rims.

▶ **1970 Ducati 50 Scrambler,** 49cc single-cylinder piston-port 2-stroke, alloy head and barrel, flywheel magneto ignition, high-level exhaust, 3.25bhp at 6,500rpm, 4-speed gearbox, 19in wheels, full duplex frame, 50mph top speed, original and unrestored.
£600–700 / $870–1,000 ⊞ **MW**
The 50 Scrambler was only built in 1969 and 1970.

1969 Ducati 160 Monza Junior, 156cc overhead-camshaft single, 61 x 52mm bore and stroke, flywheel magneto ignition, 4-speed gearbox, battery for parking lights and horn.
£900–1,000 / $1,300–1,500 ⚒ **Bon**
Introduced in 1964, the Monza Junior was an interesting machine. Aimed at the American youth market, it combined an overbored Ducati 125cc engine with the frame of the 250 model. The wheel diameter was 16in, ensuring a low seat height. During 1966, the styling was revised, becoming more angular with a squared headlight surround. However, by this time, the demand from the American market had evaporated, resulting in large numbers of the final variant being offered on the British market at discounted prices well into the early 1970s.

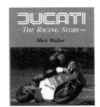

1972 Ducati 750GT, 748cc overhead-camshaft 90-degree V-twin, 80 x 74.4mm bore and stroke, wet-sump lubrication, 65–70bhp, 5-speed gearbox, 115mph top speed, US export model with Amal 930 (30mm) Concentric Mk I carburettors, Conti silencers, Lockheed front disc brake, full-width drum rear brake, Aprilia headlamp, side reflectors, larger rear lamp and stainless-steel mudguard.
£2,800–3,000 / $4,000–4,400 ⊞ **MW**

1974 Ducati 750 Sport, 748cc, standard specification apart from Lucas Rita ignition and 36mm (instead of 32mm) Dell'Orto PHF carburettors.
£5,000–6,500 / $7,250–8,700 ➢ Bon
Designed by the legendary Fabio Taglioni, Ducati's first road-going V-twin – the 750GT – arrived in 1971. The engine looked like two of the Bologna firm's bevel-driven overhead-camshaft singles on a common crankcase (which, in essence, it was), although the coil valve springs represented a departure from Ducati's traditional hairpins. The 90-degree layout made for exceptional smoothness and a lengthy wheelbase, a handicap more apparent than real, which failed to stop the fine handling Ducati V-twins from notching up a succession of wins in Formula 750 events, beginning with Paul Smart's famous victory at Imola in 1972. Smart's bike was based on th 750 Sport introduced that year. Built only until 1974, the Sport underwent minor changes to its front fork and disc brake, but otherwise changed little, and was only ever sold in the classic yellow/black livery shared with the Desmo singles. First of a line of sporting Ducati V-twins, the 750 Sport is a true landmark machine; much rarer than, for example, the later Mike Hailwood Replica, it is one of the most sought after of all Ducatis.

1977 Ducati 860GTS, 864cc overhead-camshaft valve-spring 90-degree V-twin, 86 x 74.4mm bore and stroke, electronic ignition, Conti silencers, twin-disc front brake, alloy rims.
£1,150–1,300 / $1,500–1,900 ⊞ PS
The GTS came from the débâcle of unsold 860GT models, which cluttered the Bologna factory during 1975. Some early models were converted GTs, others purpose-built machines. Later, the GTS became the 900 (still 864cc), with improvements to the engine and cycle parts.

1978 Ducati 900SS, 864cc 90-degree V-twin, desmodromic valve gear, aftermarket wire-wheel conversion, side panels missing, non-standard paint scheme.
£3,600–4,500 / $5,000–6,500 ➢ COYS
Ducati's road-going motorcycles have always reflected the Italian company's competition pedigree and, as a result, these high-performance machines have always been sought after. Much of the credit for the success of Ducati's road and racing machinery – particularly the lightweight singles and V-twins – is due to the legendary engineer Fabio Taglioni, who was responsible for the desmodromic valve actuation. Introduced in 1976, the 900SS, with a top speed of over 130mph, was tough competition for the Japanese, particularly in view of the beautiful Italian styling. This thoroughbred racing image was strengthened when Mike Hailwood rode a race prepped version to victory at the Isle of Man TT.

◀ **1978 Ducati 250 Strada,** 247cc overhead-camshaft valve-spring single, 74 x 37.8mm bore and stroke, 21bhp at 8,000rpm, 5-speed gearbox, in need of cosmetic restoration.
£800–900 / $1,150–1,300 ⊞ MW
The 250 Strada was Mototrans' own development of Ducati's 250 bevel single. There were many differences compared to the Italian version, including the frame, front forks, rear suspension, silencer, electrics, instrumentation and bodywork.

1979 Ducati Darmah SS, 864cc overhead-camshaft 90-degree V-twin, desmodromic valve gear, unrestored.
£3,200–3,800 / $4,700–5,500 ⊞ IVC
The SS version of the Darmah was only offered for some 18 months, approximately 550 being built. Changes to the original SD included a fairing, clip-ons, rear-sets, paintwork (metallic ice blue) and graphics.

1981 Ducati 900SS, 864cc 90-degree V-twin, desmodromic valve gear, Gold Line Brembo brake calipers, 6-bolt-hole discs, FPS cast alloy wheels.
£3,500–4,000 / $5,000–5,800 ✗ Bon
For 1981, Ducati updated its long running 900SS (Super Sport). This was essentially a cosmetic operation and centred on the design of a new dualseat, revised graphics and a silver paint finish for the fairing, tank, seat tail and side panels.

◄ **1981 Ducati 500SL Pantah,** 499cc belt-driven overhead-camshaft V-twin, desmodromic valve gear, 52bhp at 9,000rpm, original Conti 2-into-1 exhaust with central collector box, 5-speed gearbox, electric starter, mechanically operated clutch.
£1,900–2,300 / $2,750–3,350 ⊞ MW
This is a Series 2 machine, which used the 600SL-type fairing.

▶ **1982 Ducati Mike Hailwood Replica 900,** 864cc unit-construction 90-degree V-twin, desmodromic valve gear, Silentium silencers, 5-speed gearbox, wet multiple clutch, triple Brembo 6-bolt-hole disc brakes, FPS cast alloy wheels, 38mm Marzocchi front forks, rear swinging arm with twin shock absorbers, dual/single seat, multi-piece fairing, 130mph top speed, very original.
£5,500–6,000 / $8,000–8,700 ⊞ NLM
The MHR was offered originally in 1979 in recognition of Mike Hailwood's famous comeback victory in the Isle of Man that year.

 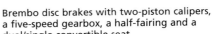

Miller's
Motorcycle Milestones

Ducati 500SL Pantah (Italian 1979)
Price range: £1,500–2,400 / $2,200–3,500
During the mid-1970s, Ducati's state owned corporate body decided it had to have a middleweight parallel twin so that the Italian marque could take on the Japanese. However, chief designer Fabio Taglioni was against this plan from the start, wanting instead to build a scaled-down version of his existing 90-degree V-twin. Just as Taglioni had believed, the parallel twin proved a major sales disaster. This resulted in him finally being given authority to proceed with his smaller-capacity V-twin. The outcome was the Pantah, which became father to all the belt-driven overhead-camshaft Desmo V-twins that followed, including today's superbike family of street and racing bikes.
First seen in prototype guise during 1977, the Pantah entered production in 1979 as the 500SL. It featured 74 x 58mm bore and stroke dimensions, Ducati sources claiming 50bhp at 9,000rpm. Other standard features included an electric starter, 18in cast alloy wheels, triple

Brembo disc brakes with two-piston calipers, a five-speed gearbox, a half-fairing and a dual/single convertible seat.
The 1979 machine was finished in red with silver lining, but it was not imported into the UK. From the 1980 model year, a new metallic ice blue colour scheme was used with red and blue striping. A Mk 2 version was introduced for 1981; this employed new fairing (with a bottom 'lip' from the 600SL, which had also arrived that year), improvements to the gearbox and some other minor changes. The new 600 version, still coded SL, was the first Ducati production model to feature a hydraulic clutch.
By 1983, a 350SL had been added. Also new that year were the touring-specification 350XL and 600TL versions, and the 650SL (the last of the line). Production ceased in 1986.
The other Pantah was the 600TT F2 racer. This version sported a special Verlicchi-made frame, with monoshock rear suspension. The Englishman Tony Rutter won no fewer than four world championship titles during the early 1980s on the TT F2.

Dunelt *(British 1919–35, 1957)*

◄ **1924 Dunelt,** 246cc 2-stroke single, hand-change gearbox, chain final drive, electric lighting.
£1,150–1,380 / $1,500–2,000 ✓ Bon
Marketed as 'the supercharged two-stroke', the Dunelt featured a double-diameter piston and had a power output that exceeded many comparable four-stroke machines. By 1925, all Dunelt models featured chain drive and mechanical lubrication via a Pilgrim pump.

1926 Dunelt Model G, 499cc 2-stroke split single.
£3,600–4,000 / $5,000–5,800 ⚙ BTSC
Thanks to the engine design and a massive external flywheel, the Dunelt Model G could pull like a steam engine from very low speeds. This made it an ideal motorcycle for sidecar work; in fact, it was offered as a complete outfit by the company.

Excelsior *(British 1896–1964)*

1922 Excelsior V-twin, 770cc JAP side-valve V-twin engine.
£6,000–7,000 / $8,750–10,250 ✓ Bon
An early manufacturer in both the motorcycle and car fields, the Coventry firm of Bayliss and Thomas was an established concern before WWI, at one time making an 800cc single-cylinder motorcycle under the name of Excelsior. In common with many marques, Excelsior used proprietary engines made by Blackburne and J. A. Prestwich. By 1914, it was listing a JAP powered twin, and in 1915–16 had prepared prototypes and production 8hp models for supply to the Imperial Russian government, although it seems that the firm was left with many machines. Post-war, to avoid confusion with the American Excelsior, Bayliss and Thomas christened its twin the 'British Excelsior'. It was fitted with the 6hp side-valve engine and a Sturmey Archer gearbox. For the 1922–23 season, this was replaced by JAP's 8hp twin. This example is the much rarer first version of the post-war twin.

◀ **1935 Excelsior Manxman E12,** 349cc bevel-driven overhead-camshaft single, 75 x 79mm bore and stroke, fully enclosed valve gear.
£7,000–8,000 / $10,500–11,500 ⮷ **EXM**
This early long-stroke engine was conceived by Excelsior's managing director, Eric Walker, designed by Ike Hatch and made at Blackburne's factory at Bookham, Surrey.

1954 Excelsior Consort, 98cc Villiers 2-stroke single, rigid frame.
£400–480 / $580–700 ⮷ **PS**

◀ **1954 Excelsior D12 Condor,** 122cc Villiers 13D 2-stroke engine, girder forks, rigid frame.
£400–500 / $580–720 ⮷ **BTSC**
This model was only produced for 1954.

FB Mondial *(Italian 1948–79)*

A known continuous history can add value to and enhance the enjoyment of a motorcycle.

▶ **1952 FB Mondial 125 MT,** 124cc overhead-valve unit single, 4-speed gearbox, plunger rear suspension, blade girder front forks, full duplex frame.
£1,800–2,400 / $2,600–3,500 ⊞ **MW**
'MT' stood for Milan-Taranto, which, like the equally famous Moto Giro, was a long-distance road event held in Italy every year until the end of the 1950s.

Francis-Barnett *(British 1919–64)*

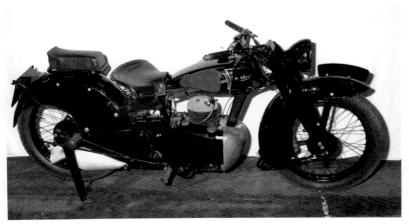

◀ **1934 Francis-Barnett Cruiser Model 39,** 249cc Villiers 2-stroke single, 63 x 80mm bore and stroke, 4-speed hand-change gearbox, blade girder front forks.
£540–600
$785–870 ⊞ **PS**
The frame of the Cruiser featured an I-section forging that formed the head lug and downtube. From the lug, two channel-section members ran back under the tank to the rear wheel. The engine was enclosed.

1957 Francis-Barnett Falcon, 197cc Villiers 8E 2-stroke single-cylinder engine, one owner from new.
£225–250 / $325–360 ⊞ PS

1959 Francis-Barnett Light Cruiser 79, 171cc AMC 2-stroke single, telescopic front forks, swinging-arm rear suspension, good condition.
£270–300 / $400–450 ⊞ PS

▶ **1961 Francis-Barnett Cruiser Twin,** 247cc Villiers 2T 2-stroke engine, 4-speed foot-change gearbox, full-width brake hubs.
£800–1,200 / $1,150–1,750 ⊞ BLM

Gilera *(Italian 1909–)*

1950 Gilera Saturno Sport, 498.76cc overhead-valve single, 84 x 90mm bore and stroke, hairpin valve springs, alloy head, iron barrel, forward mounted mag/dyno, 22bhp at 3,000rpm, 4-speed foot-change gearbox with rocking pedal, 78mph top speed.
£5,500–6,000 / $8,000–8,700 ⊞ NLM

1953 Gilera 150 Sport, 150cc overhead-valve unit-construction single, wet-sump lubrication, 4-speed gearbox, one owner from new.
£1,700–2,200 / $2,500–3,200 ⋏ Bon
This particular bike was given by Guiseppe Gilera to Austin Monks, who had arranged Geoff Duke's ride with the Italian company; it was offered with its original log book recording Austin Monks as its sole owner.

1959 Gilera B300, 305cc overhead-valve unit-construction parallel twin, parallel valves, rear-facing spark plugs, 60 x 54mm bore and stroke, alloy head, iron barrel, wet-sump lubrication, 15bhp at 6,800 rpm, 4-speed gearbox, full-width brake hubs, Silentium chrome-steel silencers, 78mph top speed.
£1,200–1,500 / $1,750–2,200 ⊞ NLM
The B300 ran from 1953 until 1969.

1959 Gilera Giubeleo, 98cc overhead-valve unit-construction single, 50 x 50mm bore and stroke, 7.8:1 compression ratio, 5.8bhp at 7,000rpm, 4-speed gearbox, primary drive by gears, final drive chain, 49mph top speed, concours condition.
£1,200–1,900 / $1,750–2,750 ⊞ IMOC

Greeves *(British 1952–78)*

1960 Greeves 24 DB Sports, 246cc Villiers 31A 2-stroke single-cylinder engine, 66 x 72mm bore and stroke, completely restored 1995.
£1,200–1,400 / $1,750–2,000 🏍 **GRA**
The 24 DB ran from 1959 through to 1961.

1964 Greeves Essex, Villiers 2T 2-stroke twin-cylinder engine, piston-port induction, alloy heads, iron barrels, finished in Greeves Morland blue, concours condition.
£1,200–1,400 / $1,750–2,000 🏍 **CGC**

Harley-Davidson *(American 1903–)*

The Harley-Davidson marque's logo is a proud 'Number 1', and this is fully deserved, as in terms of American motorcycles, it reflects the company's position. In fact, Harley has become a true icon. From movie stars to GIs, from Hells Angels to policemen, from farmers to politicians, anyone who wants to enhance their image rides a Harley-Davidson. More than any other motorcycle, the Harley-Davidson evokes unsurpassed style and glamour. And the Harley story is unique; from humble beginnings in a small shed in Milwaukee, the marque has conquered the world. During its 100-year history, the company has survived the ravages of depression, an influx of foreign imports from Europe and Japan, and take-over. Perhaps most amazing is that the machines Harley-Davidson has created rarely used the most up-to-date technology. Instead, the American company has generated its own traditions of styling and engineering, consistently building motorcycles that have appealed to the rugged individualism that is at the heart of American culture. The popular J-series V-twin range, for example,

saw Harley-Davidson through some of its most difficult times during the late 1920s, while the classic WL (A-America/C-Canada) military bikes were built in countless thousands during the 1940s. By the 1950s, the Harley brand name was well established, and classic bikes such as the Duo-Glide, Electra Glide and Sportster helped seal the reputation. Additionally, first the side-valve and later the overhead-valve V-twins garnered much racing success on both dirt and tarmac. Harleys have been raced since the early days. The great Joe Petrali in the 1930s, Joe Leonard in the 1950s, Cal Rayborn in the 1960s and 1970s, and after that the wonderful Jay Springsteen, have all added to the Harley aura. Even that master showman Evil Knievel used Harley machinery in his death-defying stunts. Finally, mention must be made of the customisers who have created dream bikes for the masses of Harley-Davidson enthusiasts at the annual gatherings at Sturgis and Daytona, not forgetting the various Harley-Davidson owners' clubs, which have sprung up around the globe to foster a unique camaraderie among enthusiasts.

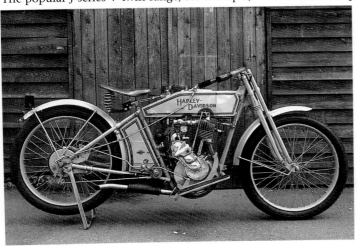

◄ **1914 Harley-Davidson CI0 Single,** 499cc 4-stroke single, integral iron cylinder and head, heat treated steel piston, chrome steel I-beam conrod, separate camshafts for inlet and exhaust valves, Bosch high-tension magneto, concours condition.
£70,000+ / $100,000+ ⊞ **Warr**
This series of single-cylinder models was known collectively as the 5-35, which stood for 5hp and 35cu.in (or 3,500rpm). This example is one of the rare two-speed models, which appeared in 1914 as a single (the CI0) and a V-twin. This was for one year only, as the singles and twins were all equipped with a three-speed transmission by 1915. The 5-35 series ran from 1913 to 1918.

◀ **1917 Harley-Davidson 17J,** 987.67cc V-twin engine.
£20,000–25,000 / $30,000–36,000 ↗ **Bon**
By 1917, Harley-Davidson had already established a certain formula for the vast majority of its motorcycles. The engine was a V-twin, which is still the case with Harley-Davidsons rolling out of Milwaukee and York, Pennsylvania, 84 years later. In the case of the 17J, the engine featured a 45-degree layout and was an F-head configuration. For the first time, however, the valve springs were enclosed. The 987.67cc engine produced 16bhp at 3,000rpm, breathing through a Schebler carburettor. This model benefited from Harley-Davidson's racing experience, being fitted with the four-lobe camshaft designed for the company's eight-valve racing bikes. In addition, like all Harley V-twins since 1915, a gear-driven oil pump took care of lubrication.

1927 Harley-Davidson Model U, 1200cc inlet-over-exhaust V-twin engine, chain final drive, drum rear brakes, footboards, fully restored to concours condition.
£12,300–13,500 / $18,000–20,000 ⊞ **NLM**

Cross Reference
For more Harley-Davidsons see Dirt Bikes, Racing Bikes, Sidecars & Colour Reviews

1964 Harley-Davidson Service Car, 1213cc V-twin, foot-change gearbox, tank mounted instruments.
£5,200–6,200 / $7,500–9,000 ↗ **COYS**
The Harley-Davidson has become a legendary symbol of American design in the same league as the Coca-Cola bottle and Levis jeans. Because we associate the Harley with its *Rebel Without a Cause* image (even though Brando actually rode a Triumph), we forget that American public services used this icon of rebellion for much more mundane purposes. This particular service car is just such an example. The three-wheeler was made in small numbers for meter maids and police departments. It came with reverse gear and an electric starter, which was not available on standard bikes of that period.

1965 Harley-Davidson Electra Glide, 1200cc overhead-valve V-twin, 4-speed foot-change gearbox, screen, spot lamps, crash bars, top box and panniers, whitewall tyres, direction indicators, concours condition.
£8,000–10,000 / $11,500–14,500 ⊞ **MW**
This was the first year of electric starting, hence the Electra name.

1969 Harley-Davidson Sprint H, 344cc overhead-valve unit-construction flat single, fully enclosed alloy cylinder head, wet-sump lubrication, 5-speed gearbox, concours condition.
£2,500–2,800 / $3,600–4,000 ⊞ MW
This open-frame model was built in the Italian Aermacchi factory for sale in the USA.

Healey *(British 1968–74)*

1973 Healey 1000/4, 995cc Ariel 4G Mk 2 Square Four engine, 65 x 75mm bore and stroke, 42bhp at 5,800rpm, 4-speed foot-change gearbox, Italian Grimeca brakes, spine frame.
£11,000–12,000 / $16,000–17,500 ⊚⊚ AOM
The Healey was built in small numbers in Redditch by brothers Tim and George Healey during the 1960s and early 1970s. This particular machine was the first production bike of approximately 12 constructed.

Henderson *(American 1912–31)*

1913 Henderson, 1068cc inlet-over-exhaust 4-cylinder inline engine, hand-change gearbox, Cowey 0–80mph speedometer, P&U acetylene headlamp and generator, Gloriaphone hand klaxon.
£31,000–37,000 / $45,000–54,000 ✗ Bon
W. G. 'Bill' Henderson's first four-cylinder motorcycle appeared in 1911, a sensational new design with four separate, air-cooled cylinders arranged in line and featuring overhead inlet valves with side exhaust valves. It was mounted in a particularly long-wheelbase frame, and early models had a cylinder capacity of 1086cc. On the British market, the Henderson was priced at £81 18s in 1913, by no means inexpensive. Transmission was by chain in conventional manner, and the elastic double front fork was simple and pleasing in appearance, 'there being no complication of trusses, exposed springs and projecting parts'. The Henderson was commonly accepted to be the Rolls-Royce of American motorcycles, and in the UK it had no equal. The footboards in place of conventional footrests allow the rider to sit in a more comfortable position with feet forward, thus avoiding the heat of the motor.

Hesketh *(British 1981–)*

1987 Hesketh V1000, 992cc double-overhead-camshaft unit-construction V-twin, 5-speed constant-mesh gearbox, 43mm forks with custom yokes machined from solid aluminium with full preload and damping adjustment, rear Marzocchi suspension with two-way damping, twin front disc brakes, single rear disc.
£5,000+ / $7,250+ ✗ C

In the early 1980s, Lord Hesketh, following his privateer success in Formula 1, channelled his enthusiasm and engineering facilities into buildng a motorcycle of the highest quality, in an attempt to revive the British bike industry. Developed on the Hesketh estate at Easton Neston, the prototype appeared in spring 1980. In many ways, it was a revolution in British manufacture, as it was powered by a four-valve-per-cylinder, double-overhead-camshaft engine among other innovative high-tech features. However, the project lacked funding, and while some support came from the City of London to establish Hesketh Motorcycles, there was not enough money or time to organise production properly before the company fell victim to the early 1980s recession. Only 100 V1000 motorbikes were actually built, but the buyers of these required support and back-up, so the decision was made for the development team to continue to provide this. Between 1982–84, further V1000s were constructed under the name Hesleydon. Since that time, all development, production and support has been provided by Broom Development Engineering, and today production still continues with an output of approximately 12 machines per year.

► **1985 Hesketh Vampire,** 992cc double-overhead-camshaft 90-degree V-twin, 5-speed gearbox, Brembo brakes, 38mm Marzocchi front forks, nickel plated Reynolds 531 frame.
£3,000–4,000 / $4,400–5,800 ✗ Bon
The Vampire evolved after the main Hesketh production had come to an end. Built by Mick Broom at Easton Neston, the stately home of Lord Hesketh, the Vampire was noted for its comprehensive body panels and large fairing, which afforded the rider excellent weather protection.

Honda *(Japanese 1946–)*

1964 Honda C50 Cub, 49cc overhead-valve horizontal 2-stroke single, dualseat, leg shields, unrestored, original specification.
£250–400 / $360–580 ⊞ MAY
The C50 was the first of the famous 'step-thru' models, and it really put Honda on the map when it first appeared towards the end of the 1950s. Subsequently, millions were sold all around the world.

1965 Honda C102, 49cc overhead-valve horizontal single, enclosed final drive chain, leg shields, indicators, mirrors, original specification, concours condition.
£1,000–1,200 / $1,500–1,750 ⚙ VJMC
The Honda 'step-thru' series was responsible for the Honda advertising slogan, 'You meet the nicest people on a Honda'. Eventually, the range embraced 50, 70 and 100cc versions.

1972 Honda CL360, 360cc single-overhead-camshaft parallel twin, 2 CV carburettors, chrome mudguards, mirror, indicators, matching speedometer and rev-counter, US model with high-level exhaust.
£1,700–1,900 / $2,450–2,750 ⊞ NLM

◄ **1968 Honda CB250,** 249cc single-overhead-camshaft parallel twin, wet-sump lubrication, 5-speed gearbox, wet multiple clutch, electric starter, full-width alloy brake hubs, front gaiters, matching speedometer and rev-counter, fully restored, concours condition.
£800–1,200 / $1,150–1,750 ⅄ Bon
Introduced in 1968 alongside a street scrambler variant, a touring CD version and two similar models displacing 350cc, the CB250 featured new styling and a revised set of cycle parts. The frame was a full loop, instead of the spine type that had graced the CB72, and housed an engine that, although similar to the previous model in general layout, had been revised slightly with the cylinders in a more upright position.

1976 Honda CB750, 736cc single-overhead-camshaft across-the-frame four, electric starter, dry-sump lubrication, disc front brake, unrestored, very good original condition.
£2,000–2,500 / $3,000–3,600 ⅄ Bon
One of the last of the original sohc CB750s in four-pipe European guise to be sold, this machine was recently imported from Holland, where it had been kept since new.

Miller's
Motorcycle Milestones

Honda CB750 (Japanese 1969)
Price range: £2,000–4,000 / $3,000–5,800
The Honda CB750 of 1969 ushered in the era of the affordable modern superbike in the UK and created standards for the big-bike market that the opposition – mainly British at the time – simply couldn't match.
Not only was there a 750 four-cylinder engine, but also a five-speed gearbox, front disc brake, full-cradle frame, large matching speedo and tacho, four-pipe exhaust, electric starter, indicators and twin mirrors.
Moreover, the 736cc (61 x 63mm) across-the-frame four could reach 125mph in total comfort, so it was a bike with wide appeal. As one journalist reported, 'It was reliable, clean and civilized, as well as docile at low speed.' The only area in which the big Honda couldn't match the likes of the BSA Rocket 3 or Triumph Trident was in handling.

The new engine used well-tried Honda technology, such as horizontally-split crankcases, two valves per cylinder and a single overhead camshaft driven by a cam chain (placed centrally between the cylinders). There were also four carburettors and reliable 12 volt electrics.
The CB750 was so successful that not only did it sire a series of Honda four-cylinder models, but also created the UJM (Universal Japanese Motorcycle), with Kawasaki, Suzuki and Yamaha all eventually employing the same across-the-frame, four-cylinder design formula.
Honda also produced its own variations on the theme, including a version of the single-overhead-camshaft four in detuned 47bhp form. By the late 1970s, the company had introduced a double-overhead-camshaft, 16-valve replacement. To many, however, the original CB750 is a historic motorcycle – the first of a new breed.

◄ **1980 Honda CB900F Super Sport,** 900cc double-overhead-camshaft four, 4 valves per cylinder, 64.2 x 69mm bore and stroke, air-assisted 39mm front forks, Comstar-type wheels, 128mph top speed.
£1,800–2,000 / $2,600–3,000 ⅄ CGC
Introduced in 1979, the CB900F was a larger-engined version of Honda's highly regarded CB750F double-overhead-camshaft, 16-valve model, the two machines sharing the same basic chassis design. The CB900F's engine was developed from a version of the existing CB900 Custom's powerplant, but with a 530 chain replacing the C-model's shaft.

1980 Honda CB650, 650cc, chopper style with 4-into-1 exhaust, peanut tank, Comstar wheels, raked and extended front forks, leather saddle bags, fork mounted custom roll, custom-made saddle, small chrome headlamp, one-off side panels, pillion grab rail and disc brakes.
£1,200–1,500 / $1,750–2,200 ⊞ MAY

Miller's is a price GUIDE not a price LIST

1982 Honda XL 500S, 498cc overhead-camshaft 4-valve twin-port single, alloy head and barrel, 5-speed gearbox, branched exhaust header pipe, plastic front mudguard, non-welled alloy front rim, knobbly tyres, rev-counter, direction indicators, original specification.
£1,500–1,700 / $2,150–2,450 ⊞ MW

Humber *(British 1900–30)*

▶ **1924 Humber 2¾hp,** 349cc side-valve vertical single, hand-change gearbox, flat tank, rigid frame, original, unrestored.
£4,000–4,600 / $5,800–6,500 ⊁ Bon
Humber Motorcycles of Coventry enjoyed a glorious success in 1923 with the 2¾hp model, which, following its successes in the Scottish Six Days Trials and the ACU English Six Days Trials, was designated the 'Six Days' Model. In the English Trials, each rider in the Humber team secured the coveted First Class Gold Medal, while the team was nominated as the winners in the 'Crack' Class of the Trials.

Husqvarna *(Swedish 1903–)*

1929 Husqvarna V-Twin, 600cc narrow-angle side-valve V-twin, rear mounted magneto, chain final drive, footboards, carrier, leather side bags, single sprung saddle, complete but in need of restoration.
£4,500–5,500 / $6,500–8,000 ⊞ VER

Indian (*American 1901–53*)

◄ **1925 Indian Wall of Death Scout,** 750cc narrow-angle V-twin, hand-change gearbox, leaf-spring front suspension, rigid frame.
£4,400–4,700 / $6,400–6,800 ➶ Bon
Indian's 1920s Scout was the work of Charles B. Franklin, the company's prolific designer. It was a success from the start, being a mainstay of the range for years and providing the basis for the WWII 741B. The Indian motorcycle, in particular the Scout, became synonymous with one once-famous area of motorcycle sport, the circus or fairground Wall of Death. Short, relatively light and with enormous 'grunt', the invariably red Indians rumbled around the vertical wooden cylinders, many still being in use in the trade.

1939 Indian Chief, 1200cc, side-valve twin, unrestored, excellent mechanical condition.
£4,000–5,000 / $5,800–7,250 ⊞ MW

1940 Indian Chief, 1200cc side-valve V-twin, drum brakes, sprung saddle, front and rear crash bars.
£35,000–42,000 / $50,000–60,000 ➶ Bon
Indian revised the styling of their V-twin range leader, the Chief, for the 1940 model season, and in doing so created a style icon that endures to this day. New mudguards with deep skirts combined with an elegant chain enclosure to produce a smooth, flowing line. The alterations to the model's appearance were complemented by changes to the cycle parts, which enhanced rider comfort. Wider-section tyres became a standard fitting, and undamped, plunger rear suspension replaced the earlier rigid rear end. The frame geometry was also altered to enhance stability at high speeds. This Chief was previously owned by the actor Steve McQueen, who represented the United Stated at the International Six Days Trial riding a Triumph.

1942 Indian 741B, 500cc, restored after WWII for civilian use.
£5,400–6,000 / $8,000–8,700 ⬥ IMC

Miller's Motorcycle Milestones

Indian Four (American 1928)
Price range: £5,000–20,000 / $7,250–29,000
Some 12,000 Indian Fours were built between the late 1920s and early 1940s, and even though it had rather strange origins and was far from perfect, remaining examples are highly prized today. Actually, the design dates back to 1912 and the Henderson badge, and at the time, there was no connection with its ultimate home. But Henderson was under-capitalized, resulting in a buy-out by the Schwinn concern, which made the American Excelsior machines. As for William Henderson, he created a new machine, the Ace, which was launched in 1920.
Even then, that was not the end of the saga, as the Ace company was sold in 1924 to Michigan Motors – before finally ending up in the hands of Indian during 1927.
The first Indian Four (marketed as the Collegiate Four) was essentially the Ace with a different tank badge, but it was slowly developed by Indian, receiving an S-bearing crankshaft in 1929; then, in 1932, a new frame arrived.
The engine was always a 1265cc (69.9 x 82.6mm) unit and air cooled. At first, it featured an inlet-over-exhaust (ioe) arrangement for the valves, but in 1936 an unusual exhaust-over-inlet (ioe) set-up was adopted.
Finally, in 1938, the motor was redesigned for improved reliability with better cooling and lubrication as priorities.
The Four's main attributes were connected with the powerplant's great flexibility, top-gear performance ranging from 5 to 100mph. But its main drawback – overheating – remained. Weighing in at around 440lb (200kg), the machine had its cylinders arranged lengthways, a chain final drive and a three-speed hand-change gearbox.
Production came to an end in 1942.

Italjet *(Italian 1966–)*

◄ **1977 Italjet Buccaneer,** 124cc 2-stroke twin, 43 x 43mm bore and stroke, pump lubrication, 16bhp at 8,500rpm, 5-speed gearbox.
£1,200–1,600 / $1,750–2,300 ⚙ IMOC
Designed by Italjet boss Leo Tartarini, the Buccaneer had a full-cradle duplex frame, a Yamaha RD125 air-cooled twin-cylinder engine, disc front brake and drum rear brake. This machine is probably the only example in the UK.

Itom *(Italian 1944–67)*

1966 Itom Mk 8 Competition, 49cc 2-stroke single, alloy head, iron barrel, 4-speed foot-change gearbox, telescopic forks, rear swinging arm, racing seat, clip-ons, tyre pump, concours condition.
£2,200–2,650 / $3,200–3,800 ➹ RM
The first Itom engine was designed just before the end of the war and was fitted on top of the front wheel to create the 'clip-on' moped. A second version was made to fit over the rear wheel, and this unit was copied exactly in moped-mad post-war Britain as the Power Pak. In 1955, the first Itom 50cc motorcycle appeared. This machine had a pressed-steel frame and telescopic forks with a three-speed transmission. Later in 1955, a tubular frame was introduced. This machine was called the Sports Model and had larger-diameter 22in wheels. February 1957 saw the introduction of the new Super Sport and Competition models. The Mark 8 Competition model, or Mighty Itom as it was called in the Italian promotional material, was very competitive as a 50cc over-the-counter racer. Ride to the track or hill, remove the tool box, lights, speedo and exhaust pipe, and you were ready to race.

IZH *(Russian 1933–)*

Restored values
The cost of a professional restoration will have an influence on, but no direct relation to, a motorcycle's market value. A restored motorcycle can have a market value lower than the cost of its restoration.

▶ **1981 IZH 350,** 346cc 2-stroke single, alloy head and barrel, 4-speed gearbox, full-width brake hubs.
£270–300 / $390–440 ⚙ CMAN

Colour Review

1960s Aermacchi Ala Verde, 246cc overhead-valve horizontal single, megaphone exhaust, twin-leading-shoe front brake, Hagon rear shock absorbers, alloy rims, Veglia racing tachometer, café-racer styling.
£2,500–3,000 / $3,500–4,500 ⊞ **MW**

▶ **1960 AJS Model 31,** 646cc overhead-valve parallel twin, siamesed exhaust, fitted with sports CSR engine, otherwise standard specification.
£2,700–3,200 / $4,000–4,750 ⊞ **BLM**

1951 Ariel 4G Mk I Square Four, 998cc overhead-valve 4-cylinder engine, 2-pipe exhaust, distributor electrics, 4-speed foot-change gearbox, plunger rear suspension, correct valanced front mudguard, restored.
£4,000–4,500 / $5,800–6,500 ⊞ **BLM**

◄ **1951 BSA Bantam D1,**
123cc 2-stroke single,
piston-port induction,
3-speed gearbox, plunger
rear suspension, undamped
telescopic front forks,
concours condition.
**£1,000–1,200
$1,500–1,750 ⊞ BLM
The Bantam was derived
from the 1939 DKW RT125.**

► **1969 BSA Rocket 3 Mk I,**
744cc overhead-valve
triple, 4-speed gearbox,
immaculate example.
**£4,500–5,000
$6,500–7,250 ⊞ PM
This was the first year
of production with
a twin-leading-shoe
drum front brake and
'ray-gun' silencers.**

◄ **1992 Cagiva Mito Lawson Series 1,**
124cc single-cylinder liquid-cooled
2-stroke, reed-valve induction and
power valve, 30bhp, 100mph, 7-speed
gearbox, monoshock rear suspension,
3-spoke cast alloy wheels.
**£900–1,100 / $1,300–1,600 ⊞ MW
The Mito Lawson was a limited-
production machine intended for
sports-racing or fast road work.**

1959 Ceccato 125T, 124cc overhead-valve unit single, wet-sump lubrication, 9bhp, 4-speed gearbox, 63mph top speed,
concours condition.
£1,600–1,800 / $2,300–2,600 ⊞ MW

1966 Ducati 160 Monza Junior, 156cc bevel-driven overhead-camshaft single, narrow-case engine, Dell'Orto 22UB carburettor, wet-sump lubrication, 4-speed gearbox, 16in wheels, full nut-and-bolt restoration.
£1,200–1,400 / $1,750–2,000 ⊞ MW

1970 Ducati 350 Mk 3D, 340cc wide-case engine, 31.5mm front forks, stainless-steel mudguards, matching speedometer and rev-counter, concours condition.
£2,800–3,000 / $4,000–4,500 ⊞ MW
Towards the end of the 1960s, the Italian Ducati company became the first motorcycle manufacturer in the world to offer series-production models with desmodromic (Desmo) engines.

◄ **1972 Ducati 24 Hours,** 246cc overhead-valve single, 69 x 66mm bore and stroke, Spanish Amal carburettor, 5-speed gearbox, concours condition.
£2,000–2,100
$2,900–3,000 ⊞ MW
Built at the Spanish Mototrans factory in Barcelona, the 24 Hours was considerably different from the conventional Italian made Ducati overhead-valve singles. Not only was the bore and stroke different, but so were many of the cycle parts, including the front forks, wheels, tank, seat and mudguards.

1974 Ducati 250 Desmo Disc, 248cc single, bevel-driven camshaft, desmodromic valve gear, 74 x 57.8mm bore and stroke, Marzocchi 35mm forks, Grimeca 180mm double-sided drum front brake, subject of nut-and-bolt restoration, concours condition.
£4,000+ / $5,800+ ⊞ MW

1973 Harley-Davidson SS 350, 344cc overhead-valve unit-construction horizontal single, 5-speed foot-change gearbox, twin-leading-shoe front brake, 12 volt electrics, electric start, full cradle frame.
£2,000–2,600 / $3,000–3,800 ⊞ MW
This model was built at the old Aermacchi plant in Varese, Italy.

1978 Laverda Jota, 981cc triple, 3-into-1 exhaust, cast alloy wheels, triple Brembo disc brakes, ND Denso instrumentation, one owner from new, original condition.
£3,150–3,500 / $4,500–5,000 ⑯ ILO

1974 Laverda 750 SFC, 744cc overhead-camshaft twin, 4-bearing 360-degree crankshaft, 80 x 74mm bore and stroke, basically standard apart from black painted exhaust, front mudguard and drilled aluminium footrests.
£8,000–8,800 / $11,600–12,750 ⊞ MW
This was the first year of the disc-braked SFC model.

1960 Matchless G80, 498cc overhead-valve pre-unit single, 4-speed foot-change gearbox, Amal Concentric carburettor, otherwise standard specification.
£2,500–3,000 / $3,600–4,400 ⊞ BLM
This heavyweight AMC single gained an excellent reputation for reliability, achieving success in both trials and scrambles.

◄ **1961 Matchless G2,** 248.5cc overhead-valve semi-unit single, 69.85 x 64.85mm bore and stroke, very good condition.
£800–1,000
$1,200–1,500 ⊞ BLM
The 'Lightweight' series (which also included the 350G3/Model 16) was never as popular as the 'Heavyweight' 350/500 range.

► **1962 Matchless G50 CSR,** 496cc overhead-camshaft single, Amal GP carburettor, kickstarter, 4-speed foot-change AMC gearbox, full lighting equipment, dualseat, alloy mudguards, concours condition.
£15,000+ / $22,000+ ⊞ MW
The G50 CSR was built in very small numbers to homologate it for AMA (American Motorcycle Association) events in the United States. It employed a G50 racing engine in a road-going Matchless chassis. Today, examples are extremely rare.

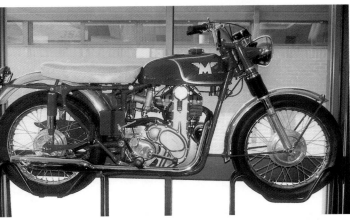

1982 Moto Guzzi V50 Mk III, 490cc overhead-valve 90-degree V-twin, 47bhp (crank reading), 5-speed gearbox, shaft final drive, triple Brembo disc brakes.
£1,600–1,800 / $2,300–2,600 ⊞ NLM
The much improved V50 III went on sale in 1981. It had points instead of electronic ignition – needed to cure a flat spot that blighted the earlier V50 series. The carburettor size increased from 24 to 28mm, and the machine had a new seat and silencers.

1976 Moto Guzzi Le Mans I, 844cc overhead-valve 90-degree V-twin, 70bhp, 5-speed gearbox, shaft final drive, 125mph top speed, cast alloy wheels, 'bikini' fairing, indicators, original specification.
£4,000–4,500 / $5,800–6,500 ⊞ MW
This was the first year of production for the Le Mans, and to many it was the best of the series.

1975 Moto Morini 3½ Strada 1st Series, 344cc overhead-valve 72-degree V-twin, Heron heads, parallel valves, drum brakes, wire wheels, stainless-steel mudguards and chainguard.
£2,200–2,500 / $3,200–3,600 ⊞ NLM
The Strada was jointly designed by Gianni Marchesini and Franco Lambertini Jnr.

◄ **1984 Moto Morini 500 Camel SIA,** 478.6cc V-twin, 6-speed gearbox.
£2,200–2,500
$3,200–3,600 ⊞ **NLM**
This is the Mk 2 version with revised styling from the 350 Kanguro, but without the latter's mono-shock rear suspension. It was replaced at the end of 1984 by the 507cc Camel 501 with monoshock rear end.

1975 MV Agusta 750S, 743cc double-overhead-camshaft across-the-frame 4-cylinder engine, 65 x 56mm bore and stroke, Magni exhaust, shaft final drive, twin front discs, wire wheels with alloy rims.
£13,000–14,000 / $19,000–20,000 ⊞ **VER**

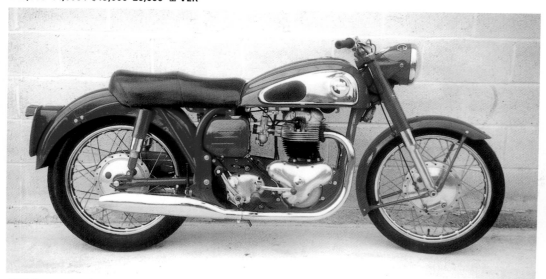

1958 Norton Dominator 88, 497cc overhead-valve pre-unit twin, 4-speed gearbox, Roadholder front forks, wideline frame, full-width hubs, dualseat, concours condition.
£3,750–3,950 / $5,500–5,800 ⊞ **BLM**

◄ **1975 Norton Commando Roadster,** 828cc overhead-valve twin, twin Amal Concentric Mk I carburettors, 4-speed gearbox, front and rear disc brakes, JPS colour scheme, original specification.
£3,500–4,000 / $5,000–5,800 ⊞ **BLM**

1963 Parilla Sports Special, 174cc high-camshaft unit single, Dell'Orto carburettor, telescopic front forks, rear swinging arm, full-width aluminium brake hubs, dualseat.
£2,500–2,800 / $3,600–4,000 ⅗ **IMOC**
This machine is designed so that the engine is used as a stressed member.

1911 Premier, 499cc side-valve single, iron head and barrel, rear mounted magneto ignition, pedal starting, belt final drive, caliper brakes.
£5,500–6,000 / $8,000–8,700 ⊞ **VER**

◄ **1961 Royal Enfield Constellation,** 692cc overhead-valve parallel twin, separate cylinders and heads, dry-sump lubrication with oil container inside engine, 4-speed gearbox with neutral finder, original specification apart from painted mudguards and crash bars.
£2,700–3,200 / $4,000–4,700 ⊞ **PM**

1965 Royal Enfield Turbo Twin Sports, 249cc Villiers 4T twin-cylinder engine, Crusader 250 cycle parts, restored.
£2,200–2,400 / $3,200–3,500 ⊕ **REOC**

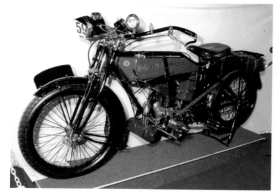

◄ **1922 Rudge Multi,** 499cc, 85 x 88mm bore and stroke, inlet-over-exhaust valves, Rudge multi gears (variable pulleys, belt), 650 x 65mm wheels, 26 x 3in tyres, caliper pads operating on wheel rim, brake shoe operating on flange integral with belt pulley, concours condition.
£8,000+ / $11,600+ ⊕ **AMCA**

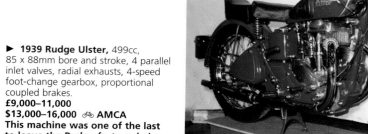

► **1939 Rudge Ulster,** 499cc, 85 x 88mm bore and stroke, 4 parallel inlet valves, radial exhausts, 4-speed foot-change gearbox, proportional coupled brakes.
£9,000–11,000
$13,000–16,000 ⊕ **AMCA**
This machine was one of the last to leave the Rudge factory, being registered 14 days before the outbreak of WWII.

1935 Sunbeam Model 8, 346cc overhead-valve twin-port single, 70 x 90mm bore and stroke, hand-change gearbox, enclosed final-drive chain, girder forks, rigid frame.
£4,200–4,600 / $6,000–6,650 ⊞ **VER**
The Model 8 was offered between 1933 and 1937.

James *(British 1902–66)*

1924 James 500 V-Twin, 499cc side-valve V-twin, 64 x 77.5mm bore and stroke, forward mounted magneto, single carburettor between cylinders, hand-change gearbox, James inscribed aluminium silencer, spring forks, full lighting equipment, original specification.
£5,000+ / $7,250+ ⊞ **MW**

1956 James L1 Comet, 99cc Villiers 4F 2-stroke single-cylinder engine, unrestored, completely original.
£400–600 / $580–870 ⊞ **BLM**
The L1 Comet appeared for the 1956 model year. It used the new Cadet frame and forks to house the 4F engine.

1962 James L15A Flying Cadet, 149cc AMC 2-stroke single, 3-speed foot-change gearbox, complete but unrestored.
£200–400 / $300–580 ⊁ **Bon**
The Flying Cadet with the AMC engine was introduced in the autumn of 1959. The engine was the same as that found in the Francis Barnett Plover.

Jawa *(Czechoslovakian 1929–)*

c1952 Jawa 500 Twin, 489cc overhead-camshaft unit-construction parallel twin, shaft and bevel gears, dry-sump lubrication, telescopic front forks, plunger rear suspension, very original, good condition.
£1,700–2,000 / $2,500–3,000 ⊁ **Bon**
Jawa became known as a manufacturer of two-stroke twins that provided reliable, if unexciting, transport. However, the Czech firm has a long sporting history. In recent years, its efforts have been directed towards speedway and enduros, but in the period following WWII it was a regular competitor in Grand Prix racing with double-overhead-camshaft twins. The production machines of the period consisted of a number of two-strokes together with an advanced single-overhead-camshaft 500cc twin.

1972 Jawa 90 Roadster, 89cc disc-valve 2-stroke single, unit construction, alloy head and barrel, 4-speed gearbox, fully enclosed final drive chain, beam frame, full-width alloy hubs, telescopic forks, swinging-arm rear suspension, completely original specification.
£1,600–1,800 / $2,300–2,600 ⊛ **JCZ**

Auction prices

Miller's only includes motorcycles declared sold. Our guide prices take into account the buyer's premium, VAT on the premium, and the extent of any published catalogue information relating to condition and provenance. Motorcycles sold at auction are identified by the ⊁ icon; full details of the auction house can be found on page 167.

Kawasaki *(Japanese 1962–)*

◄ **1973 Kawasaki HIA,** 499cc piston-port 2-stroke triple, 60 x 58.8mm bore and stroke, 5-speed gearbox, twin-leading-shoe drum front brake, restored.
£2,200–2,500 / $3,200–3,600 ⊞ CotC
The Kawasaki 500 triple appeared in September 1968. Initially named the Mach 3, it created something of a cult following thanks to its 125mph and near-12 second standing quarter-mile performance.

1974 Kawasaki KV75, 74cc 2-stroke single, piston-port induction with rear vertical cylinder, alloy head, iron barrel, 3-speed gearbox, automatic clutch.
£900–1,100 / $1,300–1,600 ⚙ CGC
The KV75 was popular as a paddock bike, and even was used at American air force bases to avoid long walks in the enormous hangers!

1979 Kawasaki Z650 Series B, 652cc double-overhead-camshaft across-the-frame four, electric starter, 5-speed gearbox, twin hydraulically operated front disc brakes, duplex steel frame.
£1,600–1,800 / $2,300–2,600 ⊞ NLM
The Series B is instantly recognizable from the Series A machine due to its cast alloy, rather than wire, wheels. Production finally ceased in 1983.

Laverda *(Italian 1949–)*

◄ **1970 Laverda 750 SF 1st Series,** 743.92cc single-overhead-camshaft twin, slightly inclined cylinders, 4-bearing 360-degree crank, 80 x 74mm bore and stroke, humped tank, single seat, wire wheels, concours winner and Best Classic at Stafford 2000.
£3,600–4,000 / $5,000–5,800 ⊞ ILO
The code 'SF' (standing for Super Freno – super brake) referred to the adoption of entirely new drum brakes designed by the company's founder, Dr Francesco Laverda. The 1st Series machines had Smiths instruments, whereas the 2nd Series, which appeared in 1971, had ND Denso instruments.

1972 Laverda 750 SF 2nd Series, 743.92cc single-overhead-camshaft twin, Lafranconi silencers, balance pipe at front of cylinders, wire wheels, Bosch headlamp.
£1,700–1,900 / $2,500–2,750 ⊞ NLM
For the 1971 model year, the SF underwent a number of changes, including ND Denso clocks and switchgear and a new fuel tank. This machine has a dualseat (most SFs had a single seat) and a twin disc brake conversion.

1979 Laverda 500 Alpino, 496.7cc double-overhead-camshaft twin, 4 valves per cylinder, 72 x 61mm bore and stroke, cylinders slanted forward 20 degrees from vertical, 6-speed gearbox, horizontally-split crankcases, cast alloy 18in wheels, 105mph top speed, standard apart from aftermarket megaphone silencers.
£1,600–1,800 / $2,300–2,600 ⊞ NLM

Levis *(British 1911–40)*

◀ **1923 Levis Model T,** 211cc 2-stroke single, 2-speed gearbox.
£1,600–1,900 / $2,300–2,750 ⊞ **PS**
Levis dated from 1911, and in its early days was best known for its excellent range of two-strokes. During 1920 and 1922, it also gained some excellent racing successes, including the 250cc TT, and French and Belgian GPs. Because of this success, Levis used the slogan, 'The Master Two-Stroke'. The engine in this example is a Levis designed unit.

McKenzie *(1921–25)*

▶ **1923 McKenzie Ladies' Model,** 169cc 2-stroke single.
£1,800–2,000 / $2,600–3,000 ⌁ **PS**
The McKenzie was a featherweight model and little more than a motorized bicycle, weighing only 80lb (36.2kg). Powered by a Hobart two-stroke engine, it had only two controls – a decompressor and a throttle lever. The rear brake was of the coaster type, while at the front was a bicycle type using brake blocks. This is a rare machine, there being only 13 listed on the Vintage MCC's register

Maserati *(Italian 1953–61)*

Of the six Maserati brothers, one, Marco, became a painter while the other five, Alfieri, Bindo, Carlo, Ernesto and Ettore, became engineers. Carlo, the eldest, raced motorcycles and won several events in 1899 and 1900 on a Cancano machine, which he had designed, built and ridden himself under the colours of the Marquis Cancano de Anzano del Parco. Carlo Maserati also raced cars and worked as an engineer for Bianchi, Fiat and Junior, but he died in 1911.

Alfieri worked as a test driver for Isotta-Fraschini and raced for the marque. Alfieri, together with Bindo and Ettore, set up Officine Alfieri Maserati SpA in Bologna during December 1914.

WWI saw Maserati manufacturing spark plugs and overhauling aero engines. In 1919, the youngest brother, Ernesto, joined the firm. In the 1920s and 1930s, Maserati concentrated on building and racing cars, but in 1938 the company was taken over by the Modenese industrialist Adolfo Orsi, although Bologna was retained as its base.

Post-war, Maserati moved to Modena, built more Grand Prix cars and undertook a new venture by producing motorcycles. The first models, a 123cc (52 x 58mm) two-stroke and a 158cc (60 x 56mm) overhead-valve four-stroke arrived in 1953. The following year, 1954, these were joined by new 175 and 200cc overhead-valve singles based on the existing 158cc machine. Then, at the Milan show late in 1955, Maserati staged a major coup when it unveiled what it claimed was the world's first production motorcycle to sport a front disc brake. This machine was a new 246cc (70 x 64mm) overhead-valve single.

Later in the 1950s came a particularly neat 50cc machine, which, although road legal, was clearly mainly aimed at the racing fraternity. This machine was also exported to other European countries including the UK. After 1961, Maserati axed its motorcycle arm to concentrate on expensive supercars.

◀ **1956 Maserati 50/T2/SS Il Rospo,** 48cc unit-construction 2-stroke single, all-steel tubular frame, engine supported at rear of crankcase and cylinder head, full-width aluminium brake hubs, rare, concours condition.
£5,500–6,000 / $8,000–8,700 ⌁ **Bon**
The famous Modena car manufacturer entered motorcycle production during 1953 with two models, which were offered in de luxe, sports and standard forms. The following year, 175cc and 200cc four-stroke machines joined the range, followed in 1955 by a 250. At the opposite end of the capacity scale was the 48cc T2/SS two-stroke, which, despite its diminutive size, was built to the same high standards.

Matchless
(British 1901–69, 1987–)

◄ **1955 Matchless G9,** 498cc overhead-valve parallel twin, 4-speed gearbox, AMC 'jampot' rear shocks, megaphone silencers, 19in wheels, full-width hubs, completely restored 2000, fewer than 300 miles since.
£2,500–3,000 / $3,600–4,400 ➚ Bon
The introduction and subsequent success of the Speed Twin forced the other major manufacturers to produce machines of a similar configuration. Associated Motor Cycles, owners of the AJS and Matchless brands, announced their new parallel twins in 1948, typed the Model 20 and G9 respectively. Producing 29bhp at 6,800rpm, they offered performance that was comparable to their rivals which combined with good handling and an excellent finish.

► **1956 Matchless G11 Super,** 593cc overhead-valve twin, alloy head, iron barrel, 72 x 72.8mm bore and stroke, 33bhp at 6,800rpm, full-width alloy hubs, megaphone silencers, AMC 'jampot' rear shocks, Teledraulic front forks.
£2,500–2,800
$3,600–4,000 ⊞ CotC
The 600 G11 was built between 1956 and 1958, before being superseded by the 650 G12.

1958 Matchless G3, 348cc overhead–valve single, 72 x 85.5mm bore and stroke, ac electrics, ignition coil under tank, small timing cover with points, rectifier under seat, full-width alloy hubs.
£1,800–2,000 / $2,600–3,000 ⊞ BB
Coil ignition was introduced on the G3 for 1958.

1961 Matchless G12 De Luxe, 646cc overhead-valve parallel twin, 72 x 79.3mm bore and stroke, alloy head, iron barrel, nodular crank, coil ignition, alternator and distributor, 19in wheels, full-width hubs, good original condition.
£2,400–2,800 / $3,500–4,000 ⊞ MW

◄ **1963 Matchless G2,** 248.5cc semi-unit construction overhead-valve single, 69.85 x 64.85mm bore and stroke, alloy head, iron barrel, 18bhp, coil ignition, alternator, separate 4-speed gearbox housing, 17in wheels, 75mph top speed.
£360–400 / $500–580 ➚ PS
The lightweight range of AMC singles was introduced in 1958. The G2 was a better bike than usually it is given credit for; examples are still available for little money.

Mi-Val *(Italian 1950–67)*

Metalimeccanica Italiana Valtrompia, of Brescia, was essentially a machine-tool manufacturer, which also produced motorcycles for a number of years under the Mi-Val brand. At first, it built 125cc two-strokes; then in 1954, it was granted the right to build the Messerschmitt three-wheel microcar. In fact, the Italian version was considerably different to the German original. In 1956, Mi-Val made history by displaying a new 125cc overhead-valve motorcycle with a five-speed gearbox – a world's first in a production roadster. Mi-Val also produced a number of competition models for most branches of motorcycle sport. For example, in the 1950s ISDT, the company entered a team that included

sidecar racing champion Eric Oliver and the famous woman trials rider Olga Kevelos. In events such as the Milano-Taranto, Mi-Val fielded a special version of its 125cc two-stroke and a new 175cc four-stroke single. But it enjoyed most success in motocross during the late 1950s, with a range of exotic, double-overhead-camshaft 250, 350 and 500cc singles, with five- or even six-speed gearboxes. In 1966, its last full year of bike production, the Mi-Val marque offered no fewer than ten individual models, from a commuter moped through to the 200cc overhead-valve Principe (Prince) motorcycle. The following year, the company axed motorcycle production to concentrate on its machine-tool business.

1954 Mi-Val 125 Sport, 124cc unit-construction 2-stroke single, piston-port induction, swinging-arm rear suspension, telescopic front forks, dualseat, heel-and-toe gear-change, flywheel magneto ignition and lighting.
£1,100–1,200 / $1,600–1,750 ⊞ NLM
Clearly, the Mi-Val was yet another machine inspired by the much-copied German DKW RT125.

1955 Mi-Val 125MT, 123cc piston-port 2-stroke single, 12bhp, telescopic front forks, swinging-arm rear suspension, alloy rims, alloy brake hubs, 75mph top speed.
£1,600–1,800 / $2,300–2,600 ⊞ MW
'MT' stood for Milano-Taranto. Built in small numbers, it differed from the standard 125 Sport in many ways, including a more highly tuned engine, more heavily-finned head and barrel, close-ratio gears, alloy wheel rims, Dell'Orto SS1 racing carburettor and much more.

MM *(Italian 1924–57)*

◄ **1951 MM 51A,** 247cc overhead-valve unit-construction single, Dell'Orto SS carburettor, full-cradle frame, plunger rear suspension, telescopic front forks, largely original specification, concours condition.
£4,000–4,500 / $5,800–6,500 ⊞ NLM
MM was founded by Mario Mazzetti and Alfonso Morini (the latter left to set up what was to become Moto Morini in 1937). MM was known in Italy as the Rolls-Royce of Bologna.

> A known continuous history can add value to and enhance the enjoyment of a motorcycle.

► **1956 MM 54A Turismo,** 247.70cc unit-construction overhead-camshaft single, 64 x 77mm bore and stroke, 4-speed gearbox, not entirely original.
£2,200–2,500 / $3,200–3,600 ⊞ NLM

Motobi *(Italian 1949–76)*

1960 Motobi Catria, 174cc overhead-valve unit-construction horizontal single, alloy head, iron barrel, wet-sump lubrication, 16bhp, 4-speed foot-change gearbox, Silentium silencer, full-width polished alloy brake hubs, 80mph top speed, fully restored, concours condition.
£2,000–2,200 / $3,000–3,200 ⚙ IMOC
The Catria was successful in Junior racing events, capturing championship titles in several countries, including Italy, Belgium and Chile.

Moto Guzzi *(Italian 1921–)*

c1924 Moto Guzzi 500 Sport, 498.4cc inlet-over-exhaust horizontal single, 88 x 82mm bore and stroke, 13bhp at 3,800rpm, girder forks, rigid frame, acetylene lighting, handlebar klaxon horn, luggage rack, sprung saddle.
£6,000–7,500 / $8,500–11,000 ⚖ Bon
Now extremely rare, the 500 Sport was one of the first models produced by Moto Guzzi.

1937 Moto Guzzi PE, 238cc overhead-valve horizontal single, 68 x 64mm bore and stroke, 9bhp at 4,000rpm, blade girder forks, 67mph top speed.
£2,700–3,000 / $4,000–4,500 ⚙ IMOC

1955 Moto Guzzi Galletto 192, 192cc overhead-valve single, 65 x 58mm bore and stroke, 4-speed foot-change gearbox, kickstarter, leading-link fork, swinging-arm rear suspension,
£600–800 / $870–1,150 ⊞ MW
All three wheels were interchangeable. When originally conceived at the beginning of the 1950s, the Galletto (Cockerel) displaced 147cc; by 1951, it was 160cc; in 1952, it had grown to 175cc, before gaining the definitive 192cc capacity in early 1954.

1956 Moto Guzzi Cardinello 73cc rotary-valve 2-stroke single, 45 x 46mm bore and stroke, alloy head, iron barrel, 2.6bhp at 5,200rpm, 3-speed gearbox, telescopic front forks, spring-and-friction rear suspension.
£900–1,200
$1,300–1,750 ⚙ BTSC
The larger-engined Cardinello arrived for 1957.

1956 Moto Guzzi Zigolo Series I, 98cc horizontal 2-stroke single, rotary-valve induction, alloy head and barrel, 50 x 50mm bore and stroke, 6.8bhp at 5,400rpm, 3-speed gearbox, 17in wheels, 50mph top speed.
£850–1,000 / $1,250–1,500 ⊞ NLM

1959 Moto Guzzi Zigolo 98 Series II, 98cc 2-stroke horizontal single, rotary-disc-valve induction, 4.6bhp at 5,200rpm, 3-speed foot-change gearbox, chrome tank, dualseat.
£1,000–1,250 / $1,500–1,800 ⊞ CotC

1961 Moto Guzzi Galletto 200 Elettrico, 192cc overhead-valve single, manual advance and retard mechanism, electric starter, dualseat.
£1,400–1,600 / $2,000–2,300 ⊞ NLM
The 1961 model offered a power increase to 7.7bhp, different final-drive gear ratio, new rear suspension, revised bodywork and 12 volt electrics (including electric start) and a smaller headlamp.

1962 Moto Guzzi Lodola GT, 235cc overhead-valve unit-construction single, inclined cylinder, 68 x 64m bore and stroke, 11bhp at 6,000rpm, 4-speed foot-change gearbox, telescopic front forks, swinging-arm rear suspension, restored.
£2,200–2,250 / $3,200–3,350 ⊞ CotC
'GT' stood for Gran Turismo.

1957 Moto Guzzi Falcone, 499cc overhead-valve single, 88 x 82mm bore and stroke, magneto ignition, 4-speed foot-change gearbox, telescopic front forks, Lafranconi fishtail silencer sport specification.
£5,500–6,500 / $8,000–9,500 ⚡ Bon
Carlo Guzzi's first prototype motorcycle of 1919 was unconventional in so far as its single-cylinder engine was installed horizontally, and by the end of the 1930s the flat single had established itself as a Guzzi trademark. Guzzi began post-war production with a range of updated pre-war designs, the 500cc touring GTV and sportier GTW soon gaining telescopic front forks and hydraulic rear suspension, before being replaced for 1949 by the Astore. The latter incorporated several features pioneered on the successful 250cc Airone, principally an aluminium cylinder barrel and head with enclosed valve gear, and remained in production until 1953. By then, the ultimate expression of Guzzi's classic vintage-style single had arrived – the legendary Falcone. Introduced in 1950, the Falcone took over the GTW's mantle of Guzzi's top sports bike, its tunable engine being closely related to that of the Dondolino racer. Offered in Sport, Turismo and military/police specifications, the Falcone outlived all its contemporaries, the Turismo civilian version remaining in production until 1963.

1963 Moto Guzzi Lodola 235, 235cc overhead-valve unit-construction single, inclined cylinder, alloy head, iron barrel, 7.5:1 compression ratio, 11bhp at 6,000rpm, 4–speed gearbox, original and unrestored.
£1,100–1,400 / $1,600–2,000 🏍 Bon
The Lodola was Carlo Guzzi's last design. When it arrived in 1956, it displaced 174.5cc (62 x 57.8mm) and had a chain-driven overhead camshaft. Then, in 1959, the engine was revamped to 235cc, but with pushrod operated valves.

1971 Moto Guzzi Nuovo Falcone, 498.4cc overhead-valve unit-construction single, 5-speed gearbox, electric starter.
£1,850–2,000 / $2,700–3,000 ⊞ NLM
Civilian models of this machine are rare, since most Nuovo Falcones were supplied to government departments, including the armed forces and police.

▶ **1978 Moto Guzzi V35 Series I,** 346.23cc overhead-valve 90-degree V-twin, 27bhp at 7,750rpm, alloy front engine (generator) cover, wet-sump lubrication, electric starter, alloy swinging arm, 18in cast alloy wheels.
£900–1,100 / $1,300–1,600 ⊞ NLM
The V35 and V50 were introduced at the Cologne show in September 1977.

1978 Moto Guzzi 254, 231cc unit-construction across-the-frame four, wet-sump lubrication, 27.8bhp at 10,500rpm, 5-speed gearbox, 12-spoke alloy wheels.
£800–1,600 / $1,150–2,300 🏍 Bon
The Guzzi 254 and its Benelli sibling (also called 254) were built at Guzzi's Mandello del Lorio plant, but today the Benelli version is far better known.

▶ **1979 Moto Guzzi 1000SP,** 948.8cc overhead-valve 90-degree V-twin, 88 x 78mm bore and stroke, 55bhp at 6,250rpm, 120mph top speed.
£2,100–2,300 / $3,000–3,350 ⊞ NLM
Known as the Spada (Sword) in the UK, the 1000SP was a direct competitor of the BMW R100RS.

1968 Moto Guzzi Stornello 160, 153.2cc overhead-valve unit-construction single, inclined cylinder, wet-sump lubrication, 12.6bhp, full-width alloy brake hubs, 17in wheels, 65mph top speed, unrestored.
£700–800 / $1,000–1,150 ⊞ IVC
The four-speed 160 Stornello was produced from 1968 to 1970. Then it continued in updated guise (with five speeds) until 1974.

1974 Moto Guzzi 850T, 844cc overhead-valve V-twin, 83 x 78mm bore and stroke, 5-speed gearbox, shaft final drive, electric starter, drum rear brake, 38mm Guzzi-made front forks, front crash bars, twin front disc brake conversion, handlebar fairing.
£2,500–2,700 / $3,500–$4,000 ⊞ BLM

Miller's
Motorcycle Milestones

Moto Guzzi 1000SP (Italian 1978)
Price range: £1,800–3,000 / $2,600–4,400
With the SP, known as the Spada (Sword) in the UK, Moto Guzzi set out to offer a machine that could break BMW's stranglehold on the long-haul, luxury touring market. In fact, the model was a genuine attempt by the Italian factory to steal the clothes from that Teutonic flagship, the R100RS Boxer Twin. One look at the SP's fairing gives the game away. At Guzzi in mid-1976, the management had realized that a logical move to attract a percentage of BMW's potential customers would be to offer a similar bike, but one that appealed to Italian enthusiasts. Thus plans were laid for what was to emerge as the 1 litre SP. It was a clever move, as the luxury sports/tourer project was able to draw heavily on existing technology and therefore could not only be put into production after a relatively short period, but also at a much lower cost than if it had been built from scratch.

In fact, as far as the main chassis and engine components were concerned, the SP was largely a marriage of convenience between the 850T3 and V1000 models. The increased engine displacement was necessary to give Guzzi a competitive motorcycle in the, by then, vital 1000cc class and make use of the work already carried out on the 948.8cc (88 x 78mm) engine originally created for the largely unsuccessful

V1000 automatic back in 1975. This was simply given a conventional clutch and five-speed gearbox from the T3, and housed in the frame and suspension package from the same motorcycle.

But if these measures smacked of convenience engineering, the same couldn't be said of the fairing. In fact, a considerable chunk of the project's R&D budget was set aside to confront BMW head on – and in an area where the German giant hitherto had led the industry. This meant not only rider protection, but a high level of instrumentation.

To achieve its aim of giving SP buyers true weather protection, Guzzi was able to make use of its own in-house wind-tunnel facilities. First developed in the early 1950s for its GP racing team, these were put to use for the production model. The result was a large handlebar fairing with separate side panels. This arrangement was not only efficient, but also provided mechanics with easier access than the BMW fairing. Besides the usual speedometer and rev-counter, there were also an analogue clock, volt meter and an array of hazard warning lights. The result was a motorcycle that ran until the beginning of the 1990s, and stretched to a defined series: SP1000 1978–80; SP NT 1981–83; SP II 1984–87; and finally the SP III, which was sold from 1988 until stocks ran out towards the end of 1992.

Cross Reference
See Colour Review (page 53)

◄ **1982 Moto Guzzi Le Mans III,**
844cc overhead-valve V-twin, 76bhp (crank) at 6,200rpm, shaft final drive, dual 300mm front/single 242mm rear disc brakes, 18in cast alloy wheels, cylinder-head protection bars, front fork brace.
£2,400–2,700
$3,500–4,000 ⊞ NLM
The Le Mans III was a major redesign with a new fairing, tank, seat, footrest supports, exhaust system, side panels and modified engine top end. It was built from 1981 to 1984.

▶ **1989 Moto Guzzi Mille GT,**
948.8cc overhead-valve 90-degree V-twin, 88 x 78mm bore and stroke, twin Dell'Orto PHF 30mm accelerator-pump carburettors, 5-speed gearbox, electric starter, standard apart from Goodridge hoses, unlinked brakes, Malossi polished carburettor bellmouths and straight handlebars, only 5,000 miles from new, original, unrestored, concours condition.
£2,700–3,000 / $4,000–4,500 ⊞ MW
The Mille GT appeared at the Milan show in November 1987. It was offered with a choice of cast alloy or wire wheels, the majority of customers requesting the latter. The Mille GT was what people would later label a retro bike. Production ceased in 1991.

Motom
(Italian 1947–early 1960s)

◄ **1957 Motom 98TS,** 98cc overhead-camshaft unit-construction single, horizontal cylinder, wet-sump lubrication, ducted cooling.
£1,200–1,500 / $1,750–2,200 ⊞ **MW**
The 98TS was introduced in 1956 and created a stir because of its unique, cantilever, rubber-in-torsion swinging-arm suspension at both front and rear. Today, it is a rare sight, even in Italy.

Moto Morini *(Italian 1937–)*

1955 Moto Morini 175GT, 172.6cc overhead-valve unit-construction single, battery/coil ignition, single Silentium silencer, 4-speed gearbox, single-sided drum brakes, telescopic front forks, swinging-arm rear suspension, dualseat.
£1,800–2,200 / $2,600–3,200 ⊞ **IVC**

1958 Moto Morini Sprint, 172.6cc overhead-valve unit-construction single, 60 x 61mm bore and stroke, wet-sump lubrication, 4-speed foot-change gearbox, dual Silentium silencers with bridge piece from single exhaust header pipe, 82mph top speed.
£2,200–2,400 / $3,200–3,500 ⊞ **IVC**

◄ **1964 Moto Morini Corsarino,** 48.82cc overhead-valve unit-construction single, inclined cylinder, 41 x 37mm bore and stroke, 4-speed foot-change gearbox, original, largely unrestored.
£400–450 / $580–650 ⊛ **MORI**
The Corsarino Sport appeared in the mid-1960s, entering a class largely dominated by two-strokes. It was expensive, but sold well thanks to its four-stroke engine and reliability. Street scrambler and touring versions were also offered.

► **1969 Moto Morini 250 Settebello GTI,** 248cc pushrod single, all original, unrestored Italian import.
£1,350–1,500
$2,000–2,200 ⊛ **MORI**
This is the touring version. It broke from traditional Italian small-bike lines with high handlebars, substantial mudguards and a relatively sedate performance. It has the largest capacity of the pre-V-twin Morinis.

1971 Moto Morini Corsaro Country, 123cc overhead-valve unit-construction single, 56 x 50mm bore and stroke, full-width alloy brake hubs, upswept silencer, rev-counter, restored.
£1,350–1,500 / $2,000–2,200 ⚙ MORI
The Corsaro (Corsair) was a development of the smaller 98cc Sbarazzino (Rogue or Rascal). The Country version was a green lanes-type machine. There was also a more specialized ISDT version intended for serious competition.

▶ **1974 Moto Morini 3½,** 344cc overhead-valve 72-degree V-twin, twin Dell'Orto VHB carburettors, 35bhp at 8,250rpm, capacitor-discharge ignition, 12 volt 100 watt alternator, original wire wheels, drum brakes, full-cradle duplex frame, 99mph top speed.
£1,800–2,000
$2,600–3,000 ⊞ NLM
A feature of the Morini V-twin engine was the camshaft, which was located high in the crankcase – in the crutch of the V – so it was necessary to space the cylinders apart to allow room for it. This method of cylinder placement is know as désaxé.

1975 Moto Morini 3½ Sport Series I, 344cc overhead-valve 72-degree V-twin, 39bhp at 8,500rpm, wire wheels with alloy rims, drum brakes, hydraulic steering damper, chrome headlamp, clip-ons, stainless-steel mudguards and chainguard, single seat, polished engine covers, 108mph top speed.
£3,200–3,500 / $4,600–5,000 ⊞ NLM
To many, this machine is the best of the Morini V-twin family.

1976 Moto Morini 125H, 119.75cc overhead-valve unit-construction single, inclined cylinder, 59 x 43.8mm bore and stroke, 24mm carburettor, 13.75bhp at 9,000rpm, 6-speed gearbox, disc front/drum rear brakes, wire wheels, 73mph top speed, early example.
£900–1,100 / $1,300–1,600 ⊞ NLM

1976 Moto Morini 3½ Sport, 344cc overhead-valve 72-degree V-twin, alloy heads and barrels, 7-spoke cast alloy wheels, single disc front brake, unrestored.
£1,800–2,200 / $2,600–3,200 ⊞ IVC

1977 Moto Morini 3½ Strada, 344cc, 7-spoke cast alloy wheels, Grimeca disc front brake, drum rear brake, stainless-steel chainguard and mudguard, chrome round CEV indicators, pillion footrests, original specification.
£1,100–1,200 / $1,600–1,750 ⊶ MORI

1977 Moto Morini 3½ Sport, 344cc overhead-valve V-twin, 5-speed gearbox, full-cradle frame, front mudguard, non-standard paintwork.
£1,700–1,950 / $2,500–2,750 ⊞ NLM
By 1977, not only had a disc front brake been added to this machine, but also seven-spoke cast alloy wheels.

1979 Moto Morini 3½, 344cc overhead-valve V-twin, Heron combustion chambers, gas rear shocks, Marzocchi front forks, disc front/drum rear brakes, 7-spoke alloy wheels, plastic chainguard.
£1,600–1,800 / $2,300–2,600 ⊞ MW

◄ **1980 Moto Morini Camel Series II,** 478.6cc 72-degree V-twin, twin 26mm Dell'Orto PHBH carburettors, high-level exhaust, Grimeca conical brake hubs, Marzocchi competition front forks, gas rear shocks, full-cradle frame, 3.00 x 21in front/4.10 x 18in rear tyres.
£1,900–2,100 / $2,750–3,000 ⊞ NLM
Morini's first six-speed production 500 was the Camel enduro-styled trail bike, which arrived in 1981 and was a development of factory entries in such events as the ISDT. It featured kickstarting only and had 6 volt electrics; this is the Mk II version, sold as the Sahara in the UK.

1980 Moto Morini 2502C, 239.4cc overhead-valve 72-degree V-twin, 59 x 43.8mm bore and stroke, 26.8bhp at 9,000rpm, 6-speed gearbox, 31.5mm Paioli front forks, 6 volt electrics, Grimeca cast alloy wheels, black exhaust, 87mph top speed.
£1,100–1,300 / $1,600–2,000 ⊞ NLM
Built from 1980 to 1984, the 2502C suffered from a high price and cost cutting. However, it was still a fine motorcycle with a particularly smooth engine.

1982 Moto Morini 350 Kanguro, 344cc overhead-valve 72-degree V-twin, high-level exhaust, fork gaiters, Marzocchi long-travel leading-axle front forks, 21in front/18in rear wheels.
£1,000–1,250 / $1,500–1,800 ⊞ NLM
Launched at the Milan show in November 1981, the 350 Kanguro went on sale in early 1982; it was Morini's first motorcycle with monoshock rear suspension. It was also the Bologna company's best seller in the early/mid-1980s.

1985 Moto Morini 500 Sei V, 498cc 72-degree V-twin, 6-speed gearbox, electric starter, Marzocchi front forks and rear shocks, 7-spoke cast alloy wheels, hydraulic steering damper, belly pan and small fairing.
£3,000–3,300 / $4,400–4,750 ⊞ NLM
The 500 Sei V was updated in line with the new 350 K2 at the end of 1983. The alterations were mostly cosmetic, but there were a few technical changes, the electrics being the most notable – a more powerful 24 amp/hour battery and stronger 160 watt alternator were introduced.

1984 Moto Morini 350 K2, 344cc overhead-valve 72-degree V-twin, electric starter, 6-speed gearbox.
£1,900–2,100 / $2,750–3,000 ⊞ NLM
The 350 K2 was a major revision of the 3½ concept. It was also the first Morini to sport Nikasil cylinder bores; it had a left-hand gear-change. Not everyone liked its styling.

MV Agusta
(Italian 1945–78, 1998–)

◀ **1955 MV Agusta 175 Turismo Lusso,** 172.4cc overhead-camshaft unit-construction single, 59.5 x 62mm bore and stroke, 10bhp at 6,500rpm, 4-speed gearbox, telescopic front forks, swinging-arm rear suspension, full-width alloy brake hubs, dualseat.
£1,600–1,800 / $2,300–2,600 ⊞ CotC

1955 MV Agusta 175CS Sport, 172cc overhead-camshaft unit-construction single, 59.5 x 62mm bore and stroke, wet-sump lubrication, 12bhp, 4-speed gearbox, full-width alloy hubs, fully restored.
£1,700–2,800 / $2,500–4,000 ⚸ Bon
Having started motorcycle production late in 1945 with a 98cc two-stroke, Meccanica Verghera (MV) introduced its first production four-strokes – the single-cylinder 175CST and CSTL – at the Milan show in 1952; the newcomer's advanced overhead-camshaft, unit-construction engine set them apart from most of the opposition. A year later, the 175CS Sport joined the line-up, featuring an engine in a higher state of tune; the modifications raised top speed to over 70mph. Production of this very successful model continued until 1958.

◀ **1967 MV Agusta 600 Four,** 591.5cc double-overhead-camshaft across-the-frame four, gear-driven camshafts, 4 Dell'Orto 24mm carburettors, 52bhp at 8,200rpm, 106mph top speed.
£12,000–14,000 / $17,500–20,500 ⊞ MW
Only 135 examples of the 600 Four were built over seven years, ensuring the rarity of surviving examples. Only its ugly looks and relative lack of performance count against it.

1972 MV Agusta Sport, 743cc double-overhead-camshaft across-the-frame four, 65 x 56mm bore and stroke, 4 Dell'Orto UB24 carburettors, 65bhp at 8,500rpm, 5-speed gearbox, shaft final drive, 4-leading-shoe front brake, stainless-steel mudguards, 125mph top speed, concours condition.
£15,000–20,000 / $22,000–30,000 ◯ **CME**

▶ **1972 MV Agusta 750S**, 743cc double-overhead-camshaft across-the-frame four, gear-driven camshafts, 5-speed gearbox, battery/coil 12 volt ignition, electric starter, 18in wire wheels.
£15,000–20,000 / $22,000–30,000 ⊞ **MW**
The first prototype of the 750S was displayed on the MV Agusta stand at the 1969 Milan show to great acclaim. However production did not get under way until 1971.

◀ **1973 MV Agusta 350B GT Elettronica**, 349cc overhead-valve unit-construction twin, 65 x 56mm bore and stroke, 5-speed gearbox, full-width brake hubs.
£2,200–2,400
$3,200–3,500 ⊞ **NLM**
The 350B was produced in two versions, the Sport and the Turismo. Both were introduced at the Milan show in November 1971. For the 1973 model year, they received 12 volt electrics and electronic ignition.

1999 MV Agusta F4 Serie Oro, 749.4cc liquid-cooled double-overhead-camshaft across-the-frame four, electronic fuel injection, wet-sump lubrication, 126bhp at 12,200rpm, 6-speed cassette gearbox, 171mph top speed.
£20,000–22,000 / $30,000–32,000 ⚲ **COYS**
Like its British counterparts, MV Agusta succumbed to the severe and growing competition from Japanese manufacturers in the late 1970s. The return of the MV Agusta name has to be one of the most dramatic marque resurrections in the motorcycling world. Claudio Castiglioni of Cagiva commissioned Massimo Tamborini (already possessing an impressive cv with Bimota, Ducati and Ferrari) to head the design project. The result of his labour was the exquisite F4 Serie Oro (Gold Series). A limited run of 300 was made and sold rapidly. The much more affordable Silver Series was produced in sufficient numbers to be available to the merely rich biker.

MZ *(German 1953–)*

1977 MZ TS250 Series I, 247cc piston-port 2-stroke single, 18bhp, drum brakes, fully enclosed final drive chain, alloy wheel rims, 75mph top speed.
£500–600 / $720–870 ⚒ **Bon**
Built in the former DKW works in Zschopau, East Germany, MZ motorcycles were constructed in prolific numbers, production being centred on a series of lightweight two-stroke singles, mainly in 125, 150 and 250cc engine sizes.

1980 MZ TS250, 247cc piston-port 2-stroke single, 5-speed gearbox, matching speedometer and rev-counter, rubber drive-chain gaiter, fork gaiters, completely standard apart from rear carrier and bar-end mirror.
£500–650 / $720–1,000 ⊞ **NLM**
The rubber gaiter gives excellent final-drive-chain protection.

New Hudson *(British 1909–57)*

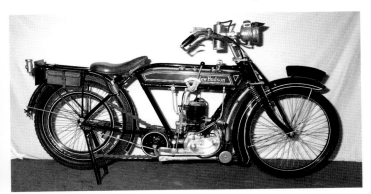

◀ **1914/20 New Hudson 2¼hp,** 225cc 2-stroke single.
£2,000–2,250 / $3,000–3,250 ⚒ **PS**
There are some serious doubts about the authenticity of this machine. Although the frame is of 1914 manufacture, the engine number prefix and the number itself suggest 1920 to be the date of the engine's manufacture. A Vintage MCC dating certificate confirms this mismatch of parts.

New Imperial *(British 1910–39)*

1933 New Imperial Model 30, 247cc overhead-valve unit-construction single, 67 x 70mm bore and stroke, blade girder forks, very original.
£2,000–3,000 / $3,000–4,400 ⚒ **Bon**
Builder of the last British machine to win the Lightweight (250) TT, New Imperial was unsurpassed for innovation during the early 1930s, its models featuring pivoted-fork rear suspension and unitary construction of engine and gearbox. Introduced for 1933, the Model 30 was based on the early 148cc Model 23 and featured helical primary drive gears, pushrod overhead valves and coil ignition. Production continued until 1936.

Norman *(British 1937–61)*

A known continuous history can add value to and enhance the enjoyment of a motorcycle.

◀ **1960 Norman B3 Roadster,** Villiers 2T piston-port twin-cylinder engine, 4-speed gearbox, leading-link front forks, swinging-arm rear suspension.
£750–1,250 / $1,100–1,800 ⊕ **NORM**
Norman Motorcycles were built in Ashford, Kent.

Norton *(British 1902–)*

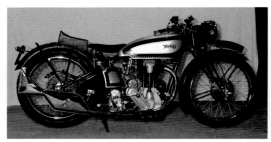

1928 Norton CS1, 490cc single-overhead-camshaft single, exposed coil valve springs, 79 x 100mm bore and stroke, chain final drive, drum brakes, girder forks, rigid frame.
£7,000–8,000 / $10,000–11,500 ⋩ **Bon**
CS1 stood for Cam Shaft I, the machine having been designed by Walter Moore who subsequently left Norton to join NSU in 1929. After Alec Bennet gave his CS1 a TT debut victory, the design was sold to paying customers, both in racing and road-going guises.

1934 Norton Model 30 International, 490cc single-overhead-camshaft single, 79 x 100mm bore and stroke, 4-speed gearbox, girder forks, rigid frame, restored, largely original specification.
£7,000–8,000 / $10,000–11,500 ⋩ **Bon**
The name 'International' was first used by Norton for its top-of-the-range sports roadster in 1932. Its Arthur Carroll designed overhead-camshaft engine had been developed in the works racers for the preceding two years. Although it retained the classic 79 x 100mm bore and stroke dimensions, and the shaft-and-bevels cam drive of the existing SC1, it was entirely new. Although intended for racing, the International could be ordered with refinements such as lights and a kickstart equipped gearbox, and by the time production halted in 1939, it was being built with a four-speed foot-change box and plunger rear suspension. This machine was first owned by Jock West, noted Brooklands and Isle of Man TT competitor, and a works rider for both AJS and BMW.

c1934 Norton Model 50, 348cc overhead-valve single, 71 x 88mm bore and stroke, non-original paintwork.
£2,200–2,800 / $3,200–4,000 ⋩ **Bon**
During the 1920s, having enjoyed continued success with its camshaft sporting singles, Norton continued to produce a quality range of overhead-valve and side-valve machines to suit the varying requirements of a developing market. In 1933, two new models appeared in a smaller size – the single-port Model 50 and the twin-port Model 55. Both had bore and stroke dimensions of 71 x 88mm to give 348cc, but otherwise they were the same as the Models 18 and 20. The transmission continued to be Sturmey Archer, the four-speed being offered as standard on the overhead-valve models.

1937 Norton Model Big Four, 634cc side-valve single, iron head and barrel, 82 x 120mm bore and stroke, enclosed valve gear, 4-speed foot-change gearbox, girder forks, rigid frame, gearbox rebuilt, forks rebushed, speedometer reconditioned.
£1,000–1,500 / $1,500–2,200 ⋩ **Bon**
This machine is not original. It features an industrial version of the Norton side-valve engine fitted into a period chassis. However, it is equipped with the correct cylinder head and other components.

◀ **1938 Norton ES2,** 490cc overhead-valve single, 79 x 100mm bore and stroke, 4-speed foot-change gearbox, girder forks, rigid frame, unrestored.
£1,100–1,250 / $1,600–1,800 ⋩ **PS**

1949 Norton 16H, 490cc side-valve single, 79 x 100m bore and stroke.
£2,000–2,400 / $3,000–3,500 ⚞ Bon
The 16H had a long career, having been developed from the original Model 16 back at the beginning of the 20th century. During WWII, it proved one of the most popular military bikes, some 100,000 examples being built between 1939 and 1945. In the immediate post-war years, the 16H received Roadholder hydraulically-damped front forks. For 1948, a number of improvements were introduced, including revised tappet adjusters and enclosed valve gear. The 16H finally bowed out in 1954.

1952 Norton Big Four, 634cc side-valve engine.
£2,500–3,000 / $3,600–4,400 ⊞ BLM
The Big Four received a cast aluminium enclosure for the valve gear in 1948, a laid-down gearbox in 1950, and new tanks in 1951, together with an aluminium front brake plate. There was no change for 1962. Equipped with telescopic front forks and a rigid rear end, it was ideal for sidecar work.

1953 Norton Model 7, 497cc overhead-valve parallel twin, 66 x 72.6mm bore and stroke, iron head and iron barrel, 30bhp at 7,000rpm.
£3,000–3,300 / $4,400–4,800 ⊞ CotC
Swinging-arm rear suspension was introduced on the Model 7 for the 1953 season. Prior to this, from its launch in 1948, the machine had a plunger frame. The first of the Norton twin-cylinder series, it was designed by Bert Hopwood.

◄ **c1946 Norton ES2,** 490cc overhead-valve single, 79 x 100mm bore and stroke, upright gearbox, good original example.
£2,500–3,000 / $3,600–4,400 ⊞ PM
The 1946 ES2 models had girder forks, but in 1947 they received telescopic front forks and a plunger frame.

1952 Norton Dominator Model 7, 497cc overhead-valve parallel twin, 66 x 72.6mm bore and stroke, iron head and barrel, 4-speed foot-change laid-down gearbox, telescopic front forks, subject of complete nut-and-bolt restoration.
£3,000–3,300 / $4,400–4,800 ⚞ CGC
The Model 7 was the first of the Dominator series and ran from 1948 to 1952 in plunger-frame guise. Then, from 1953 until production ceased in 1956, it gained a swinging-arm frame.

◀ **1955 Norton Dominator 88,** 497cc overhead-valve twin , alloy head, iron barrel, 4-speed laid-down gearbox, completely restored to concours condition.
£5,000–6,000 / $7,250–8,700 ⚲ Bon
This was the first year that the Dominator 88 had a welded-up sub-frame and full-width rear brake, while the frame was based on the Manx racing model, modified for series production. The frame was known as a 'wideline' until the end of 1959, when it was redesigned and renamed 'slimline'.

1956 Norton 19S, 597cc overhead-valve single, 82 x 113mm bore and stroke, alloy head, iron barrel, single downtube, non-Featherbed frame, full-width alloy hubs.
£2,250–2,500 / $3,200–3,600 ⚲ PS
The 19S and 19R were added to the Norton range for 1955. The main difference between them was the frame: swinging-arm on the S, rigid on the R.

1958 Norton Dominator 99, 597cc overhead-valve pre-unit twin, AMC gearbox, wideline frame, Roadholder forks, full-width hubs, several non-standard parts including aluminium cylinder barrel.
£2,700–3,200 / $3,900–4,600 ⊞ BLM

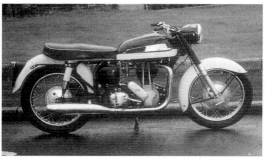

1960 Norton ES2, 490cc overhead-valve single, alloy head, iron barrel, AMC gearbox, slimline frame, Roadholder forks, full-width hubs, original specification, very good condition.
£3,000–3,500 / $4,400–5,000 ⊞ PM
This was the first year of the slimline frame.

1960 Norton Dominator 99, 597cc overhead-valve twin, 68 x 72mm bore and stroke, AMC gearbox, slimline Featherbed frame, revised silencers, fitted optional rev-counter, non-standard dualseat.
£3,400–5,000 / $5,000–7,250 ⚲ Bon
The 99 arrived for 1956 and continued through to 1962. For 1960, it received the slimline frame and revised silencers. Compared to the smaller 88, both the bore and stroke sizes were different.

1961 Norton Model 50, 348cc overhead-valve pre-unit single, 71 x 88mm bore and stroke, AMC 4-speed foot-change gearbox, original, unrestored.
£1,800–2,200 / $2,600–3,200 ⊞ MAY
The slimline-framed Model 50 ran from 1960 until 1963. A Mk 2 version appeared in 1964, but with AMC engine and cycle parts, Roadholder forks and Norton brakes.

1961 Norton Dominator 99SS, 597cc overhead-valve twin, twin Amal Monobloc carburettors, alternator/coil ignition, siamesed exhaust, 49bhp at 6,800rpm, non-standard period alloy wheel rims.
£3,600–4,500 / $5,000–6,500 ⚲ Bon
The 99SS was the forerunner of the 650SS and was only produced for a short period in 1961 and early 1962.

◄ **1962 Norton 650SS,** 646cc overhead-valve parallel twin, twin Amal Monobloc carburettors, slimline frame, rev-counter, dualseat.
£2,700–3,600 / $4,000–5,000 ↗ **Bon**
At the beginning of the 1960s, the Norton parallel twin, which had begun with the 497cc Model 7 of the late 1940s, was stretched from 597cc to 646cc. This was achieved by increasing the stroke from 82 to 89mm, the bore remaining unchanged at 68mm. Initially named the Manxman, it was intended for the American market. Then, in 1963, the range was slimmed down to just the 88 and 650, with SS (Super Sport) variants of both.

1967 Norton Atlas, 745cc overhead-valve twin, 73 x 89mm bore and stroke, 49bhp at 6,800rpm, rev-counter, 115mph top speed.
£3,000–3,500 / $4,400–5,000 ⊞ **PM**
The Atlas took the Norton twin one stage further in the displacement stakes. Introduced in 1962, it was basically the 650SS, but with a larger bore size. Its main benefit over the smaller engine was torque, the disadvantage being more vibration. This machine was one of the last Atlas models built before the Isolastic mounted Commando took over in an attempt to beat the vibes.

1970 Norton 750 Commando Roadster, 745cc overhead-valve twin, 73 x 89mm bore and stroke, 4-speed gearbox, diaphragm clutch, triplex primary drive chain, twin-leading-shoe front brake.
£2,500–2,900 / $3,600–4,200 ⊞ **MW**
The Commando was first shown to the public at the 1967 Earls Court show, although it was not until April 1968 that the first examples began to roll off the line. The new machine was an instant success, securing the *Motor Cycle News* Machine of the Year award in 1968, an accolade it would continue to hold up to 1972.

1974 Norton 850 Commando Interstate, 829cc overhead-valve parallel twin, 60bhp at 6,200rpm, 10.7in front disc brake, full-width drum rear brake.
£2,500–2,600 / $3,600–3,800 ⊞ **MAY**
The Interstate was added to the Commando range in 1972, featuring a larger petrol tank and disc front brake. The 850 version was launched the following year.

1975 Norton 850 Commando Roadster, 829cc overhead-valve twin, 77 x 89 mm bore and stroke, twin carburettors, 4-speed gearbox, some non-standard parts including front disc brake, fork sliders, fork gaiters and front mudguard.
£1,700–1,900 / $2,450–2,750 ↗ **Bon**
Introduced in 1973, the 850 provided more mid-range urge than the 750 Commando, even though power output and maximum speed were little different. The non-standard parts on this machine led to its lower value.

► **1978 Norton 850 Commando Interstate Mk III,** 829cc overhead-valve twin, twin Amal Concentric 932 32mm carburettors, 58bhp at 5,900rpm, electric starter, front and rear disc brakes with 2-piston calipers, one of only 30 Commandos built in 1978.
£2,800–3,100
$4,000–4,500 ⊞ **NLM**

NSU *(German 1901–65)*

1957 NSU Supermax, 247cc overhead-camshaft single, 69 x 66mm bore and stroke, 18bhp at 6,500rpm, 5-speed gearbox, fully enclosed rear chain, 79mph top speed, completely restored by Dave Livesey.
£3,600–4,000 / $5,000–5,800 ⊞ MW
The Supermax was the final development of the Max. It came on to the market in 1956 and incorporated several improvements over the original, mainly aimed at providing a more luxurious specification.

OK-Supreme *(British 1899–1939)*

◄ **1934 OK-Supreme Model G250 Flying Cloud,** 245cc overhead-valve single-port single, 62.5 x 80mm bore and stroke, iron head and barrel, foot-change gearbox, girder forks, rigid frame.
£1,100–1,300 / $1,600–2,000 ⚒ Bon
During the early 1930s, OK-Supreme offered an extensive range of 250-class machines catering for all tastes within that sector of the market. During 1934, three models were offered, all utilizing a proprietary JAP overhead-valve, single-cylinder engine, with the choice of either three- or four-speed gearbox.

Panther *(British 1900–66)*

► **1957 Panther Model 10,** 197cc Villiers 9E single-cylinder 2-stroke, piston-port induction, swinging-arm rear suspension, full-cradle frame.
£400–500 / $580–720 ⚒ Bon
Panther, of Cleckheaton, West Yorkshire, introduced a series of Villiers powered lightweights in 1956, three of which had 197cc 9E engines. The model offered a choice of three- or four-speed gearboxes. The most unusual feature was the front forks, which were of the Earles type, styled in such a way as to appear similar to contemporary telescopic designs.

◄ **c1947 Panther Model 60,** 249cc overhead-valve single, inclined cylinder, iron head and barrel, 60 x 80mm bore and stroke, restored.
£1,200–1,500 $1,750–2,150 ⚒ Bon
The overhead-valve 250 Redwing and Red Panther machines had been marketed during the inter-war years by London dealer Pride & Clarke, being the cheapest machines then readily available. The post-war 250 was a direct development of these motorcycles.

Parilla *(Italian 1946–67)*

1954 Parilla 175 Turismo, 174cc unit-construction single, wet-sump lubrication, 4-speed gearbox, Triumph-style tank-top parcel grid, completely restored by Dave Livesey, concours condition.
£3,000–3,200 / $4,400–4,650 ⊞ MW
The high-cam engine makes the Parilla almost as fast as an overhead-cam model. This machine is a very rare example of the classic Italian lightweight.

1960 Parilla Olimpia, 98cc overhead-valve horizontal single, alloy head, iron barrel, 52 x 46mm bore and stroke, 6.5bhp at 7,200rpm, 4-speed foot-change gearbox, fully restored.
£1,200–1,300 / $1,750–2,000 ⬧ BTSC
Developed from the unorthodox Slughi (Greyhound), the Olimpia was also available in 125 (114cc) two-stroke guise.

Premier *(British 1908–21)*

The Premier motorcycle was made by a company that had been founded in the days of the penny-farthing cycle, which was such an awkward device that many attempts were made to ease the lot of the rider. One of these was a high-wheel bicycle, the front wheel of which was driven by a system of levers. This machine was named Kangaroo, and its inventors were also involved in the creation of the Premier

Cycle Company. When that company began making motorcycles, as a tribute to the earlier venture, it adopted the motif of a kangaroo holding a glittering crown; thus was born the Premier tank badge. Making its own engines, Premier adopted some quite technically innovative ideas, but unfortunately, due to poor management, the company only existed until 1921.

Miller's is a price GUIDE not a price LIST

◄ **1914 Premier Pioneer,** 246cc, belt final drive, chain-driven pedal starting, gas lighting set, bulb horn, pump, sprung saddle, tool bags.
£4,500–4,700 / $6,500–7,000 ⚒ Bon

Puch *(Austrian 1903–)*

▶ **1965 Puch Allstate SGS 250,** 248cc 2-stroke split single, 2 pistons on one connecting rod, 2 carburettors, 4-speed foot-change gearbox, concours condition.
£2,000–2,300
$3,000–3,200 ⊞ MW
Puch machines were sold in the USA under the Allstate banner.

◄ **1960 Puch SGS 250,** 248cc 2-stroke split single, unrestored, in need of cosmetic attention.
£900–1,100 / $1,300–1,600 ⚒ **Bon**
The Austrian Puch singles were high-quality, well-built motorcycles. The engine of the SGS had been developed from the SGSH scrambler; its unusual split single-cylinder configuration provided an equally unique exhaust note.

Raleigh *(British 1899–1970s)*

► **1922 Raleigh 2¾hp,** 328cc side-valve single.
£2,250–2,500
$3,300–3,600 ⚒ **PS**
Now only associated with bicycles, Raleigh never quite achieved the prestige enjoyed by many other motorcycle manufacturers.

1924 Raleigh Model 6, 348cc side-valve single, forward mounted magneto, chain final drive, hand gear-change, caliper front brake, carrier, leather saddle.
£3,200–3,500 / $4,650–5,000 🚲 **RSS**

1927 Raleigh 174, 174cc side-valve single.
£2,250–2,500 / $3,300–3,600 🚲 **RSS**
This machine was the smallest of the Raleigh range.

1928 Raleigh Overhead Cam, 250cc overhead-camshaft single.
£2,700–3,000 / $4,000–4,400 🚲 **RSS**
This machine is one of only three known overhead-cam Raleighs. It is not known whether they were works prototypes or specials. Although the model was never in a Raleigh catalogue, subsequently its chassis was used for a 298cc side-valve machine, while the engine was sold to Dunelt.

1929 Raleigh Model MJ, 248cc side-valve single, hand-change Sturmey Archer gearbox, chain final drive, drum brakes, girder forks, rigid frame.
£3,200–3,500 / $4,650–5,000 🚲 **RSS**

Ratier *(French 1959–62)*

1950s Ratier Twin, 348cc overhead-valve flat-twin, 4-speed gearbox, shaft final drive, full-width drum brakes, telescopic front forks, rear swinging arm with twin shocks.
£5,000–6,000 / $7,250–8,750 ⊞ MW
Based on the BMW, the Ratier is now extremely rare. Ratier took over CEMEC (1948–55), which itself had taken over production of the BMW-style flat-twins from CMR (1945–48). The bikes were mainly sold to the police and army in France.

Rickman *(British 1959–80s)*

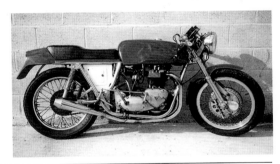

▶ **1971 Rickman Métisse Triumph,** 649cc Triumph T12OR Bonneville overhead-valve unit-construction twin, alloy head, iron barrel, twin carburettors, 4-speed gearbox, Rickman nickel plated frame, 4-leading-shoe front brake.
£3,500–4,000 / $5,000–5,800 ⊞ BLM
Brothers Don and Derek Rickman made their name campaigning a series of Métisse (French for mongrel dog) motocrossers. By the mid-1960s, their fame had led to orders for replica machines. From then on, Rickman made small batches of machines for motocross, road-racing and the street – and even some Zündapp powered lightweights for police duties.

Rover *(British 1902–25)*

1914 Rover, 550cc side-valve single, iron head and barrel, belt final drive, hand-pump lubrication, pedalling gear, caliper brakes.
£6,000–6,800 / $8,750–9,850 ⊞ VER

Royal Enfield *(British 1901–70)*

1914 Royal Enfield 350 V-Twin, 348cc, dry-sump lubrication, front mounted Bosch magneto, chain final drive, pedal starting, caliper brakes, sprung saddle, footboards, very original with correct period components, full running order.
£3,000–4,000 / $4,400–5,800 ⊞ MW
A racing version of this machine finished third in the 1914 Junior TT.

▶ **1921 Royal Enfield 225,** 221cc 2-stroke single, 2-speed gearbox, chain final drive, caliper brakes.
£1,200–1,800 / $1,750–2,600 ⚒ Bon

Auction prices

Miller's only includes motorcycles declared sold. Our guide prices take into account the buyer's premium, VAT on the premium, and the extent of any published catalogue information relating to condition and provenance. Motorcycles sold at auction are identified by the ⚒ icon; full details of the auction house can be found on page 167.

▶ **1922 Royal Enfield 2¼hp,** 221cc 2-stroke single, fitted optional kickstarter and 2-speed gears.
£1,400–2,800 / $2,000–4,000 ⚒ PS
Once a very popular machine with women, for whom a special version was available with a lowered frame, this model was powered by one of the company's own engines.

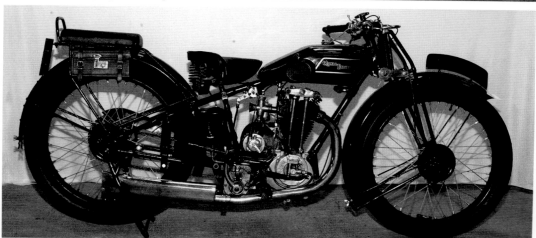

1928 Royal Enfield Model 35, 346cc overhead-valve single, 70 x 90mm bore and stroke.
£3,000–3,400 / $4,400–4,850 ⚒ Bon
For its 1928 range of motorcycles, Royal Enfield adopted saddle tanks for the first time. Additionally, the Druid-pattern front forks were replaced by girder forks employing a central spring in compression. In fact, 1928 was to be a good year for the factory: many trials successes were gained, and a venture to the Isle of Man resulted in a credible performance by the company's machines in both the Junior and Lightweight races.

◀ **1934 Royal Enfield Model S,** 248cc overhead-valve single, 64 x 77mm bore and stroke, inclined cylinder, dry-sump lubrication, 4-speed gearbox.
£1,400–1,650 / $2,000–2,400 ✗ Bon
This was the first year of production for the Model S.

▶ **1953 Royal Enfield Meteor,** 692cc overhead-valve parallel twin, separate cylinders and cylinder heads, 70 x 90mm bore and stroke, 36bhp at 6,000rpm.
£2,700–3,000 / $4,000–4,400 ⚙ REOC
The Meteor was in full production for 1953, and the only larger-capacity machine made in Britain at the time was the far more expensive Vincent twin. Its only fault was the new dual 6in (15.2cm) front brake; experience shows that this brake needs to be set up carefully, then run in for perhaps 1,000 miles, after which it can be extremely effective. The original Meteor was equally suited to solo and sidecar duties.

◀ **1955 Royal Enfield Clipper,** 248cc overhead-valve single, 64 x 77mm bore and stroke, iron head and barrel, 11bhp at 5,500rpm, 19in wheels, telescopic forks, swinging-arm rear suspension.
£1,200–1,500 / $1,750–2,150 ✗ CGC
The pre-unit Clipper ran from 1953 until 1957, when it was effectively replaced by the new unit-construction Crusader. A budget version of the Crusader, labelled Clipper II, was marketed from 1958 to 1965 and should not be confused with the original.

▶ **1956 Royal Enfield 350 Clipper,** 346cc overhead-valve single, 70 x 90mm bore and stroke, iron head and barrel, dry-sump lubrication, 15bhp at 5,500rpm, 4-speed gearbox, telescopic forks, swinging-arm rear suspension, single saddle, in need of cosmetic restoration.
£700–850
$1,000–1,250 ✗ PS
Basically a budget version of the Bullet, the 350 Clipper ran from 1955 to 1957.

◀ **1957 Royal Enfield 350 Clipper,** 346cc overhead-valve single, 70 x 90mm bore and stroke, iron head and barrel, 15bhp at 5,500rpm, 4-speed Albion gearbox, single-sided brakes, dualseat, very original, good running order.
£1,200–1,400 / $1,750–2,000 ✗ Bon
Introduced initially in 1953 as a 250cc model, the Clipper was available also as a 350 from 1955 onwards. It used the familiar Model G engine with 70 x 90mm bore and stroke dimensions, and was almost indistinguishable from the smaller bike.

Cross Reference
See Colour Review (page 56)

◄ **1958 Royal Enfield Crusader,** 248cc unit-construction single, 70 x 64.5mm bore and stroke, alloy head, iron barrel, 4-speed gearbox, chrome mudguards and tank panels, 17in wheels, headlamp nacelle.
£1,200–1,500 / $1,750–2,150 ⊞ NLM
This is a standard Crusader fitted with the engine from a Sports model.

Miller's
Motorcycle Milestones

Royal Enfield 350 Bullet (British 1949)
Price range: £1,800–3,000 / $2,600–4,400
The original Bullet models appeared in the early 1930s and comprised a range of Royal Enfield singles. However, the really important Bullet, the 350 swinging-arm model, arrived during the late 1940s.

Three prototypes were entered in the Colmore Trial during February 1948, and apart from the frame and some minor details (such as the bolted-up Albion gearbox and a revised crankcase-cum-oil container) the remainder of the motorcycle was much as before. The basic 346cc displacement (70 x 90mm bore and stroke) and general overhead-valve engine design came from the late 1930s, whereas the Enfield-made telescopic front forks had first appeared in prototype form in 1941, and had entered series production with the Model G in late 1945.

A revised bottom end for the engine reduced the assembly's length, made shorter still by the bolted-up gearbox, which, with its fixed chain centres, meant semi-unit construction.

But what made the 1948 350 Bullet such an important motorcycle was its new frame and suspension, which came at a time when rival manufacturers were still using either rigid or, at best, the relatively primitive plunger type. The compactness and good handling of the post-war 350 Bullet made it a bike that was largely ahead of its time, even though its mechanical roots were set in previous decades. The result was a much copied formula during the 1950s, which played a major part in ensuring that the machine ultimately outlived its peers in the British motorcycle industry. It has survived into the 21st century, courtesy of ongoing production in India.

► **1960 Royal Enfield Meteor Minor,** 496cc overhead-valve twin, 70 x 64.5mm bore and stroke, 4-speed Albion gearbox, telescopic forks, swinging-arm rear suspension, 17in rims, full-width alloy hubs, dualseat, headlamp nacelle.
£1,700–2,300 / $2,450–3,350 ⊞ MW
The Meteor Minor was built between 1958 and 1963, having been developed from the earlier 500 Twin (1949–58), but with several changes, including bore and stroke dimensions, wheel size, brake hubs and styling.

1960 Royal Enfield 350 Bullet, 346cc overhead-valve semi-unit-construction single, coil ignition, 4-speed bolted-up Albion gearbox with neutral finder, 17in wheels, full-width alloy brake, complete and original, in need of cosmetic restoration.
£1,000–1,100 / $1,500–1,600 ⟋ Bon
This machine is a late-type British-made Bullet.

► **1959 Royal Enfield Crusader,** 248cc overhead-valve unit-construction single, 70 x 64.5mm bore and stroke, 4-speed foot-change gearbox, full-width aluminium brake hubs, 17in wheels, dualseat, restored to original specification.
£1,400–1,600 / $2,000–2,300 ⊞ MW

1961 Royal Enfield Crusader Sports, 248cc overhead-valve unit-construction single, 70 x 64.5mm bore and stroke, 17bhp at 6,250rpm, 4-speed gearbox, chrome mudguards and tank, 17in wheels, full-width aluminium hubs.
£1,500–2,000 / $2,200–3,000 ⊞ MW
The original Crusader, designed by Reg Thomas, made its appearance towards the end of 1956. It was the first of the modern British post-war four-stroke 250s.

1961 Royal Enfield Prince, 148cc 2-stroke single, piston-port induction, 56 x 60mm bore and stroke, 6bhp at 4,750rpm, 3-speed gearbox, undamped telescopic forks, swinging-arm rear suspension, complete but in need of some cosmetic restoration.
£400–600 / $580–870 ⊞ BB
The Prince was offered between 1958 and 1962. It was the final development of the wartime Flying Flea RE125. Today, it is quite rare.

1963 Royal Enfield Turbo Twin Roadster, 247cc Villiers 4T 2-stroke twin-cylinder engine, 50 x 63.5mm bore and stroke, cycle parts from Crusader model, completely restored to original specification.
£1,800–2,000 / $2,500–3,000 ⊛ BTSC

1966 Royal Enfield Crusader Sports, 248cc overhead-valve unit-construction single, 70 x 64.5mm bore and stroke, 17bhp at 6,250rpm, 4-speed gearbox, telescopic forks, swinging-arm rear suspension, full-width alloy hubs, 17in wheels, chrome mudguards and tank, 2-tone dualseat, concours condition.
£1,800–2,000 / $2,600–3,000 ⊛ REOC
This machine was one of the final Crusader Sports models to be built before the Redditch factory's closure.

1966 Royal Enfield Continental GT, 248cc overhead-valve unit-construction single, 9.5:1 compression ratio, 21.5bhp at 7,500rpm, 5-speed gearbox, 85mph top speed, completely restored.
£1,800–2,000 / $2,600–3,000 ⚲ **REOC**
The Continental GT was launched in November 1964, when a team of riders rode from John O'Groats to Land's End in under 24 hours. On the way, they put in some laps of the Silverstone racing circuit, one of the machines being ridden by John 'Moon-eyes' Cooper.

1969 Royal Enfield Series II Interceptor, 736cc overhead-valve semi-unit twin, 71 x 93mm bore and stroke, 52.5bhp at 6,500rpm, fitted optional 4 gallon (18 litre) tank, original front drum brake replaced by a disc unit.
£3,600–4,000 / $5,000–5,800 ⚲ **PBM**
The Series II model was launched in 1968. New features included wet-sump lubrication, points in the timing case, capacitor ignition, vertical oil filter, Norton forks and Norton 8in (200mm) front drum brake.

1988 Royal Enfield India 350 Bullet, 346cc overhead-valve semi-unit single, 70 x 90mm bore and stroke, 18bhp at 5,600rpm, 75mph top speed.
£800–1,000 / $1,200–1,500 ⊞ **BLM**
Based on the 1955 British 350 Bullet, this machine was made in India.

1990 Royal Enfield India 500 Bullet, 499cc overhead-valve single, 84 x 90mm bore and stroke, alloy head, iron barrel, 4-speed foot-change gearbox with neutral finder, full-width drum brakes, original apart from Gold Star-pattern silencer.
£900–1,000 / $1,300–1,500 ⊞ **BLM**
The 500 easily outsells the 350 version in export markets, but in India the reverse applies.

Royal Ruby *(British 1909–33)*

c1921 Royal Ruby Lightweight, 269cc 2-stroke single.
£2,600–3,000 / $3,800–4,400 ⚲ **PS**
Today, Royal Ruby is an almost forgotten make. This is probably a 1915 model, despite its 1921 registration date. Only one other 1915 model is recorded in the Vintage MCC's register, so this may be the only existing machine fitted with a two-speed gearbox.

Rudge *(British 1911–40)*

◄ **1911 Rudge,** 499cc side-valve single, magneto ignition, Mabon variable gear system, belt final drive, front-wheel speedometer drive, caliper brakes, lighting equipment.
£6,200–6,700 / $9,000–9,750 ⊞ VER

1923 Rudge Multi, 499cc inlet-over-exhaust single, 85 x 88mm bore and stroke, forward mounted magneto, variable transmission, belt final drive, pedal starting, unrestored, mechanically sound.
£4,800–5,000 / $7,000–7,250 ⚴ RRN
The Multi first appeared in 1911 and remained in production until 1922.

► **1928 Rudge Special,** 493cc, overhead-valve single, 84.5 x 88mm bore and stroke, one owner for 31 years, believed to have been raced during 1950s and 1960s, very original.
£3,500–3,800 / $5,000–5,500 ⚴ Bon
The 1927 racing season had been one of mixed fortunes for the formidable Rudge team of Ashby, Longman, Nott, Walker and Tyrell Smith, but 1928 saw improved fortunes, with Walker riding to an outstanding victory in the Ulster Grand Prix. The production models that year consisted of the Standard, Special and Sports models, the 500cc Special featuring radially disposed exhaust valves.

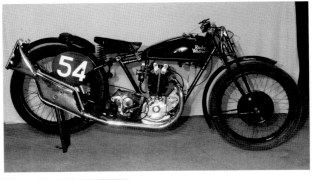

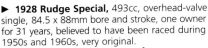

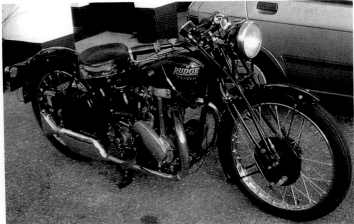

◄ **1931 Rudge Ulster,** 499cc overhead-valve twin-port single, 85 x 88mm bore and stroke, drum brakes, girder forks, rigid frame, engine, gearbox, carburettor, speedometer and wheels professionally rebuilt.
£5,000–5,500 / $7,250–8,000 ⚴ Bon
Rudge entered the 1930s in a strong position; sporting success at Brooklands, on 'the Island' and in events such as the Ulster Grand Prix had enhanced the company's reputation. Its name was was further improved in 1930, at the TT, where Rudge machines secured the first three places in the Junior, and the first two in the Senior. However, this would be the high-water mark in the firm's fortunes.

1934 Rudge Ulster, 499cc overhead-valve single, 85 x 88mm bore and stroke, 4-valve bronze cylinder head, twin exhaust ports, good condition.
£4,800–5,000 / $7,000–7,250 ⊞ VER

1936 Rudge Ulster Grand Prix Competition, 499cc overhead-valve single, twin-port high-level exhausts.
£10,000–12,000 / $14,500–17,500 ➴ Bon
This rare Ulster was found dismantled some years ago and was painstakingly restored to its correct specification. A variation of the standard Ulster, it is one of only two believed to exist. It was featured in *Classic Bike* magazine of October 1988. Its unusual high-level exhaust system is complemented by a crankcase shield plate, deemed necessary because of the 5½in (14cm) ground clearance. An additional feature is the lift-over rear stand, which is pivoted from the rear frame.

1937 Rudge Ulster, 499cc overhead-valve single, semi-radial 4-valve cylinder head, 4-speed foot-change gearbox, restored.
£4,300–4,800 / $6,250–7,000 ➴ Bon
In 1936, for the third successive year, only 2,000 Rudge machines were sold. This necessitated drastic changes to be made for 1937. In respect of the top-of-the-range Ulster, the redesigned enclosed valve gear of the bronze cylinder head, which had been introduced at the Olympia show, became standard specification. Fortunately, the machine became popular with the buying public, and all the combined changes to the various models saw sales output rise to 3,000 that year.

1938 Rudge Rapid, 245cc overhead-valve single-port single, 62 x 81mm bore and stroke, completely restored, unmodified.
£2,500–3,300 / $3,600–4,750 ➴ Bon
The Rapid was sold between 1936 and 1939. It replaced the more exotic, but rather fragile, 248cc Radial four-valve model.

Rumi *(Italian 1949–late 1950s)*

Officine Fonderie Rumi was founded by Donnino Rumi in Bergamo, just before WWI. During the inter-war years, the company built textile machinery. During WWII, Rumi specialized in the design and construction of midget two-man submarines and torpedos – hence the anchor in the marque's logo. After the conflict – like others such as Agusta and Macchi, who had built military hardware – Rumi diversified into motorcycles. The first design was a 180-degree-crank, parallel twin-cylinder two-stroke with forward-facing horizontal cylinders. Displacing 124.68cc (42 x 45mm bore and stroke), this power unit would become a Rumi trademark throughout its years as a motorcycle and scooter manufacturer. By 1950, Rumi was exhibiting its products outside Italy – in Geneva and Paris – and in the following year, the company made its sporting debut in the 1951 ISDT. January 1952 saw the Bergamo firm launch a sports

version, featuring twin Dell'Orto carburettors. But this was only the beginning, for soon a whole string of new two-wheelers arrived, mainly thanks to the pen of the much travelled engineer Giuseppe Salmaggi. One example of his work was an experimental 247.36cc (54 x 54mm) double-overhead-camshaft racing twin with shaft final drive. Another was Rumi's first scooter the Scoiattolo (Squirrel). These were soon followed by a new 125cc over-the-counter racer, and 175 and 200cc variants of the horizontal 125 roadster twin. In 1954, the definitive Rumi appeared, the Formichino (Little Ant) scooter. The Formichino went on not only to become the company's top seller, but also to win its class in the prestigious French Bol d'Or on more than one occasion. The engine was also utilized to power the Junior Gentleman sports/racing motorcycle; race kitted, it could exceed 100mph.

1951 Rumi Scoiattolo, 124.68cc, Dell'Orto UA15S carburettor, 6bhp at 4,800rpm, 4-speed gearbox, legshields, footboards, substantial mudguards, 50mph top speed.
£2,800–3,000 / $4,000–4,400 ⊞ NLM
The Scoiattolo (Squirrel) came about because of the success of the Lambretta and Vespa scooters. Rumi thought a better bet would be a machine that was more like a motorcycle, but with the weather protection and comfort of a scooter. Hence, the company's effort had 14in wheels and motorcycle suspension.

▶ **1955 Rumi 125 Turismo,** 124.68cc 2-stroke horizontal twin, 42 x 45mm bore and stroke.
£5,000–5,500 / $7,250–8,000 ⊞ NLM

1954 Rumi Bicarburatore, 124.68cc horizontal twin, 10.5:1 compression ratio, 2 Dell'Orto 18mm (or optional 22mm) carburettors, 9bhp at 7,300rpm.
£6,500–7,000 / $9,500–10,500 ⊞ NLM
The Bicarburatore (twin carburettor) was virtually a cross between the racing and road-going Rumi 125s. The model ran from 1953 through to 1956.

Sarolea *(Belgian 1896–1963)*

◀ **c1925 Sarolea 500,** 499cc overhead-valve single-port single, exposed valve gear, iron head and barrel, forward mounted magneto, hand-change gearbox, chain final drive, drum brakes, girder forks, rigid frame, full lighting kit.
£3,200–3,500 / $4,650–5,000 ⋌ Bon
Like its great rival FN, Sarolea began as a weapons manufacturer. Early motorcycles were powered by a mixture of single-cylinder and V-twin engines. During the 1920s, the firm enjoyed considerable racing success. Post-war production ranged from a 125cc two-stroke to a 600cc overhead-valve single. In 1960, following a bout of financial trouble, Sarolea merged with Gillet-Herstal; production of Sarolea machines ended in 1963.

Scott *(British 1909–late 1960s)*

Alfred Angus Scott was a true pioneer of the two-stroke motorcycle, building his first machine in 1908. This bike, a 450cc twin, set the scene for what was to be nine decades of two-stroke engine development, culminating with the near total domination of this type of engine in the smaller classes.

Alfred Scott cultivated an engine technology that many were to pursue. His basic ideas on the two-stroke cycle are still followed today, albeit modified in the light of modern thinking, with the application of acoustic theory to improve gas flow and modern materials to withstand the increases in power that his new science gave. Scott was a natural engineer, who originally designed his creation as a gas cycle-engined boat, his early experiments being carried out on the Clyde during 1900, and later in the cycle frames. The Scott practice of using a central flywheel, overhung cranks, deflector pistons and detachable transfer ports came about from these early experiments, one motor being built with a grooved flywheel that drove the front wheel of a pedal cycle.

The specification of the 450 twin was far in excess of anything available at the time. In the days of belt final drive and push starting, the Scott showed the way ahead by featuring chain drive and a kickstarter, being further enhanced by a two-speed gearbox with a central neutral finder.

Rival manufacturers were really worried, so much so that they complained to motorcycle sport's organizing body the ACU. However, officials did not ban the Scott, but they imposed a rule that as the two-stroke engine fired twice as often as its four-stroke rivals, it must be twice the size. But the ACU ruling gave Scott a brilliant advertising opportunity, which it seized, proclaiming, 'The bike which all other manufacturers feared'; Scott went on to even more competition successes.

To rub salt into the wounds of its rivals, and to further enhance the potential of the handicapped bike, the Scott Trial was formulated, an arduous open-to-all test of both man and machine, which is still run today. The other manufacturers knew the prestige that a Scott Trial victory would give them and tried their hardest, but to no avail; Scotts won the event from 1914 though to 1924.

The Isle of Man TT of 1911 saw the feared Scott, now using rotary inlet and transfer valves on the works racers, break the lap record. Wins were recorded at the 1912 and 1913 TT races, with a further lap record gained in 1914.

Sadly, Scott himself left the Shipley works he had founded in 1915 to set up an experimental workshop near Bradford. Thereafter, Scott motorcycle development stagnated, and the lead gained under the founder's guidance slowly dwindled as rival manufacturers slowly made advances themselves.

As for Scott, he worked throughout the war, developing several important inventions. But when hostilities ended, he launched the Autocar, which proved a financial disaster, and he relinquished his directorship in the project; he died shortly afterwards of pneumonia. A sad end for such a great engineering genius.

1909 Scott Two-Speeder, 333cc liquid-cooled 2-stroke twin, 2-speed gearbox, chain final drive.
£5,500–6,000
$8,000–8,700 ⚙ SCOT

▶ **1914 Scott TT,** 532cc, rotary-valve inlet, 2 spark plugs per head, 2-speed foot-change gearbox, pressurized pannier fuel tank, only surviving example of 3 made, recently rebuilt to concours condition.
£25,000+ / $36,000+ ⚙ SCOT

1930 Scott Power Plus Replica, 596cc 2-stroke twin, engine rebuilt by Scott expert.
£3,500–4,000 / $5,000–5,800 ✈ **PS**

1932 Scott Squirrel Sports, 596cc, Power Plus detachable head, foot-change gearbox.
£5,000–6,000 / $7,250–8,750 🚲 **APM**

▶ **1938 Scott Flying Squirrel,** 497cc liquid-cooled twin, inclined cylinders, drum brakes, foot-change gearbox, chain final drive, unrestored.
£2,300–2,800 / $3,350–4,000 ✈ **Bon**
By the mid-1930s, the Scott range consisted of the Flying Squirrel, in either 497cc or 596cc engine sizes, and a three-cylinder model to special order.

◀ **1947 Scott Squirrel,** 596cc liquid-cooled 2-stroke twin, telescopic front forks, rigid frame, full-width brake hubs, largely original, unrestored.
£2,000–2,500
$3,000–3,600 ⊞ **NLM**
This machine was one of the last Scotts to be built in Yorkshire, before the move south to Birmingham at the end of the 1940s.

Sparkbrook *(British 1912–25)*

◄ **1926 Sparkbrook 2¼hp,** 269cc 2-stroke single-cylinder engine.
£2,200–2,450 / $3,200–3,500 ⚒ PS
This relatively rare Villiers-engined two-stroke is one of only six post-1920 models listed in the Vintage MCC's register. It is understood to have a 1924 engine fitted identical to the original.

Sun *(British 1911–61)*

1955 Sun Challenger, 197cc Villiers 8E 2-stroke single-cylinder engine, piston-port induction, 3-speed foot-change gearbox, fully restored.
£900–1,000 / $1,300–1,500 ⚒ Bon
The 8E-engined Challenger was offered between 1954 and 1957, the Sun Cycle & Fittings Company having re-entered production in 1946 with the 98cc Autocycle. Motorcycles made a return in 1949. All post-war Sun machines were powered by the ubiquitous Villiers two-stroke engine family.

1914 Sun Villiers, 250cc 2-stroke single, side mounted carburettor, belt final drive, caliper brakes, full lighting equipment.
£3,500–3,800 / $5,000–5,500 ⊞ VER

> A known continuous history can add value to and enhance the enjoyment of a motorcycle.

Sunbeam *(British 1912–57)*

1917 Sunbeam 3½hp, 499cc side-valve single.
£3,870–4,300 / $5,500–6,250 ⚒ PS
Known as the gentleman's motorcycle, the Sunbeam was built to a very high standard and was renowned for the quality of its finish – and its correspondingly high price! Most 1917 models were made for War Department use during WWI, although a few could be purchased for civilian use by special permit.

1922 Sunbeam 3½hp, 499cc side-valve single, 85 x 88mm bore and stroke, 3-speed hand-change gearbox.
£5,000–5,700 / $7,250–8,250 ⚒ Bon

The first Sunbeam motorcycle – a 350cc side-valve single – left the Wolverhampton premises of John Marston, hitherto a manufacturer of high-quality enamelled goods, bicycles and – latterly – cars, in 1912. Equipped with a two-speed countershaft gearbox and fully enclosed all-chain drive, the 2hp Sunbeam was an instant success in an era when hub gears and belt drive were commonplace. Like Marston's other products, his motorcycles soon established a reputation for sound construction and superb finish. Their race-track performance did nothing to discourage sales either. Howard Davies finished second in the 1914 Senior TT on a Sunbeam, and Tommy De La Hay took victory in the 1920 Senior, after George Dance, also Sunbeam mounted, retired while leading. Sunbeam's second model was the 3½hp of 1913. A side-valve single like its predecessor, the 3½hp came with a three-speed hand-change gearbox and fully enclosed oilbath chaincases. Although effectively superseded by the famous 'long-stroke', which appeared in 1921, the short-stroke (85 x 88mm) 3½hp model remained in production until 1926.

1923 Sunbeam Model 5, 491cc side-valve single, 77 x 105.5mm bore and stroke, fully enclosed final drive chain, caliper brakes front and rear, full lighting equipment, leather pannier bags, good original example with correct tinware.
£4,800–5,000 / $7,000–7,250 ⊞ VER

1925 Sunbeam Model 1 2¾hp, 346cc side-valve single, 70 x 90mm bore and stroke, chain final drive, girder forks, rigid frame, drum brakes.
£2,400–2,700 / $3,500–4,000 ⚒ Bon

1927 Sunbeam Model 5 Light Tourist, 491cc side-valve single, 77 x 105.5mm bore and stroke, mag/dyno, fully enclosed final drive chain, fully restored to original specification.
£4,000–4,200 / $5,800–6,000 ⚒ CGC
The Model 5 remained in production until 1930.

1927 Sunbeam Model 9, 493cc overhead-valve single, 80 x 8mm bore and stroke, rear mounted magneto, unrestored, excellent condition.
£4,500–5,000 / $6,500–7,250 ⊞ VER
Sunbeam's long-running Model 9 was still in production as late as 1937.

▶ **1928 Sunbeam Model 2,** 346cc side-valve single, 70 x 90mm bore and stroke, P & H acetylene headlamp, Holdtite rear lamp, leather pannier, only 2 owners from new.
£4,200–4,500 $6,000–6,500 ⚒ Bon
When sold in 1928, the Model 2 was priced at £66.3s with Lucas mag/dyno; electric lighting cost an additional £10.10s.

1932 Sunbeam Model 9, 493cc overhead-valve twin-port single.
£5,500–6,000 / $8,000–8,700 ⚒ Bon
Sunbeam's range of machines for 1932 comprised four models: the 350cc Model 10, the 500cc Lion Long-stroke, the sporting Model 90 and the touring 500cc Model 9. The long-running and hugely popular, overhead-valve-engined Model 9 was gradually developed over its production run, a saddle tank appearing for 1929, while by 1932 electric lighting had become standard. The Model 9 came with either a single-port or twin-port head; pushrod enclosure was standard by 1930.

1932 Sunbeam Lion, 599cc side-valve single, 85 x 105.5mm bore and stroke, fully enclosed final drive chain, original condition, variety of spares including cylinder barrels, crankcases and flywheels.
£1,700–1,900 / $2,500–2,750 ⚒ PS
This powerful side-valve single was often seen attached to a sidecar. The Lion ran from 1932 to 1937.

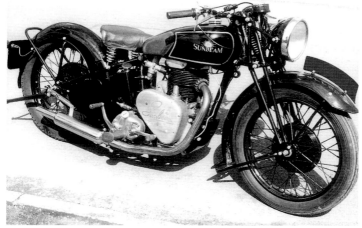

◄ **1939 Sunbeam B28,** 598cc overhead-valve single, 90.48 x 93mm bore and stroke.
£3,500–4,000
$5,000–5,800 ⊞ AtMC
Following AMC's acquisition of Sunbeam in 1937, a new range of high-cam models was developed for introduction during 1938. The new range was offered in four different capacities, from 245cc to 598cc, the 348, 497 and the 598cc models sharing the same stroke. During 1939, the larger machines acquired a form of pivoted-fork rear suspension, which used captive spring boxes that were similar in appearance to a plunger system.

▶ **1950 Sunbeam S7,** 489cc overhead-camshaft inline twin, 70 x 63.5mm bore and stroke, 4-speed foot-change gearbox, shaft final drive, standard specification apart from Burgess silencer.
£2,000–2,800 / $3,000–4,000 ⊞ MW
Designed by Erling Poppe, the S7 was built between 1947 and 1954.

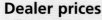

Dealer prices

Miller's guide prices for dealer motorcycles take into account the value of any guarantees or warranties that may be included in the purchase. Dealers must also observe additional statutory consumer regulations, which do not apply to private sellers. This is factored into our dealer guide prices. Dealer motorcycles are identified by the ⊞ icon; full details of the dealer can be found on page 167.

▶ **1951 Sunbeam S7,** 489cc overhead-camshaft unit-construction inline twin, front mounted generator, 4-speed foot-change gearbox.
£2,000–2,800 / $3,000–4,000 ⊞ BB

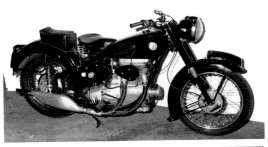

◄ **1952 Sunbeam S7 De Luxe,** 489cc overhead-camshaft inline twin, fully restored.
£2,500–3,000 / $3,600–4,400 ⚒ Bon
BSA bought the Sunbeam name in 1943, and the S7 was the first all-new motorcycle from the group in the post-war period. The first S7 was not without its problems, and BSA revised the machine considerably, the S7 De Luxe eliminating the earlier problems. A dynamo-smooth, overhead-camshaft twin – rubber mounted in a cradle frame – and a unique sprung saddle make the experience of riding an S7 unlike that of any other bike, and its stately progress is addictive.

► **1952 Sunbeam S8,** 489cc overhead-camshaft inline twin, 4-speed foot-change gearbox, shaft final drive, plunger rear suspension.
£1,100–1,400 / $1,600–2,000 ⚒ PS
The S8 was the sporting version of the S7, featuring narrower tyres of larger diameter (from 16in on both wheels to a 19in front and 18in rear), and front forks and brake from the BSA range.

Suzuki (Japanese 1952–)

1963 Suzuki T10, 246cc 2-stroke twin, piston-port induction, 52 x 58mm bore and stroke, alloy head, iron barrel, 21bhp at 8,000rpm, 4-speed gearbox, fully enclosed final drive chain, electric starter, spine frame, telescopic front forks, swinging-arm rear suspension, 17in wheels, 80mph top speed, fully restored, concours condition.
£3,200–3,500
$4,650–5,000 🚲 VJMC
The T10 was a luxury touring machine, not a sportster like the T20 that followed it. An interesting feature was the hydraulically operated rear brake. This bike is now very rare.

◄ **1976 Suzuki K50,** 49.9cc 2-stroke single, 37.8 x 49.9mm bore and stroke, near-vertical cylinder, pump lubrication, alloy head, iron barrel, 17in wheels, only 16 miles from new.
£800–900 / $1,150–1,300 ⚒ Bon
The K50 ultra-lightweight motorcycle was in production for a decade, from 1966 to 1976. It was also sold in some markets (including the UK) with pedals as the AP50 moped.

1977 Suzuki GT550, 544cc piston-port 2-stroke triple, pump lubrication, alloy heads and barrels, Ram Air System, 53bbhp at 7,500rpm, 5-speed gearbox, electric starter, disc front brake, chrome mudguards, unused, 'as new' condition.
£2,000–2,300 / $3,000–3,350 ⚒ Bon

1978 Suzuki GT250, 247cc, concours condition.
£900–1,100 / $1,300–1,600 ⚒ Bon
The GT250 could trace its ancestry back to the T20 Super Six of the mid-1960s. This version has had the full period café-racer conversion, including Koni rear shocks, rear-sets, clip-ons, fairing, and racing alloy tank and seat; the oil tank has been relocated into the tail fairing of the seat.

▶ **1979 Suzuki GS1000,** 998cc double-overhead-camshaft across-the-frame four, 70 x 64.8mm bore and stroke, 87bhp at 8,000rpm, 5-speed gearbox, electric starter, telescopic front forks, swinging-arm rear suspension, triple disc brakes, cast alloy wheels, 135mph top speed.
£2,000–2,500 / $3,000–3,600 ⊞ NLM

Restored values

The cost of a professional restoration will have an influence on, but no direct relation to, a motorcycle's market value. A restored motorcycle can have a market value lower than the cost of its restoration.

1981 Suzuki GSX750, double-overhead-camshaft across-the-frame four, 75bhp, aftermarket 4-into-1 exhaust, cast alloy wheels, triple disc brakes, full instrumentation, 125mph top speed.
£1,200–1,500 / $1,750–2,150 ⊞ NLM

1977 Suzuki RE5, 497cc liquid-cooled single-rotor Wankel engine, 62bhp at 6,500rpm, pump lubrication, 5-speed gearbox, electric starter, fewer than 900 miles from new.
£3,000–3,500 / $4,400–5,000 ⚒ Bon
During the early 1970s, both Suzuki and Yamaha explored the potential of the Wankel rotary engine for motorcycle use. Although Yamaha did not put it into production, Suzuki eventually released the RE5 in 1975. Although the engine design is inherently simple, the ancillary systems required added a degree of complexity and weight that many potential purchasers found off-putting, especially when the performance was compared to the multi-cylinder machines available of similar nominal capacity. The model continued in production for a few years, eventually fading from the range. Today, the machine is viewed as an astonishing technical tour de force. This example is the final version with conventional instrumentation in place of the original pop-up, barrel-shaped instrument cover.

1980 Suzuki SP370, 370cc overhead-camshaft unit-construction single, full-cradle frame, high-level exhaust.
£700–900 / $1,000–1,300 ⚒ CGC
After its unrivalled success in the 1976 Motocross World Championships – where it won all three titles (125cc, 250cc and 500cc) – Suzuki was in an excellent position to offer the public an increasing number of trail bikes for on/off-road use. One of its best bikes of the period was the four-stroke SP370, which offered unusually good performance and a high degree of comfort.

Triumph *(British 1902–)*

c1907 Triumph 3½hp, 499cc side-valve single.
£6,000–7,000 / $8,700–10,200 ⚲ Bon

▶ 1910 Triumph Model D, 499cc side-valve
single, double-barrel carburettor, forward
mounted magneto, belt final drive, lighting set,
front-wheel speedometer drive.
£5,000–6,000 / $7,250–8,750 ⊞ VER

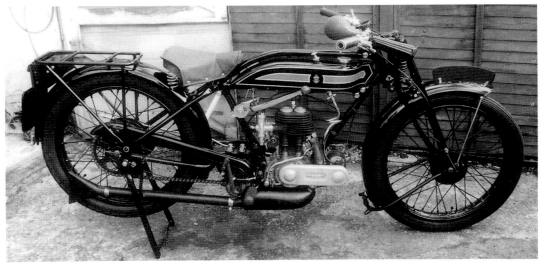

1921 Triumph 550, 549cc side-valve single, 84 x 99mm bore and stroke, chain final drive, drum brakes, girder forks, rigid
frame, rear carrier.
£2,500–2,700 / $3,600–4,000 ⊞ MAY

▶ 1931 Triumph Model WL, 348cc side-valve single,
72 x 85.5mm bore and stroke.
£1,000–1,200 / $1,500–1,750 ⚲ Bon
Triumph's new 350cc side-valve Model WL was
current for the 1931 and 1932 seasons. It was a stylish
bike with an inclined single-cylinder engine with
enclosed valve gear, a fashionable saddle tank;
electric lighting was an optional extra. It was one of
11 different models catalogued by Triumph in 1931
and sold for £38 / $55.

◀ **1927 Triumph Model N,** 549cc side-valve single, double-barrel carburettor, girder forks, rigid frame, fully restored.
£3,000–4,000
$4,400–5,800 ⊞ BLM

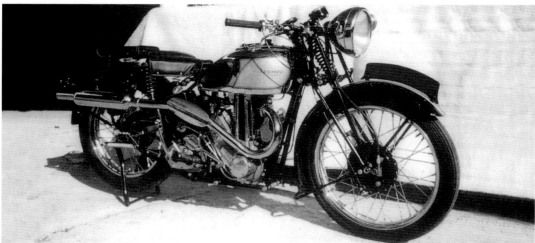

1937 Triumph Tiger 80, 343cc overhead-valve single, 70 x 89mm bore and stroke, rear mounted mag/dyno, 4-speed foot-change gearbox, concours condition.
£4,000–4,800 / $5,800–7,000 ⊀ Bon
During 1936, Edward Turner took over the ailing Triumph factory and decided to update the range. Initially, this was done by enhancing existing machines to produce an interim Tiger series, to be followed eventually by new models. This meant that for approximately five months there was a short production run of what can only be referred to as prototype new Tiger 80s. This version was manufactured between April and August 1936, and differs from the later Tiger 80 in retaining the twin-downtube frame, pre-series gearbox, petrol tank and tank panel (which has an oil pressure indicator instead of a gauge) and adjusters at the top of the forks. Additionally, the tool box was mounted adjacent to the top of the rear mudguard.

1939 Triumph Tiger 100, 499cc overhead-valve pre-unit twin, 63 x 80mm bore and stroke, mag/dyno, girder forks, rigid frame, finished in chrome and silver.
£5,000–6,000 / $7,250–8,750 ⊞ MW
The original Edward Turner designed 5T Speed Twin appeared in time for the 1938 season, the more sporting Tiger 100 arriving for 1939. Today, the latter is very rare.

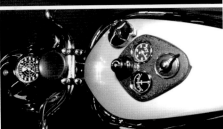

1946 Triumph Tiger 100, 499cc overhead-valve parallel twin, 63 x 80mm bore and stroke, 8-stud iron head and barrel, 38bhp, telescopic front forks, rigid frame, tank mounted gauges and switches, 95mph top speed.
£4,000–4,500 / $5,800–6,500 毾 RRN

Miller's
Motorcycle Milestones

Triumph Speed Twin (British 1938)
Price range: £3,000–5,500 / $4,400–8,000
The Speed Twin was like the Honda CB750 three decades later, a real trendsetter. Designed by Edward Turner, almost overnight it made the traditional big singles and V-twins seem old hat. A key factor in the Speed Twin's success was its lightness – it actually tipped the scales 5lb (2.25kg) lighter than the company's Tiger 90 single! Turner had joined Triumph from Ariel, where he had been responsible for the Square Four design. He had been brought to Triumph by Charles Sangster, who had recently acquired the Coventry marque.
Originally, Turner had wanted to build an overhead-cam engine, but in the end this was abandoned in favour of the more basic and cheaper overhead-valve layout. Moreover, the Speed Twin had the same 63 x 80mm bore and stroke dimensions as Triumph's existing 250 single, thus further reducing production costs. An iron cylinder head and barrel were features of the design, the latter with a six-stud base flange, updated to an eight-stud layout in 1939 following a spate of problems associated with cracks. In prototype form, the Speed Twin engine put out around 30bhp, while the early production versions, built in 1937, gave 3–4bhp less, but still good enough to propel the machine to 90mph. Just like the CB750, the Speed Twin left the opposition standing, not only in performance, but also in sophistication, being quicker, easier to start, flexible and comfortable. Turner and Triumph really had struck gold.

◀ **1947 Triumph 5T Speed Twin,** 499cc overhead-valve pre-unit twin, iron head and barrel, 4-speed foot-change gearbox, telescopic front forks, rigid frame, single-sided brakes, complete but in need of restoration.
£1,700–1,850 / $2,500–2,750 ⚘ Bon
Triumph was one of the first British manufacturers to announce a range of machines following WWII, offering five models, one of which was the Speed Twin. The major revision in comparison to the pre-war models concerned the front forks, which were of the telescopic type instead of the girder pattern used previously. In other respects, the model continued much as it had before; the instruments were still located in the tank top, and no provision was made for rear suspension.

▶ **1950 Triumph 3T,** 349cc overhead-valve twin, 58.25 x 65.5mm bore and stroke, iron head and barrel, telescopic front forks, rigid frame, sprung single saddle, chrome tank, fork mounted speedometer, original specification.
£1,800–2,000
$2,600–3,000 ⊞ MW

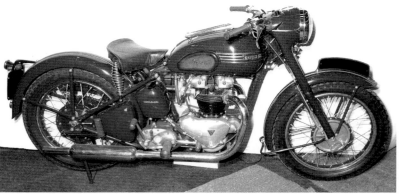

◄ **1952 Triumph 5T Speed Twin,** 499cc overhead-valve pre-unit twin, 63 x 80mm bore and stroke, single carburettor, 4-speed foot-change gearbox, sprung hub, single seat, headlamp nacelle, tank-top parcel grid, 84mph top speed, original and unrestored.
£4,500–5,000
$6,500–7,250 ⚙ **VMCC**

1952 Triumph Tiger 100, 499cc, overhead-valve parallel twin, spring-hub rear suspension.
£4,000–5,000 / $6,500–7,250 ➹ **Bon**
The sporting vanguard of the Triumph range in the early 1950s was the 500cc Tiger 100. As part of an effort to provide a substitute for the Grand Prix racer, the Tiger 100 was offered with a die-cast barrel and head, with close finning and splayed exhaust ports. A conversion kit was available for 1952 at £35 / $50, which included a full race kit comprising suitable cams, high-compression pistons, stronger valve springs, a rev-counter, racing pipes and megaphone silencers. With the full kit, output rose above 40bhp, giving a top speed of 120mph. That year, Bernard Hargreaves secured victory in the Senior Clubman's TT on a Tiger 100.

1954 Triumph T110, 649cc overhead-valve pre-unit twin, 71 x 82mm bore and stroke, iron head, telescopic front forks, swinging-arm rear suspension, alloy front brake plate, dualseat, headlamp nacelle, 105mph top speed, completely restored, concours condition.
£2,500–3,000 / $3,600–4,400 ⊞ **CotC**

1954 Triumph Tiger 100, 499cc overhead-valve pre-unit twin, 4-speed foot-change gearbox, original specification apart from Speed Twin iron cylinder head.
£4,600–5,000 / $6,500–7,250 ⊞ **MW**
This was the first year of the swinging-arm frame and 8in (20.3cm) front brake.

1956 Triumph T15 Terrier, 149cc overhead-valve unit single, 57 x 58.5mm bore and stroke, 4-speed gearbox, telescopic front forks, plunger rear suspension, 17in wheel rims.
£1,600–1,800 / $2,300–2,600 🚲 TCTR
The Terrier arrived in 1953, having been designed by Edward Turner; 1956 was the last year of production.

► 1956 Triumph T20 Tiger Cub, 199cc overhead-valve unit single, 63 x 64mm bore and stroke, distributor ignition at rear of cylinder barrel, 16in wheel rims, headlamp nacelle, dualseat.
£1,350–1,500
$2,000–2,200 🚲 TCTR
This early Cub has the plunger rear suspension of the T15 Terrier .

◄ 1956 Triumph T20 Tiger Cub, 199cc overhead-valve single, 4-speed foot-change gearbox, plunger rear suspension, 16in wheel rims.
£1,400–1,500 / $2,000–2,200 🏹 Bon
In 1953, the T20 Tiger Cub was added to the Triumph range. First exhibited at the Earl's Court show, it was described as the sports or Tiger version of the Terrier, and it was finished in blue, as were the other sporting versions in the line-up. A top speed of 66.7mph and a fuel consumption of 136mpg at 30mph were quoted. This is the rare early plunger-frame model.

► 1957 Triumph Tiger Cub, 199cc overhead-valve single, 4-speed gearbox, swinging-arm frame, 16in wheels, headlamp nacelle, correct blue and silver finish.
£600–800 / $870–1,150 🏹 Bon
The Tiger Cub had a simple, compact four-stroke engine built in unit with a four-speed gearbox; by 1957, the specification had changed to include a swinging-arm frame and hydraulically damped forks. A continual programme of development and change within the company saw the final versions with BSA Bantam cycle parts; production ceased in 1970.

1958 Triumph Tiger 100, 499cc overhead-valve pre-unit parallel twin, 63 x 80mm bore and stroke, alloy head and barrel, swinging-arm frame, full-width front hub.
£2,500–3,000 / $3,600–4,400 ⚓ **Bon**
The swinging-arm frame arrived for the 1955 model year and was a significant improvement, in terms of handling and comfort, over the infamous Turner designed sprung-hub system.

▶ **1961 Triumph 3TA Twenty One,** 349cc overhead-valve unit twin, 58.2 x 65.5mm bore and stroke, distributor ignition, separate exhaust pipes and silencers.
£1,500–2,000 / $2,200–3,000 ⚓ **Bon**
The 3TA introduced unit construction and the concept of partial enclosure to the Triumph twin-cylinder line when it was launched during 1957. The mildly tuned engine formed the basis for a family of machines that would include sporting 500cc twins bearing the famous Tiger 100 name, works racers that competed at Daytona, and trials bikes.

1960 Triumph T20 Cub, 199cc, 18mm Zenith carburettor, 17in wheel rims, minus partial rear enclosure panels, otherwise largely standard specification, unrestored.
£600–900 / $870–1,300 ⚓ **Bon**

1961 Triumph T120 Bonneville, 649cc overhead-valve pre-unit parallel twin, 71 x 82mm bore and stroke, 9-stud head, Amal Monobloc carburettors, 46bhp at 6,500rpm, later front forks, matching speedometer and rev-counter, 115mph top speed, fully restored, concours condition.
£6,000–6,500 / $8,700–9,500 ⊞ **CotC**

▶ **1962 Triumph 6T Thunderbird,** 649cc overhead-valve pre-unit twin, alloy head, iron barrel, Amal Monobloc carburettor, 4-speed gearbox, headlamp nacelle, tank-top parcel grid.
£2,600–3,000 / $3,800–4,400 ⚓ **Bon**
Introduced in 1950, the Thunderbird was aimed at the American market. However, it also proved popular in Britain, for both solo and sidecar use; it was a strong and flexible machine. Originally featuring sprung-hub rear suspension, it gained a swinging arm for 1955, 'bathtub' rear enclosure in 1960 and, finally, an alloy head in 1961.

◀ **1962 Triumph 5TA Speed Twin,** 490cc overhead-valve unit twin, 69 x 65.5mm bore and stroke, 27bhp at 6,500rpm, 17in wheels, original, very good condition.
£1,700–2,000 / $2,450–3,000 ⚒ Bon
Introduced in 1957, the Type 21 or 3TA was in the vanguard of the move to unit construction for the Triumph twin-cylinder models and also introduced the distinctive 'bathtub' rear enclosure. It was followed by the 5TA for 1959. The new model, which continued the Speed Twin name, was essentially the same as the smaller machine, apart from the increase in displacement achieved by increasing the bore.

1962 Triumph T100SS, 490cc overhead-valve unit twin, 69 x 65.5mm bore and stroke, 34bhp at 7,000rpm, siamesed exhaust, fork gaiters, correct metallic kingfisher blue and silver paintwork, 98mph top speed.
£3,200–3,500 / $4,650–5,000 ⊞ CotC
This was the first year of the T100SS, which replaced the T100A. The 'half-bathtub' rear enclosure only lasted until the end of 1963.

1964 Triumph T20 Cub, 199cc overhead-valve unit single, 63 x 64mm bore and stroke, points in side casing, partial rear enclosure, fully restored, concours condition.
£1,400–1,600 / $2,000–2,300 ⚒ Bon
This is a late genuine Triumph Cub, built before the Bantam-framed Cub arrived later in the decade.

◄ **1965 Triumph 3TA,** 349cc overhead-valve unit twin, 58.2 x 65.5mm bore and stroke, alloy head, iron barrel, converted to Tiger 90 specification with later twin-leading-shoe front brake, alloy rims, Lucas chrome 7in (17.8cm) headlamp, fork gaiters, finned points cover and other non-standard parts, in need of cosmetic restoration.
£900–1,200 / $1,300–1,750 ⊞ MAY

▶ **1966 Triumph T100SS,** 490cc overhead-valve unit-construction twin, separate exhaust pipes and silencers.
£2,200–2,500 / $3,200–3,600 ⚒ Bon
Introduced for 1960, the Tiger 100A was the first sports version of Triumph's unit-construction 500 twin, the 5TA. A raised compression ratio and hotter cams helped it to a top speed of about 90mph, while the retention of a single carburettor meant that fuel economy did not suffer unduly. The T100A's replacement, the Tiger 100SS, was built between 1961 and 1970. It featured an abbreviated rear enclosure, larger-diameter wheels and a slightly more powerful engine equipped with coil ignition. Changes to the Tiger for 1966 included an improved frame with stiffened top tube and the adoption of 12 volt electrics. Tested by *Motor Cycling* in 1961, a T100SS managed 98mph while returning 82mpg.

1966 Triumph T20 S/H Sports Cub, 199cc overhead-valve unit single, Amal Monobloc carburettor, dry-sump lubrication, heavyweight front forks, fork gaiters, separate headlamp, restored to original specification, concours condition.
£2,500–2,700 / $3,600–4,000 ⚙ TCTR
The T20 S/H Sports Cub is a cracking little bike. It could certainly keep up with all but the fastest 250s of the day and had excellent handling. It also garnered considerable success in trials and as a Formula Cub racer.

Miller's is a price GUIDE not a price LIST

◄ **1966 Triumph T100SS,** 490cc overhead-valve unit twin, 34bhp at 7,000rpm, 94mph top speed, correct specification apart from later twin-leading-shoe front brake and Boyer Bransden electronic ignition, concours condition.
£2,500–3,000 / $3,600–4,400 ⚒ Bon

1966 Triumph T20 Cub, 199cc overhead-valve unit single, alloy head, iron barrel, points in timing cover, partial rear enclosure, 17in wheels, concours condition.
£1,500–1,600 / $2,200–2,300 ⬥ **TCTR**
This was the final year of the conventional Cub, prior to the introduction of the Bantam-based machine in 1967.

1967 Triumph Tiger 90, 349cc overhead-valve unit twin 58.2 x 65.5mm bore and stroke, alloy head, iron barrel, single Amal Concentric Mk I carburettor, fitted Japanese twin-leading-shoe front drum brake and alloy wheel rims, in need of some cosmetic restoration.
£1,800–1,900 / $2,600–2,800 ⊞ **MAY**

▶ **1968 Triumph T100T Daytona,** 490cc overhead-valve twin, concours condition.
£2,500–2,800 / $3,600–4,000 ⌁ **Bon**
Triumph revamped its range for 1968 with the launch of the new super sports 500cc twin, the Daytona. Coded T100T, the bike was race-bred from Triumph's laurel winning bike at Daytona in 1967. Its twin-carburettor head was to an all-new design and mounted in a new frame with a slightly lower seat height. From the 1969 models, the Daytona Tiger featured a twin-leading-shoe front brake. In standard form, the Daytona developed 39bhp at 7,400rpm.

◀ **1968 Triumph TR6 Trophy,** 649cc overhead-valve unit twin, 71 x 82mm bore and stroke, 4-speed gearbox, twin-leading-shoe front brake, separate exhausts, fork gaiters.
£3,600–4,200 / $5,200–6,100 ⊞ MW
The first unit-construction 650 Triumphs were the 1963 models, including the TR6 Trophy, which was essentially a single-carburettor version of the T120 Bonneville. It continued to be a popular choice, offering owners almost as much performance, but without the hassle of setting up the Bonneville's twin instruments.

1968 Triumph T100T Daytona, 490cc overhead-valve unit twin, twin Amal Concentric Mk I carburettors with attached air cleaners, separate exhausts, exposed-spring rear shocks.
£2,600–3,200 / $3,800–4,650 ⊞ MW
For 1968, the T100T gained the 8in (200mm) full-width front drum brake from the 650 range. It was needed, as the original 5TA/T100SS 7in (178mm) drum was totally inadequate for a machine that could reach 105mph.

1968 Triumph T100T Daytona, 490cc overhead-valve unit-construction twin, 2 carburettors, 4-speed gearbox, single-leading-shoe 8in (200mm) full-width front brake.
£2,600–3,200 / $3,800–4,650 ⊞ BLM
The Daytona name came from the race victories garnered at that circuit by works 500 Triumphs in 1966 and 1967, ridden by Buddy Elmore and Gary Nixon respectively.

1969 Triumph T100T Daytona, 490cc overhead-valve unit twin, alloy head, iron barrel, twin Amal Concentric Mk I carburettors, 4-speed gearbox, fork gaiters, 7in (17.8cm) Lucas chrome headlamp, fully restored, standard apart from aftermarket alloy rims, concours condition.
£3,400–3,800 / $5,000–5,500 ⊞ BLM
From 1969, the T100T sported the more powerful twin-leading-shoe front drum brake.

1969 Triumph TR6 Trophy, 649cc overhead-valve unit twin, single carburettor, 4-speed gearbox, twin-leading-shoe front brake, fork gaiters, matching instruments, completely original specification, concours condition.
£4,000–4,500 / $5,800–6,500 ⊞ BLM

1969 Triumph T120R Bonneville, 649cc overhead-valve unit-construction parallel twin, 2 Amal Concentric carburettors, 4-speed gearbox, twin-leading-shoe front brake, US export model, original specification, concours condition.
£4,200–4,600 / $6,000–6,500 ⊞ MW

1970 Triumph T120R Bonneville, 649cc overhead-valve unit twin, twin-leading-shoe front brake, concours condition.
£4,200–4,600 / $6,100–6,700 ⋩ Bon
This was the last year of the Bonneville before production switched to the new Umberslade Hall designed, oil-in-frame range.

◄ **1971 Triumph T120 Bonneville,** 649cc overhead-valve unit twin, oil-in-frame model, 4-speed gearbox, twin-leading-shoe front brake, conical hubs, indicators, original specification.
£2,500–2,600 / $3,600–3,800 ⊞ MAY
The oil-in-frame 650 was produced in twin-carburettor Bonneville guise (as this machine) or with a single carburettor as the TR6C or TR6R Tiger, rather than the previous Trophy, a name that had been reserved for the single-carburettor 500.

► **1975 Triumph T160V,** 740cc overhead-valve across-the-frame triple, 67 x 70mm bore and stroke, indicators, chrome mudguards, matching speedometer and rev-counter, standard apart from Boyer electronic ignition and alarm/immobiliser, concours condition.
£4,000–4,500 / $5,800–6,500 ⋏ Bon
Arguably the most handsome of the Triumph triples, the T160, introduced for 1975, featured revised styling, a hydraulic rear disc brake and an electric starter.

Cross Reference
See Colour Review (page 121–122)

◄ **c1976 Triumph TR7 RV,** 744cc overhead-valve unit twin, 76 x 82mm bore and stroke, 10-stud cylinder head, 5-speed gearbox, left-hand gear-change, rear disc brake, non-standard alloy wheel rims, Koni rear shocks, Lockhart oil cooler and pressure switch.
£3,500–3,800 / $5,000–5,500 ⊞ BLM

1977 Triumph T160V Trident, 740cc overhead-valve triple, 67 x 70mm bore and stroke.
£4,500+ / $6,500+ ⊕ DSCM
This motorcycle was built at the BSA Small Heath factory in September 1975, but was not supplied to a customer until May 1977. It was restored over a two-year period by Keith Bloor, who even made the silencers himself.

◄ **1978 Triumph T140V Bonneville,** 744cc twin, export model, dualseat modified for short rider, low mileage.
£2,750–3,250 $4,000–4,700 ⊞ BLM

1978 Triumph T140 Bonneville, 744cc twin, 5-speed gearbox, left-hand gear-change, front and rear disc brakes, European specification.
£3,500–4,000 / $5,000–5,800 ⚲ Bon
The final phase of Triumph twin development began in 1972 with the first appearance of the new 750cc version of the Bonneville, the increase in bore size necessitating a new crankcase to accommodate the larger barrel. Other improvements included a ten-stud cylinder head, triplex primary chain, stronger transmission and a disc front brake. A five-speed gearbox, introduced on the preceding 650 Bonneville, was standard equipment on the 750. Despite the age of the basic design and strong competition from Japanese and European manufacturers, the Bonnie remained for many years the UK's top-selling 750; it was voted Machine of the Year by *Motor Cycle News* in 1979.

Auction prices

Miller's only includes motorcycles declared sold. Our guide prices take into account the buyer's premium, VAT on the premium, and the extent of any published catalogue information relating to condition and provenance. Motorcycles sold at auction are identified by the ⚲ icon; full details of the auction house can be found on page 167.

1980 Triumph T140 Electro, 740cc overhead-valve unit twin, 5-speed gearbox, electric starter, front and rear disc brakes, fork gaiters, indicators, fully restored, concours condition.
£3,250–3,850 / $4,700–5,600 ⊞ BLM
This Electro was first registered to the Triumph Motorcycle Ltd Workers' Co-operative.

1981 Triumph T140 Bonneville Electro, 740cc overhead-valve unit twin, 76 x 82mm bore and stroke, Amal Concentric Mk II carburettors, electronic ignition, original, unrestored.
£3,250–3,850 / $4,700–5,700 ⊞ MW
The Electro's starter motor was mounted behind the cylinders, in the old magneto position.

Velocette *(British 1904–68)*

◀ **1913 Velocette Type A,** 206cc
2-stroke single, 62 x 73mm bore and
stroke, Amal carburettor, Bosch chain-
driven magneto, direct belt drive,
original and unrestored.
£1,500–2,000
$2,200–3,000 🚲 **APM**
**The Type A was the first true
Velocette and was designed by
Percy Goodman.**

1936 Velocette MAC, 349cc overhead-valve single, 68 x 96mm bore and stroke.
£2,650–3,800 / $3,800–5,500 🔨 **Bon**
In 1933, Veloce augmented its overhead-camshaft range with an overhead-valve 250, the MOV. The
newcomer's engine was a high-camshaft design with enclosed valves, and the compact and spritely machine
featured a four-speed gearbox equipped with the company's new foot-change mechanism. The following year,
the overhead-valve 350 MAC built along MOV lines appeared. This was followed by the 500 MSS.

1939 Velocette GTP, 249cc twin-port 2-stroke single, 63 x 80mm bore and stroke, chain final drive, drum brakes.
£2,000–2,300 / $3,000–3,300 🔨 **Bon**
The first machine to bear the name Velocette was a two-stroke, and was so called to differentiate it from the
larger four-stroke Veloce model. The type was an almost permanent fixture of the company's range until WWII.
The ultimate expression of Velocette's two-stroke line – the GTP – appeared in 1930. Unlike many of its
contemporaries, the GTP was not a 'built to a price' utility model, but rather a sporting lightweight of
advanced design, incorporating coil ignition and pump lubrication controlled by the throttle.

1948 Velocette MAC, 349cc overhead-valve single, iron head and barrel, 68 x 96mm bore and stroke, 4-speed footchange gearbox, Dowty AV telescopic front forks, rigid frame, sprung saddle.
£2,200–2,500 / $3,200–3,600 ⊞ CotC

◄ **c1950 Velocette LE Mk I,** 192cc liquid-cooled side-valve flat-twin, 50 x 49mm bore and stroke, 3-speed gearbox with hand gear-change, shaft final drive, hand starter, original grey paintwork, sprung rider's saddle, pillion seat, vinyl panniers, in need of restoration.
£200–400 / $300–580 ⊅ Bon
Conceived as a motorcycle for the man in the street, rather than the dedicated enthusiast, the LE offered exceptional weather protection combined with good handling. The side-valve flat-twin engine was exceptionally quiet, thanks to its water cooling system. The LE was first offered for the 1949 season; production finally ended in 1970.

1952 Velocette LE Mk I, 192cc liquid-cooled side-valve flat-twin, shaft final drive, footboards for rider and passenger, original, unrestored.
£750–900 / $1,100–1,300 ⊞ BLM
The Mk I featured a three-speed, hand-change gearbox and hand-starter lever.

1956 Velocette Venom, 499cc overhead-valve single, 86 x 86mm bore and stroke, alloy head, iron barrel, telescopic front forks, swinging-arm frame, chrome mudguards, 105mph top speed, very original.
£3,500–4,000 / $5,000–5,800 ⊞ CotC
The Venom and its smaller sibling, the Viper, were new for 1956. They were high-performance sports versions of the MSS and MAC respectively.

1955 Velocette MAC, 349cc overhead-valve single, 68 x 96mm bore and stroke, separate 4-speed gearbox, single-sided drum brakes, dualseat.
£1,500–1,800 / $2,200–2,600 ⚒ Bon
The MAC was introduced during 1935, following the introduction of the first M-series single. By the mid-1950s, it had gained telescopic front forks and pivoted swinging-arm rear suspension, but in most other respects it remained true to the original design.

▶ **1959 Velocette Valiant,** 192cc overhead-valve flat-twin, 50 x 49mm bore and stroke, restored.
£1,700–1,800 / $2,450–2,600 ⊞ CotC
The Valiant arrived in 1957, its engine being based on that of the LE, but with air cooling, overhead valves and twin carburettors. It was coupled to a four-speed, foot-change gearbox, and the whole unit was mounted in a duplex tubular frame; the forks and wheels came from the LE.

1960 Velocette Viper, 349cc overhead-valve single, 72 x 86mm bore and stroke, full-width hubs, fishtail silencer, touring handlebars, completely restored 2001.
£3,000–4,000 / $4,400–5,800 ⚒ CGC
The 350 Viper was the smaller sibling of the 500 Venom, the machines sharing the same cycle parts.

1961 Velocette Venom Veeline, 499cc overhead-valve single, 86 x 86mm bore and stroke, 4-speed foot-change gearbox, full-width brake hubs, chrome mudguards, dualseat, concours condition.
£3,600–4,000 / $5,200–5,800 ⊞ MW
The Veeline had the bottom of the engine, together with the gearbox and primary cover, concealed by a glassfibre moulding. Otherwise, it was unchanged from the standard Venom specification.

1962 Velocette Venom, 499cc overhead-valve single, 4-speed foot-change gearbox, export model with small tank and high handlebars, Norton twin-leading-shoe front brake, aftermarket rear shocks and small chrome headlamp, concours condition.
£3,600–4,000 / $5,200–5,800 ⊞ MW

◄ **1963 Velocette Venom Clubman,** 499cc overhead-valve single, 86 x 86mm bore and stroke, alloy rims, rev-counter, dropped handlebars, 110mph top speed.
£5,500–6,000 / $8,000–8,700 ✗ Bon
Velocette continued building traditional British big singles right up to the end, the black and gold finish and thudding exhaust being known the world over. The Venom Clubman was an improved and uprated Venom with a GP carburettor, close-ratio gears and polished engine. The forerunner of the Thruxton, it was – and is – preferred to the latter by many enthusiasts.

1968 Velocette LE Mk III, 192cc side-valve flat-twin, 50 x 49mm bore and stroke, foot-change gearbox, shaft final drive, conventional kickstarter, stepped dualseat, screen, legshields, panniers, carrier, one of last LE models built.
£850–900 / $1,250–1,300 ⊞ PM
This machine is very similar to the LEs supplied to various police forces.

1966 Velocette Venom Thruxton, 499cc overhead-valve single, 86 x 86mm bore and stroke, completely restored.
£9,000–10,500 / $13,000–15,200 ✗ CGC
The Venom Thruxton went on sale in 1965 as a high-performance version of the standard Venom. It had a 8:1 compression ratio cylinder head with a 2in (50mm) diameter inlet valve fed by a 1⅜in Amal GP carburettor. A close-ratio gearbox, alloy rims and twin-leading-shoe front brake were also standard. An output of 41bhp gave the bike a top speed of over 100mph.

Cross Reference
See Colour Review (page 123)

► **1967 Velocette Thruxton,** 499cc overhead-valve single, 86 x 86mm bore and stroke.
£9,000–10,000 / $13,000–14,500 ⊞ NLM
This machine is one of the original 1,172 Thruxtons made, not a converted Venom or MSS.

1969 Velocette Thruxton, 499cc overhead-valve single, Amal GP carburettor, twin-leading-shoe front brake, fork gaiters, clip-ons, rear-sets, sweptback exhaust pipe, oil tank heat guard, racing tank and seat, rev-counter.
£9,500–10,500 / $13,800–15,250 ✗ Bon
This Thruxton is from the last batch of machines to be built.

Vincent-HRD *(British 1928–55)*

1935 Vincent-HRD Series A Comet, 499cc overhead-valve single, 84 x 90mm bore and stroke, 7.3:1 compression ratio, Amal carburettor, 26bhp at 5,600rpm, 4-speed Burman gearbox, Brampton forks, twin front brake, Vincent sprung frame, completely restored, concours condition.
£18,000–22,000 / $26,000–32,000 ⚒ Bon
HRD and Vincent are two titles well known to the motorcycle world. Howard Raymond Davis, a WWI RFC pilot and racing motorcyclist, was the founder of HRD, but the company went into liquidation in the late 1920s, and the company name was bought by Phil Vincent, who started building motorcycles at a new location in Stevenage, Hertfordshire. However, it was not until 1934 that the new Vincent Series A was born. Designed in great part by Phil Irving, a brilliant Australian engineer, and incorporating Phil Vincent's triangulated frame design, it heralded a new generation of superb single-cylinder sports machines.

1938 Vincent-HRD Meteor, 499cc overhead-valve single, 84 x 90mm bore and stroke, 4-speed foot-change gearbox, sprung frame, dual front brake, Brampton girder forks.
£11,400–12,500 / $16,500–18,000 ⊞ VER
Phil Vincent, together with chief engineer Phil Irving, built a new range of singles for 1935, with engines of their own design in place of the previous bought-in JAP and Rudge units. The machines were built in four guises: standard Meteor, Sports Comet, Comet Special and racing TT model.

1949 Vincent-HRD Rapide Series C, 988cc overhead-valve twin, 84 x 90mm bore and stroke, 4-speed foot-change gearbox, period mirrors and tank cover, original condition, unrestored.
£9,000–11,000 / $13,000–16,000 ⚒ PS
The Rapide was the bike that everyone wanted to own, but could never afford.

◄ **1949 Vincent-HRD Comet,** 499cc overhead-valve single, Girdraulic front forks, good original example.
£5,000–5,500 / $7,250–8,000 ⚒ Bon
Unlike many other bikes originally designed in the 1930s, the Comet featured front and rear suspension, Brampton girder forks being fitted at the front and a cantilever arrangement at the rear. The Comet arrived in 1935, featuring an all-new 500-class engine with a high camshaft and what one journalist described as 'widely spaced pushrods'. The four-speed Burman gearbox drove the rear wheel through a duplex primary chain.

1950 Vincent-HRD Comet, 499cc single, engine recently rebuilt, electronic ignition, Alton generator.
£3,600–4,000 / $5,000–5,800 ⚒ PS

1951 Vincent Comet, 499cc overhead-valve single, 4-speed gearbox, dualseat, alloy mudguards, original condition.
£5,000–5,500 / $7,250–8,000 ⊞ PM
Philip Vincent and Phil Irving created the Comet by using a cylinder from the Rapide V-twin. The problem was that it cost almost as much to build as the bigger bike, but it had to be sold at two-thirds the cost. Consequently, Vincent didn't make any money on the machine.

1951 Vincent-HRD Comet, 499cc overhead-valve single, inclined aluminium head and barrel, 84 x 90mm bore and stroke, 28bhp at 5,800rpm, 4-speed foot-change gearbox.
£5,000–5,500 / $7,250–8,000 ⊞ VER
The Comet used the front cylinder from the 998cc Rapide V-twin in a specially made crankcase. The cycle parts were largely those of the larger-capacity bike.

1952 Vincent-HRD Comet, 499cc overhead-valve single, original, unrestored, unused for some years.
£3,600–4,000 / $5,000–5,800 ⊞ BLM

▶ **1956 Vincent-HRD Black Knight,** 998cc overhead-valve V-twin, 4-speed gearbox, dual front brake, top and bottom fairings, engine covers, rear enclosure.
£12,000–13,000 / $17,500–19,000 ⊞ VER
The fully enclosed Series D was the final gasp for the Vincent company, being launched in 1955. Even so, it was a brave attempt to provide the discerning rider with a high-speed tourer, 'A two-wheel Bentley' as Phil Vincent described the design. With the enclosure, the Rapide became the Black Knight, and the Shadow the Black Prince.

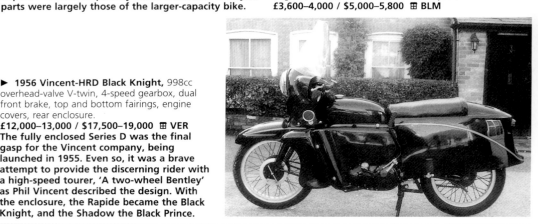

Yamaha (*Japanese 1954–*)

1971 Yamaha CS3E, 195cc twin, 52 x 46mm bore and stroke, 22bhp at 7,500rpm, Autolube, 4-speed gearbox, electric starter, twin-leading-shoe front brake, 18in wheels, 75mph top speed.
£1,800–1,900 / $2,600–2,750 ⊙ VJMC
This series of models began with the 180cc CSI in 1969.

1976 Yamaha RD250C, 247cc 2-stroke twin, reed-valve induction, 30bhp at 7,500rpm, Autolube, disc front/drum rear brakes, wire wheels, fully restored, concours condition.
£1,800–2,000 / $2,600–3,000 ⊙ VJMC

1978 Yamaha RD400E, 398cc 2-stroke twin, reed-valve induction, 64 x 62mm bore and stroke, 40bhp at 7,000rpm, Autolube, concours condition.
£1,600–1,800 / $2,300–2,600 ⊞ MW
The 'E' suffix indicated electronic ignition, but the 1978 version of the RD400 also had alloy wheels, thicker (35mm) fork stanchions, a disc rear brake to match the front, and a new paint job for the tanks and side panels.

1978 Yamaha XS750, 747cc double-overhead-camshaft across-the-frame triple, 68 x 68.6mm bore and stroke, 5-speed gearbox, double-cradle frame, triple disc brakes, cast alloy wheels, original apart from front mudguard.
£800–1,100 / $1,150–1,600 ⋏ CGC
Capable of 110mph, the XS750 soon gained an enthusiastic following as a long-distance tourer, with the emphasis on comfort and smoothness. A couple of years after its launch, the engine was overbored by 3mm to achieve 826cc, creating the XS850 for 1980.

▶ **1984 Yamaha RD500LC,** 499cc 2-stroke 4-cylinder engine, 56.4 x 50mm bore and stroke, 6.6:1 compression ratio, 87bhp at 9,500rpm, 6-speed gearbox, 16in front/18in rear wheels, totally original specification, concours condition.
£2,750–3,000 $4,000–4,400 ⊞ MW
Built between 1984 and 1986, the RD500LC is a very rare machine. It was fitted with Yamaha's patented YPVS (Yamaha Power Valve System) and monoshock rear suspension. In the USA, it was sold under the RZ500 label.

Zenith *(British 1904–50)*

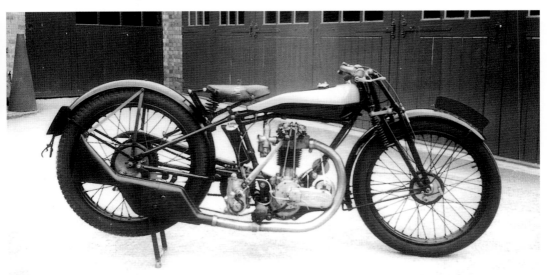

1928 Zenith 350 Blackburne, 349cc Blackburne overhead-valve single-cylinder engine, exposed valve gear, forward mounted magneto, Brooklands 'can' exhaust, girder forks, rigid diamond frame.
£4,200–5,000 / $6,000–7,250 ⊞ VER
Confusingly, Zenith offered the 350 overhead-valve single with both Blackburne and JAP engines, often at the same time.

Dirt Bikes

◀ **1948 Royal Enfield Trials Bullet,** 346cc overhead-valve semi-unit single, 70 x 90mm bore and stroke, dry-sump lubrication, magneto ignition, bolted-up 4-speed Albion gearbox, telescopic front forks.
£4,500–5,000
$6,500–7,250 ⚙ REOC
This machine is said to have been owned by Royal Enfield competition manager Charlie Rogers and also ridden by works rider Johnny Brittain. The first Bullet trials bikes pre-dated the production 350 Bullet, making their debut at the Colmore Trial in February 1948. Royal Enfield was a pioneer in developing swinging-arm rear suspension for both competition and street use.

1949 Norton 500T, 490cc overhead-valve single, 79 x 100mm bore and stroke, 21bhp at 5,000rpm, 21in front/19in rear wheels.
£3,500–3,700 / $5,000–5,400 ⚘ Bon
Norton's post-WWII trials campaign got off to a false start in 1947, due to using the iron-barrelled, overhead-valve Model 18 engine in a Roadholder-forked WD16H chassis. The result was a bike with too long a wheelbase and insufficient ground clearance. A season of extensive modification and development led to the appearance of an entirely different machine, the legendary 500T, in late 1948. An aluminium head and barrel, shortened frame stays and a modified lower fork yoke reduced the wheelbase to a more manageable 53in (1346mm), while the lighter engine components helped reduce weight to just over 300lb (136kg).

1951 BSA Bantam Trials, 123cc 2-stroke single, 3-speed foot-change gearbox, heavier oil damped front forks, alloy mudguard, revised gear, knobbly tyres, single trials seat.
£820–1,000 / $1,175–1,500 ⚘ CGC
Many Bantams were converted to road-racers and grass-trackers. However, their greatest success in competition came in the 'feet-up' trials game, where the machine's 'chuckability' easily compensated for its engine's comparatively low power output.

1952 James Trials, 197cc Villiers 2-stroke single, 8bhp, alloy head, iron barrel.
£1,800–2,000 / $2,600–3,000 ⚙ AMCA
This machine is similar to that used by the 1952 James team riders – H. W. Thorne, T. D. Reid and the great Bill Lomas – in the 1952 Scottish Six Days. They won the 200cc Cup for the second year running.

1954 Matchless G3L/CS, 348cc overhead-valve single, 69 x 93mm bore and stroke, 26bhp at 6,000rpm, mag/dyno, 4-speed gearbox, 21in front/19in rear wheels.
£2,500–3,000 / $3,600–4,400 ✗ Bon
Major differences from the standard road-going versions were confined to mudguards (alloy on the competition models); the magneto, which was a waterproof competition version; wheel sizes; and a smaller tank.

1956 Ariel HT5, 499cc overhead-valve single, 81.8 x 95mm bore and stroke, 24bhp at 5,800rpm, original Lucas Wader magneto replaced by BTH TT unit, Bultaco 35mm telescopic front forks, swinging-arm rear suspension, full-width alloy front hub, Akront wheel rims, Hagon rear shocks.
£4,000–4,500 / $5,800–6,500 ✗ Bon
The HT5 is generally considered to be one of the all-time greats of the trials world.

1957 MV Agusta Competizione, 172cc overhead-valve unit single, 59.5 x 62mm bore and stroke, 15bhp at 8,800rpm, 5-speed gearbox, full-width alloy hubs, quickly-detachable wheel spindles, 19in wheels, braced handlebars, tank-top hooks.
£8,000–9,000
$11,500–13,000 ♻ CME
Also known as the 175 Six Day Motocross, this machine is one of the rarest production MVs.

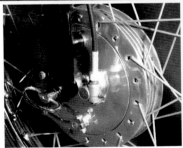
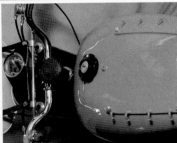

◄ **1958 Ariel HT5,** 499cc overhead-valve single, subject of complete nut-and-bolt restoration.
£4,000–4,500 / $5,800–6,500 ✗ Bon
Ariel's new sprung-frame HT5 established its credentials in 1956, when the company signed ace trials rider Ron Langston and a youthful Sammy Miller, who made his mark that year in the Scottish Six Days Trial. Lighter than most of its counterparts, the HT5 would dominate the trials scene until the arrival of the lightweight two-stroke Spanish invaders during the mid-1960s.

1958 Francis-Barnett Trials, 249cc Villiers 2-stroke single, high-level exhaust, telescopic front forks, swinging-arm rear suspension.
£750–800 / $1,100–1,250 ⊞ MW
Originally 197cc, the engine of this machine has been converted to a 250.

1959 Triumph T20 Trials Cub, 199cc overhead-valve single, completely rebuilt, modified frame, high-level exhaust, Pico alloy silencer.
£1,600–1,800 / $2,300–2,600 ⮷ TCTR
The Trials Cub was based on the Sports Cub, but with wide-ratio gears, a single seat, and different sprockets and handlebars.

1958 Triumph 5TA Trials Special, 490cc overhead-valve unit-construction twin, 69 x 65.5mm bore and stroke, 4-speed gearbox, Rickman hubs, alloy rims, high-level 2-into-1 exhaust, concours condition.
£2,100–2,200 / $3,000–3,200 ⮷ Bon
This neatly crafted trials special is based around a 5TA engine and gearbox unit. The chassis features a slimline sub-frame and an oil tank sited above the frame top tube, behind the swan neck.

1959 Dot Vale Onslow Works Replica Trials, 246cc Villiers engine.
£1,550–1,600 / $2,150–2,300 ⮷ CGC
Founded in 1903 by racing motorcyclist Harry Reed, Dot shone brightly during the 1920s, with notable successes in TT racing. However, like many manufacturers, it struggled in the following decade and production ceased in 1932. Sixteen years later, Dot resurfaced with a range of 123cc and 246cc two-strokes, many of which were motocross and trials machines. This particular example is a Works Replica Trials Model with a Vale Onslow conversion.

1960 Ducati 200 Motocross, 203cc overhead-camshaft unit-construction single, 67 x 57.8mm bore and stroke, 20bhp at 8,000rpm, 4-speed gearbox, original, unrestored.
£5,000+ / $7,250+ ⊞ MW
Now very rare, the 200 Motocross was only built for a few months and was considerably different to the series-production roadster Elite model upon which it was based. Changes included the frame, wheel sizes, brakes and hubs, fuel tank, saddle, mudguards, gearing, a Dell'Orto 27mm SSI carburettor with remote float chamber, flywheel-magneto ignition, swinging arm and handlebars.

1963 BSA C15 Trials, 247cc overhead-valve unit single, 67 x 70mm bore and stroke, 4-speed wide-ratio gearbox, modified with aftermarket trials equipment including aluminium tank, mudguards, wheel rims, high-level exhaust and silencer, curved kickstarter and inverted rear shocks.
£1,800–2,000 / $2,600–3,000 ⚙ AMCA

1964 BSA B40, 343cc overhead-valve unit single, 79 x 70mm bore and stroke.
£1,800–2,000 / $2,600–3,000 ⚙ RRN
This machine was raced in France and Holland during the mid-1980s in the first of the pre-65 scrambles. It has won many events, including hill climbs and enduros.

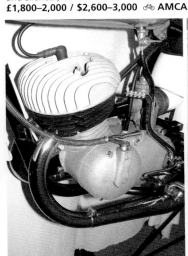

c1966 Jawa CZ, 360cc 2-stroke single, twin-port iron barrel, alloy head, piston-port induction, 4-speed gearbox, Jikov carburettor, expansion-chamber exhaust, completely restored.
£2,400–2,800 / $3,500–4,000 ⚙ JCZ

Restored values

The cost of a professional restoration will have an influence on, but no direct relation to, a motorcycle's market value. A restored motorcycle can have a market value lower than the cost of its restoration.

1967 Greeves MX5 Challenger, 246cc 2-stroke single, flywheel-magneto ignition, 4-speed Albion gearbox, full-width British Hub Company alloy brake hubs, square-section tubular swinging-arm, twin shock rear suspension, race ready.
£1,700–1,900 / $2,500–2,750 ⚙ CGC
By 1967, Greeves had adopted Italian Ceriani front forks in place of their long-running leading-link type.

1966 Husqvarna 360 Motocross, 360cc piston-port 2-stroke single, 4-speed gearbox, high-level exhaust, 23rd of 50 such models built 1966, 1st of 10 exported to USA, concours condition.
£2,500+ / $3,600+ ⚙ MW

1968 Matchless G85CS Scrambler, 497cc overhead-valve single, 86 x 85.5mm bore and stroke, alloy head and barrel, 41bhp at 6,500rpm, Teledraulic front forks, Girling rear shocks, fork gaiters, full-width front hub, braced handlebars, 7R rear hub, one of last examples built.
£6,000–7,000 / $8,700–10,000 ⊞ MW

A known continuous history can add value to and enhance the enjoyment of a motorcycle.

1969 Greeves Griffon Mk I, 380cc twin-port 2-stroke single, 82 x 72mm bore and stroke, 2-into-1 exhaust, Ceriani front forks, conical hubs, 21in front/18in rear wheels with high-tensile rims, alloy mudguards, concours condition.
£2,000–2,200 / $3,000–3,200 ⚡ CGC

1968 Greeves Challenger ISDT, 246cc 2-stroke single, 4-speed gearbox, Ceriani front forks, full-width alloy hubs, high-level exhaust.
£4,500–5,000 / $6,500–7,250 ⚡ Bon
This machine was one of four built by Greeves for its main dealer, Comerfords, who prepared them for the British Trophy team's use in the 1968 International Six Days Trial at San Pellegrino, Italy. In that event, this machine was ridden by Dennis Jones. It was entered as 257cc, although whether it was actually bored out to gain entry into the over-250cc class is uncertain. The bike was also used by the British Team in the following year's ISDT in West Germany, being ridden by Malcolm Rathemell. In 1969, the machine was used in various UK events, including the Edinburgh trial, where it was ridden by Dave Minton, before being sold to Grand Prix road-racing star Jack Findlay.

1969 Bultaco Pursang, 249cc unit-construction 2-stroke single, 5-speed gearbox, conical brake hubs, alloy wheel rims, nickel plated frame, restored.
£400–600 / $580–870 ⚡ Bon
Following the acrimonious split between Francisco Bulto and Permanyer at Montesa, the former, backed by almost the entire Montesa racing department, established a new manufacturing base near Barcelona to build motorcycles under the Bultaco name. Although initial production was based around a 125cc two-stroke roadster, the new company would establish its name in the racing world and in the manufacture of road-going and off-road bikes. The single-cylinder, two-stroke Pursang was built in the late 1960s and early 1970s.

◀ **1969 Greeves Griffon,** 380cc, fully restored to original specification.
£2,000–2,200 / $3,000–3,200 ⚡ Bon
The culmination of Greeves' long line of scrambles machines was the Griffon, introduced in 1969. Built in 246cc and 380cc variants, the two-stroke Griffon motor was a development of the preceding Challenger. Later models used a version of the engine that had been developed at Queens University, Belfast, and Greeves' own design of gearbox. Frames were constructed in Reynolds 531 tubing, and Ceriani-type Metal Profiles front forks and alloy conical hubs were fitted.

Colour Review

◀ **1954 Triumph 6T Thunderbird,** 649cc overhead-valve pre-unit twin, single carburettor, iron head and barrel, alternator, headlamp nacelle. **£4,000–4,500 / $5,800–6,500 ⊞ MW This was the final year of the sprung-hub Thunderbird.**

1959 Triumph 3TA Twenty-One, 349cc overhead-valve unit-construction twin, valanced front mudguard, bathtub rear enclosure, nacelle headlamp. **£1,500–1,800 / $2,200–2,600 ⊞ MW Introduced in 1957, the Twenty-One celebrated 21 years of the Triumph Engineering Company.**

1960 Triumph 5TA Speed Twin, 490cc overhead-valve unit-construction twin, alloy head, iron barrel, distributor ignition, 4-speed foot-change gearbox, 2-tone dualseat, original specification. **£1,800–2,200 / $2,600–3,200 ⊞ PS**

◀ **1959 Triumph Tiger 110,** 649cc overhead-valve pre-unit parallel twin, single Amal Monobloc carburettor, parcel rack on tank, headlamp nacelle, completely restored to original specification, excellent condition. **£4,500–5,000 $6,500–8,000 ⊞ MW**

▶ **1961 Triumph 6T Thunderbird,** 649cc overhead-valve pre-unit twin, alloy cylinder head, iron barrel, single Amal Monobloc carburettor, 4-speed gearbox, completely restored to a high standard. **£4,000–4,500 $5,800–6,500 ⊞ BLM**

◄ **1963 Triumph T20 S/H Sports Club,** 199cc overhead-valve unit single, 63 x 64mm bore and stroke, Amal Monobloc carburettor, 4-speed gearbox, fork gaiters.
£1,500–1,800
$2,200–2,600 ⊞ TCTR
This was the first year in which the points were fitted in the side of the engine.

► **1966 Triumph Tiger 90,** 349cc overhead-valve twin, 58.2 x 65.5mm bore and stroke, single Amal Monobloc carburettor, fork gaiters, Lucas chrome 7in headlamp.
£2,500–2,800 / $3,600–4,000 ⊞ BLM
The T90 ran from 1963 through to 1969. Essentially, it was a smaller-displacement Tiger 100SS.

1971 Triumph TR6 Trophy, 649cc overhead-valve unit-construction twin, 71 x 82mm bore and stroke, conical brake hubs, oil-in-frame model, non-standard megaphone silencers.
£3,400–3,800 / $5,000–5,500 ⊞ MW

► **1975 Triumph T160V,** 740cc overhead-valve triple, 67 x 70mm bore and stroke, Amal Concentric Mk I carburettors, 3-into-2 exhaust, 5-speed gearbox with left-hand gear-change lever, disc front brake, chrome mudguards, high bars, indicators, concours condition.
£5,000–5,500 / $7,250–8,000 ⊞ MW

1977 Triumph T140V Bonneville Jubilee, 744cc overhead-valve unit-construction twin, 71 x 82mm bore and stroke, 5-speed gearbox, chromed outer engine cover, special paintwork and decals for bodywork.
£3,000–4,000 / $4,400–5,800 ⊞ MW
The Triumph Meridan factory built a special version of the Bonneville to celebrate Queen Elizabeth's 25th year on the throne in 1977. These bikes, in original condition, are now becoming collectable.

◀ **1934 Velocette GTP,** 249cc twin-port
2-stroke single, 63 x 80mm bore and stroke,
3-speed hand-change gearbox, original
specification, good condition.
£1,800–2,200 / $2,600–3,200 ⊞ **MW**
**Late in 1934, the GRP was fitted with a four-
speed foot-change gearbox.**

1957 Velocette Viper, 349cc overhead-valve single, 72 x 86mm bore and stroke, alloy head, iron barrel, dry-sump
lubrication, fishtail exhaust, 4-speed foot-change gearbox, full-width hubs, chrome tank, standard specification,
concours condition.
£3,750–4,250 / $5,500–6,200 ⊞ **BLM**

▶ **1960 Velocette
Venom,** 499cc, Clubman
specification including
close-ratio gears, twin-
leading-shoe front brake,
alloy wheel rims, clip-ons,
rear-sets, fork gaiters,
Thruxton seat and
headlamp brackets.
**£5,000–5,500
$7,250–8,000** ⊞ **BLM**

◀ **1956 Vincent-HRD
Black Knight,** 998cc
overhead-valve 50-degree
V-twin, 84 x 90mm bore
and stroke, 4-speed
foot-change gearbox,
original specification.
**£13,000–14,000
$19,000–20,500** ⊞ **VER**
**The Black Knight was an
attempt to make the
ultimate touring bike
with full weather
protection. Although
built in 1955, this
machine was not
registered until 1956.**

c1954 BSA ZB32 Gold Star Competition Replica, 348cc overhead-valve pre-unit single, ZB engine with Gold Star camshafts, Amal Concentric carburettor, high-level competition exhaust, B33 frame, Lyta aluminium fuel tank, alloy mudguards, built regardless of cost.
£3,600–4,400 / $5,000–6,500 ⚒ TEN

c1965 Rickman-Triumph T100SS Scrambler, 490cc, Runtronic spark ignition system, Ceriani forks, alloy wheel rims on CZ hubs, nickel plated frame.
£2,500–2,800 / $3,600–4,000 ⊞ BLM

▶ **1972 Ducati 450T/S,** 436cc overhead-camshaft single-cylinder engine, desmodromic valve gear, 5-speed gearbox, original specification.
£2,500–2,700 / $3,600–4,000 ⊞ MW
Basically, the T/S was the American R/T with lighting equipment and a street-legal exhaust system. A team of riders mounted on T/S models took part in the 1972 ISDT held in the Isle of Man.

1973 Jawa 638 Enduro, 360cc single-port 2-stroke, magnesium crankcases, full duplex frame, alloy tank, quickly-detachable wheels.
£2,700–3,000 / $4,000–4,400 ⮌ JCZ

c1975 Matchless-Pykett Trials Bike Replica, 498cc overhead-valve pre-unit single, Amal Concentric carburettor, 4-speed wide-ratio AMC gearbox.
£4,000–4,400 / $5,800–6,500 ⊞ AtMC
This machine was built to a very high standard by Peter Pykett.

1978 Can-am Flat Tracker, 250cc Rotax 2-stroke single, duplex frame, steel swinging arm with twin shocks, plastic tank and seat base, competition tyres.
£2,000–2,500 / $3,000–3,600 ⊞ MW
The Can-am was built and marketed by the Canadian Bombardier organization.

1980 Cagiva RX250 Enduro, 246cc 2-stroke single, piston-port induction, alloy head and barrel, 5-speed gearbox, Sachs Hydragas rear shocks, Marzocchi front forks, completely restored.
£2,000–2,200 / $3,000–3,200 ⊞ MW

1982 Yamaha TY250 Trials, 249cc reed-valve 2-stroke single, oil-pump lubrication, 5-speed gearbox, original specification including lighting equipment, excellent condition.
£600–800 / $870–1,150 ⚲ PS

1986 Honda TL200, 198cc overhead-camshaft unit-construction single, high-level exhaust, square-section swinging arm, twin rear shocks, fewer than 170 miles from new, concours condition.
£2,000–2,200 / $3,000–3,200 ⊞ MW

◄ **1942 Norton 16H,** 490cc side-valve single, 79 x 100mm bore and stroke, 4.9:1 compression ratio, girder forks, rigid frame, restored.
£2,000–3,000 / $3,000–4,400 ⊞ MW
Over 100,000 16H models were built by Norton for the British War Department.

▶ **c1942 Harley-Davidson WLA,** 748cc side-valve V-twin, 23bhp, pedal-operated multiplate clutch (in oil bath), 3-speed gearbox, chain final drive, mechanical brakes, bottom-link fork with twin coil springs, rigid frame, 6 volt electrics.
£8,000–9,500
$11,500–14,000 ⊞ RRM
Used for messenger service, police operations, convoy control and other roles, the WLA was among the most numerous motorcycles of WWII. The US forces alone procured well over 60,000. WLC models (for Canada) differed in detail. All were derived from the civilian Model 45, but there were many periodic changes. On 1942–45 production the headlamp sat low, with the horn above, rather than the other way round, and the air filter became rectangular in shape (on WLC from 1943). Production ceased in the early 1950s.

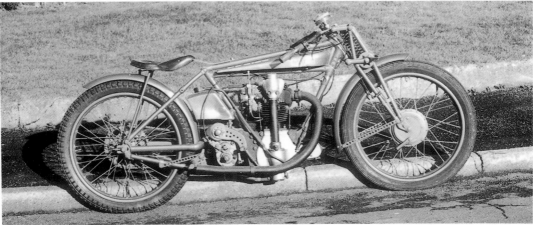

1926 Chater Lea Brooklands Racer, 349cc overhead-camshaft single, bevel shaft-driven camshaft, exposed valve gear, converted to foot-change.
£8,000–9,500 / $11,500–14,000 ⊞ PM

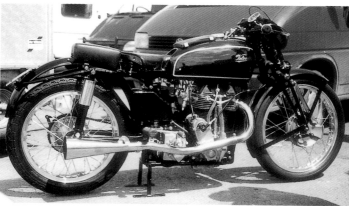

◀ **1950 Velocette KTT Mk VIII,** 348cc overhead-camshaft engine, bevel-driven camshaft, 4-speed foot-change gearbox, alloy rims, swinging-arm rear suspension, girder front forks, completely restored.
£12,000–15,000
$17,500–21,500 ⊞ MW
This was the last year of production for the KTT.

1954 Moto Guzzi Racer 350, 349.2cc double-overhead-camshaft single, 80 x 69.5mm bore and stroke, 35bhp at 7,800rpm, 5-speed gearbox, leading-link front forks, square-section rear swinging arm, alloy rims, 'bird-beak' aluminium fairing.
£75,000–90,000 / $108,000–130,000 ⊞ AtMC

1960 ESO Road Racer, 499cc unit-construction single, magneto ignition, 42mm Dell'Orto carburettor, leading-link central-spring front forks.
£9,000–10,000 / $13,000–14,500 ⚲ JCZ
The ESO racer was developed from the original speedway engine. This is the final version of the machine.

◄ **1957 Itom Competizione,** 49cc engine, restored, original specification.
£2,500–2,700 / $3,600–4,000 ⊞ RFC

► **1963 Harley-Davidson KR750,** side-valve V-twin, straight-through exhaust pipes, 4-speed close-ratio foot-change gearbox, Sportster-type front fork, alloy rims, De Carbon rear shock, Daytona fuel tank, fairing (1963 models only), original specification, concours condition.
£15,000+ / $22,000+ ⊞ MW

◄ **1968 Ducati Mk III Racer,** 340cc overhead-camshaft single, valve-spring head, 5-speed gearbox, 31.5mm front forks, narrow-case frame and engine, alloy rims, Honda twin-leading-shoe front brake, fibreglass tank, seat and mudguards.
£2,300–2,700 / $3,350–4,000 ⊞ MW

1970 Ducati 350 Desmo, 340cc overhead-camshaft single, wide-case engine, 5-speed gearbox, wet clutch, Yamaha TD1C front brake, alloy rims, Vic Camp bodywork.
£2,500–2,900 / $3,600–4,300 ⊞ MW

1973 Yamaha TZ250A, 247cc liquid-cooled piston-port 2-stroke twin, 51bhp at 10,500rpm, CDI ignition, 6-speed gearbox, concours condition.
£4,000–4,500 / $5,800–6,500 ⊞ MW
This was the first year of the TZ liquid-cooled production racer. Its cycle parts were based on the outgoing TD3 air-cooled model.

► **1977 Kreidler Van Veen GP,** 49cc disc-valve 2-stroke single, 20bhp, 6-spoke wheels, front and rear disc brakes, 105mph top speed.
£8,000+ / $11,500+ ⊞ MW
This particular machine was formally ridden by 50cc World Champion Jan de Vries.

► **1960 BSA Sunbeam B2,** 249cc, 56 x 50.6mm bore and stroke, 10bhp at 2,000rpm, 70mph top speed, fitted period options of rear carrier, spare wheel and chrome trim.
£1,700–1,800 / $2,500–2,600 ⊕ **VMSC**

1924 AJS Model D and AJS Single-Seat Sidecar, V-twin engine, front mounted magneto, drum brakes, electric lighting, footboards.
£6,500–7,500 / $9,500–10,200 ⊞ **VER**
Like many other motorcycle manufacturers in the early part of the 20th century, AJS offered its own sidecars.

► **1958 BSA A10 and Palma Sidecar,** 646cc twin-cylinder engine, Super Rocket specification with Amal Concentric carburettor and oil cooler, leading-link front forks, Windle racing wheels with Borrani alloy rims.
£3,500–3,900 / $5,000–5,750 ⊞ **BLM**

1950 Moto Guzzi Astore and Single-Seat Sports Sidecar, 498.4cc overhead-valve horizontal single, 88 x 82mm bore and stroke, 4-speed foot-change gearbox, telescopic front forks, spring-and-friction rear suspension, 19in wheels.
£10,000–11,000 / $14,500–16,000 ⊞ **NLM**

◄ **1921 ABC Skootamota,** 125cc single, inlet-over-exhaust valves, 60 x 44mm bore and stroke, 15mph top speed.
£1,200–1,300 / $1,750–2,000 ⊞ **VER**
The ABC Skootamota appeared in 1919 and was one of the most practical of early scooter designs, having a series of small-diameter tubes making up a light-weight frame. Production ended in 1923. The name ABC stood for All British Cycle.

1960 BSA A7 Shooting Star and Single-Seat Sports Sidecar, 497cc overhead-valve pre-unit parallel twin.
£2,800–3,200 / $4,000–4,650 ⊞ **MW**
The BSA twin was a good choice for sidecar use, thanks to its excellent low-down pulling power and reliability. In racing, Chris Vincent won the 1962 Sidecar TT with an A7 'kneeler' outfit.

1970 Vincent-Egli Special, 998cc overhead-valve Vincent Rapide V-twin engine, 4-speed gearbox, twin rear shock absorbers Ceriani front forks, Grimeca 4-leading-shoe front brake, Grimeca single-leading-shoe rear brake, dualseat.
£8,000–10,000 / $11,500–14,500 ⊞ **MW**
This machine was created by Swiss frame specialist Fritz Egli.

◄ **c1970 Harley-Davidson Sprint H Replica,** 344cc overhead-valve horizontal single, 74 x 80mm, 25bhp at 7,000rpm, 5-speed gearbox.
£1,800–1,900 / $2,600–2,750 ⊞ **MW**
The Sprint H was known as the Scrambler from 1965. However, this particular replica sports a 350 engine with the later-type cylinder head and massive rounded, one-piece valve inspection cover.

► **1971 Greeves Pathfinder ISDT,** 169cc Puch 2-stroke single, 62 x 56mm bore and stroke, 6-speed gearbox, one of only 16 made, converted to green-lane bike with full lighting equipment.
£750–1,500 / $1,100–2,150 ⊞ **NLM**

1971 Greeves Pathfinder, 169cc 2-stroke single, alloy tank, full-width alloy brake hubs, alloy mudguards.
£750–1,500 / $1,100–2,150 ⊅ **Bon**
Norton-Villiers' decision in 1966 to supply Villiers engines exclusively to its AJS subsidiary dealt a severe blow to a host of small independent manufacturers that had relied on these two-strokes. Those that survived turned to Continental suppliers – in Greeves' case, Puch of Austria. Powered by a 169cc Puch two-stroke single, the Pathfinder trials bike was produced during the early and mid-1970s. Despite excellent handling courtesy of a duplex-loop frame, long-travel Metal Profiles forks and three-way adjustable Girling dampers, it failed to make its mark in trials. Never intended for such use, the Puch engine lacked the necessary low-down grunt and flexibility. However, it did have ample power and a six-speed gearbox, features that made the Pathfinder a far better enduro machine than a trials iron.

► **1971 Rickman Micra ISDT,** 123cc Zündapp GS 125 2-stroke single-cylinder engine, radial-fin cylinder head, 18bhp at 7,900rpm, 5-speed gearbox, multi-plate clutch, gear primary drive, original specification.
£1,000–1,500 / $1,500–2,200 ⊞ **BLM**
The Rickman-Zündapp was an excellent combination. It sold particularly well in the USA.

1971 CZ Enduro, 246cc 2-stroke single, piston-port induction, radial-fin alloy cylinder head, 5-speed gearbox, original, excellent condition.
£1,000–1,250 / $1,500–1,800 ⊞ BLM
This rare enduro bike has never been used in anger; instead it has been in a private collection for many years.

1971 Husqvarna 360 Six Days, 360cc 2-stroke single, high-level exhaust, 5-speed gearbox, full-cradle frame, conical hubs, alloy wheel rims, braced handlebars, plastic mudguards, full lighting equipment.
£1,800–2,000 / $2,600–3,000 ⊞ MW
This enduro mount is clearly based on the world championship winning Husqvarna motocrosser.

1972 AJS 410 Stormer, 410cc 2-stroke single, piston-port induction, 4-speed gearbox, Reynolds 531 tubing full-cradle duplex frame, alloy fuel tank, original specification.
£1,600–1,900 / $2,300–2,750 ⊞ MW
The 410 Stormer was derived from the 368cc Y4 of 1970 and arrived in the following year. It had the same 83mm piston as the 370, but with the stroke increased from 68 to 74mm. In total, there were 18 modifications between the 370 and the 410.

Miller's is a price GUIDE not a price LIST

1972 Ducati 450RT, 436cc overhead-camshaft single, desmodromic valve gear, 86 x 75mm bore and stroke, alloy wheel rims, Pirelli MT73 tyres, fork gaiters, converted to street-legal enduro-type machine.
£2,600–3,000 / $3,800–4,400 ⊞ MW

1972 Harley-Davidson XR750, 748cc overhead-valve all-alloy V-twin, 85bhp, 5-speed gearbox, Ceriani front forks, alloy rims, fully restored, concours condition.
£8,000–10,000 / $11,500–14,500 ⋊ COYS
When the AMA's Grand National series began in 1954, Harley's works riders – or 'wrecking crew', as they were known – dominated the dirt track competition, winning 12 titles in the first 13 championship years. However, by the late 1960s, the threat from Great Britain had become tough, with several titles going to BSA and Triumph. The Milwaukee factory responded in 1970 with a new 750-class V-twin, the XR750. By 1971, the result was a whitewash, and in the period since, Harley has won over 20 championships.

1974 Penton Jackpiner 175, 175cc 2-stroke KTM single-cylinder engine, aluminium head and barrel, high-level exhaust, concours condition.
£2,000–3,000 / $3,000–4,400 ⊞ MW

▶ **1975 Bultaco Pursang,** 246cc piston-port 2-stroke single, 5-speed gearbox, twin rear shocks with swinging arm, alloy wheel rims, plastic mudguards and fuel tank, excellent original condition.
£500–600 / $720–870 ↗ Bon
The Pursang motocrosser was introduced into the UK during 1967, and it quickly gained a reputation for speed and reliability.

◀ **1976 Jawa Speedway 890,** 499cc single-cylinder engine.
£2,000–3,000
$3,000–4,400 ⨍ JCZ
The first Jawa speedway engine was a development of the earlier ESO design, Jawa having absorbed that company in the late 1960s. This particular machine was previously owned and restored by former World Speedway Champion Peter Collins.

1977 CZ 175 Trail, 175cc 2-stroke single, piston-port induction, pump lubrication, 4-speed gearbox, alloy wheel rims, modified with 12 volt electrics and Honda forks, front wheel and mudguard, very good condition.
£500-600 / $720–870 ↗ CGC
CZ introduced its 175 Trail in 1974, and although it was based on a commuter bike, it was capable of serious off-road use. This particular machine has been modified further to make it even more suitable for off-roading.

1980 Jawa Ice Racer, 498cc overhead-camshaft 4-valve engine, megaphone exhaust, telescopic front forks, rigid frame.
£1,200–1,500 / $1,750–2,150 ↗ Bon
This Ice Racer is said to have won the World Championships in the hands of the Russian star Anatoli Bondarengo. It produced 50bhp on alcohol fuel, and with the studded tyres was capable of fantastic angles of lean.

Military Bikes

1939 Moto Guzzi Alce, 498.4cc inlet-over-exhaust horizontal single, 88 x 82mm bore and stroke, 13.2bhp at 4,000rpm, 19in wheels, girder forks.
£1,800–2,000 / $2,600–3,000 ⊞ NLM
Developed from the earlier GT17, which had entered service during 1932, the GT20 arrived in 1938, but from 1939 it was known as the Alce (Elk). During the war years, 6,390 examples were handed over to the Italian military authorities.

1939 Gnome-Rhône AX, 804cc side-valve flat-twin, shaft final drive.
£2,800–3,000 / $4,000–4,400 ↗ Bon
One of the most famous aero engine manufacturers of WWI, the French Gnome-Rhône company began producing motorcycles in 1919, making Granville Bradshaw designed ABC's under licence. In 1923, the firm introduced single-cylinder engines of its own design. During the 1930s, a series of BMW-type flat-twins arrived and, like the German design, found favour with the military. Many AX models had shaft drive to the rear wheel and a four-speed-and-reverse gearbox. The AX was built from 1936 until 1940; some were supplied to the German forces after the fall of France.

◀ **c1939 BMW R12,** 745cc side-valve flat-twin, 78 x 78mm bore and stroke, 18bhp at 3,400rpm, shaft final drive.
£10,000–11,000 / $14,500–16,000 ⊞ AtMC
The single-carburettor R12 was produced exclusively for the German Wehrmacht between 1938 and 1942. This machine has aluminium footboards, whereas some bikes had conventional footrests. The mudguards of the military model were designed to shed mud, sand or snow much more efficiently than the deeply-valanced type found on the civilian R12.

1940 Indian Military Chief, 1200cc side-valve V-twin, hand-change gearbox, plunger rear suspension, leaf-spring front forks, footboards, original unrestored condition.
£9,000–10,000 / $13,000–14,500 ↗ IMC

Auction prices
Miller's only includes motorcycles declared sold. Our guide prices take into account the buyer's premium, VAT on the premium, and the extent of any published catalogue information relating to condition and provenance. Motorcycles sold at auction are identified by the ↗ icon; full details of the auction house can be found on page 167.

◄ **1940 BMW R35,** 342cc overhead-valve single, 72 x 84mm bore and stroke, 14bhp at 4,500rpm, coil ignition, shaft final drive, 60mph top speed.
£1,800–2,000 / $2,600–3,000 ⚒ Bon
BMW's first single-cylinder model (if one discounts the Flink of the early 1920s) was the 198cc R2 of 1930. This sold well, as did the 398cc R4, the latter being a favourite of the German Army. The R3 (300cc) and R35 appeared later in the 1930s, having telescopic front forks and shaft final drive. The R35 was more advanced than similar military bikes from other countries.

1943 Indian 741B, 500cc side-valve V-twin, girder forks, rigid frame, sprung saddle, footboards, saddlebags, restored to original specification.
£6,750–7,500 / $9,750–10,750 🚲 IMC
In Europe, 500cc was considered large enough for a military bike, so the 741 was ordered by the British government from Indian in late 1941. Some 5,000 examples were eventually sent across the Atlantic. After the end of the conflict, many were sold off to British enthusiasts.

Cross Reference
See Colour Review (page 125)

▶ **c1945 James ML,** 122cc Villiers 9D 2-stroke single-cylinder engine, flywheel-magneto ignition, 3bhp at 4,000rpm, 3-speed gearbox, blade girder forks, rigid frame, 19in wheels.
£900–1,100 / $1,300–1,600 ⚒ Bon

1950s Vespa Military Scooter, 149cc fan-cooled 2-stroke single, twistgrip operated gear-change.
£800–1,000 / $1,100–1,500 ⊞ MAY
This special version of the Vespa scooter was designed in the mid-1950s for the French Army. Its main purpose was as a bazooka carrier; thus it must rank as one of the most bizarre military vehicles of all time.

1956 Triumph TRW, 499cc side-valve parallel twin, siamesed exhaust, telescopic forks, rigid frame, alternator electrics, fully restored by David Livesey.
£2,500–2,900 / $3,600–4,000 ⊞ MW
The TRW was used mainly by the Royal Air Force, serving from the 1950s until well into the 1970s. It was not sold in civilian guise.

1972 Moto Guzzi Falcone N, 498.4cc overhead-valve unit-construction single, 20bhp at 4,800rpm, single exhaust header pipe and twin stacked silencers, rocking gear pedal, electric starter, full-width Grimeca brake hubs, single seat and pillion pad, 77mph top speed.
£1,900–2,150 / $2,750–3,000 ⊞ NLM

1971 Moto Guzzi Falcone N, 498.4cc overhead-valve unit-construction, horizontal single, 4-speed gearbox, electric starter, 18in wheels.
£2,000–2,200 / $3,000–3,300 ⊞ NLM
The Falcone N (Nuovo – new) was designed specifically for military and police work. The first prototype appeared at the Milan show in November 1969. Subsequently, it was also produced in civilian guise, albeit in small numbers compared to the military/ police machines.

Mopeds

1940 Rudge De Luxe, 98cc horizontal 2-stroke single, pedal starting, partial enclosure of engine unit.
£500–600 / $720–870 ⊞ AMCA
During WWII, this machine was used for WVS work. Subsequently, it was found in a sorry state, having been stored for over 47 years. It was restored in just eight weeks.

1958 Bianchi Amalfi, 47cc 2-stroke single, 39 x 40mm bore and stroke, 1.2bhp at 6,000rpm, 26in wheels, very original condition.
£400–750 / $580–1,100 ⊞ NLM

1957 Hercules Her-Cu-Motor, 49cc 2-stroke single.
£250–350 / $360–500 ⚲ Bon
The German Hercules concern was at the forefront of moped development during the 1950s, building high-quality products that offered years of reliable service. Leading-link front forks helped in the comfort stakes, while the crankshaft was mounted front-to-back, rather than in the more usual transverse arrangement.

1973 Motobecane Moby XI, 49cc 2-stroke single, automatic clutch.
£250–350 / $360–500 ⚲ CGC
During the 1970s, the French Motobecane company was the world's largest moped producer. No dusty French village would be complete without a game of *Pétanque* and the buzz of mopeds.

1974 Ariel 3, 49cc Dutch Anker 2-stroke single-cylinder engine.
£200–300 / $300–440 ⊞ BLM
The Ariel 3 was a sales disaster that helped seal the fate of the entire BSA group. Even after sales had bombed, the BSA computer continued to purchase thousands of engines for the machine!

Police Bikes

1952 Gilera Saturno, 498.76cc overhead-valve single, 84 x 90mm bore and stroke, 18bhp at 4,500rpm, wet-sump lubrication, Marelli magneto, Dell'Orto carburettor, 4-speed foot-change gearbox, duplex frame, girder forks, spring-box/friction rear suspension, 75mph top speed.
£5,500–6,000 / $8,000–8,700 ⊞ NLM

A known continuous history can add value to and enhance the enjoyment of a motorcycle.

◄ **1958 Velocette LE Mk III,** 192cc water-cooled side-valve flat-twin, shaft final drive, ex-Metropolitan Police, restored, retaining all original police equipment.
£1,000–1,200 / $1,500–1,750 ⊞ BLM

► **1960 Gilera B300 Police,** 305cc overhead-valve unit twin, parallel valves, 60 x 54mm bore and stroke, 15bhp at 6,800rpm, wet-sump lubrication, 4-speed foot-change gearbox, 77mph top speed, original, unrestored.
£1,200–1,600
$1,750–2,300 ⊞ MAY

1967 DMW Deemster, 247cc Villiers 4T 2-stroke engine, 50 x 63.5mm bore and stroke, siren, radio, blue warning lights.
£1,000–1,200 / $1,500–1,750 🚲 BTSC
Originally produced between 1961 and 1963 with a 2T engine, the Deemster was built with the new 4T unit from 1964 until production ceased in 1967. It combined the merits of both motorcycle and scooter.

► **1971 Moto Guzzi Falcone N,** 498.4cc, 6.8:1 compression ratio, electric starter, twin-leading-shoe front brake, swinging-arm twin-shock rear suspension, 18in wire wheels, complete with all police equipment.
£2,200–2,400
$3,200–3,500 ⊞ NLM
The Falcone Nuovo was produced between 1969 and 1976.

Racing Bikes

1926 Grindlay-Peerless, 344cc JAP overhead-valve twin-port single, complete, but in need of restoration.
£4,000–4,500 / $5,800–6,500 ⚒ Bon
One of the greatest of all Brooklands' motorcycle racers, Bill Lacey was a formidable competitor and engineering perfectionist, whose machines' impeccable presentation put his rivals to shame. The Lacey/Grindlay-Peerless combination scored countless race wins at Brooklands and set numerous world records, the most famous being the One-hour record, which he raised to over 100mph in August 1928. Lacey finished his Brooklands career with Norton, but it is for his exploits aboard the beautiful nickel plated Grindlays that he is best remembered. This example was raced by Lacey between 1926 and 1930. It continued to be raced until 1939, finishing in the hands of F. C. Stevens. Its last race is believed to have been in 1952.

1926 Sunbeam 500 Sprint Special, 493cc overhead-valve single, 80 x 8mm bore and stroke.
£11,500–13,000 / $17,000–19,000 ⚒ Bon
The 1920s started well for Sunbeam because early in the decade it began to win TT races, which settled any queries as to the machines' performance. As the decade progressed, Sunbeam achieved its greatest successes in racing and sales. By 1924, having campaigned in so-called sprint racing, which was popular and road legal at that time, Sunbeam introduced a handful of specially manufactured racers that became known as the Sprint Special. By 1926, modifications to these machines included a separate oil tank to provide more capacity in the fuel tank for longer sprints and a twin-port exhaust to enhance performance. The Sprint Special was popular in the UK for hill climbs and sprints, but it was soon to be discontinued when the use of public roads for these events was prohibited.

1927 Scott TT Model, 596cc liquid-cooled 2-stroke twin, 3-speed hand-change gearbox, siamesed exhaust, drum brakes, chain final drive, recently rebuilt.
£12,000–15,000 / $17,500–22,000 ⊞ SCOT

1928 Rudge Racer, 499cc, 4-valve single, 85 x 88mm bore and stroke, 8.5:1 compression ratio, 4-speed hand-change gearbox, 8in front/7½in (20.3cm/19.1cm) rear proportional coupled brakes,100mph top speed.
£15,000+ / $22,000+ ⊞ AMCA
Graham Walker won the 1928 Ulster Grand Prix on this Rudge. It was the first time a road race had been won at over 80mph.

1929 Grindlay-Peerless Hundred Model, 498cc overhead-valve single.
£12,000–13,000 / $17,500–19,000 ↗ Bon
When C. W. G. 'Bill' Lacey, mounted on a Grindlay-Peerless, became the first man to cover 100 miles in an hour on British soil in August 1928, the Coventry factory lost no time in producing a replica of his machine – the Brooklands 'Hundred model'. However, lacking the resources of larger rivals and perhaps over-estimating the demand for such a specialized piece of racing equipment, it sold only a handful, believed to be no more than five or six machines. Until recently, only one of these had been thought to survive. Thus, this example's emergence from long-term family ownership is of historic interest. The 'Hundred Model' replica, although different in detail, was essentially the same as Lacey's original, right down to its nickel-plated frame and cycle parts. However, as delivered to Lacey's Brooklands workshop, the replica was not capable of the 100mph lap guaranteed by the factory. The job of fettling the bikes and tweaking the JAP engine to Lacey's specification fell to his assistant, Wal Phillips, whereupon each was tested by Lacey at 100+mph and issued with a certificate.

◀ **1929 Kirby Scott Special,** 496cc liquid-cooled 2-stroke twin.
£4,000–4,500 / $5,800–6,500 ↗ Bon
David Kirby began his short-circuit racing activities in the 1950s with a 1929 Scott Flying Squirrel Tourer. At that stage, the bike was rather dated on the circuits, but Kirby's wizardry at development ensured that it stayed more or less on the pace. He engaged famous Scott racer Harry Longman to prepare a 500cc engine, and a Scott frame was fitted to the machine along with swinging-arm suspension. This machine was constantly updated during its racing life: BSA B31 front forks were fitted with Gold Star springing and front wheel, and several Velocette gearboxes were used.

1930 AJS Works Racer, 496cc.
£7,000–10,000 / $10,000–14,500 🚲 APM
This ex-factory team machine was ridden by Freddie Hicks in the 1931 Senior TT, during which he lost his life.

c1933 Ariel Supercharged Square Four Replica, 498cc overhead-camshaft Square Four engine.
£9,000–10,000 / $13,000–14,500 🏹 Bon
In 1933, Ben Bickell decided the 500cc overhead-cam Ariel Square Four was the machine to take the trophy for the first multi-cylinder 500cc motorcycle to cover 100 miles in an hour at Brooklands. When completed, his machine would lap Brooklands consistently at over 110mph. This motorcycle is an exact replica of the Ariel used.

1935 Excelsior Manxman, 246cc overhead-camshaft single, cylinder head with bronze skull and aluminium fins, Lucas TT magneto, rev-counter in top of fuel tank, straight-through exhaust pipe.
£6,500–7,500 / $9,500–11,000 🏹 Bon
Tyrell Smith, Syd Gleave and 'Ginger' Wood, among others, put the Excelsior name firmly on the racing map in the 1930s, riding the Manxman in its various forms to many successes. It was Gleave who rode the 250cc, four-valve, Hatch designed 'Mechanical Marvel' to victory in the Lightweight TT in 1933, and perhaps it was the machine's four-valve arrangement that inspired the early Manxman models. Later Manxmans reverted to the more reliable two-valve configuration in the highly-efficient overhead-camshaft engine.

1933 Excelsior Mechanical Marvel, 246cc overhead-camshaft twin-port single, 63 x 79mm bore and stroke, one of only 5 built.
£65,000–75,000 / $94,000–109,000 ⊞ BB
The frame of this machine was altered by Ronnie Mead for the 1946 Isle of Man TT.

1935 Velocette KTT Mk V, overhead-camshaft single, 71 x 81mm bore and stroke.
£7,500–8,500 / $11,000–12,500 🏹 Bon
The major change on the preceding Mk IV KTT had been the introduction of a four-speed gearbox with positive-stop foot-change and a new cylinder head incorporating hairpin valve springs and more-compact scavenge pump. Redesigning the latter enabled the spark plug to be relocated for improved combustion, and part way through production the Mk IV benefited from a change of cylinder head material from cast iron to bronze. In essence, the Mk IV frame remained the same open-diamond type as used by earlier models, with the addition of a strengthening lower sub-frame, but for the Mk V Veloce devised an entirely new frame to house a revised Mk IV engine. The new chassis featured a full lower cradle, vertical saddle tube and single front downtube. Mk V production lasted from October 1934 to October 1935, during which time slightly fewer than 70 machines were produced.

1936 Excelsior Manxman Four Valve Works Racer, 246cc.
£22,500–25,000 / $33,000–37,000 ⊞ EXM
Designed and made for the 1936 season, the first four-valver ran on 7 June 1936, H. G. Tyrell Smith riding one to second in the Lightweight 250 TT that year, then winning the 1936 German Grand Prix and Grand Prix of Europe. For 1938, the machines were cannibalized to make two-valvers and broken up. Pieces were all kept in the factory as obsolete racing bits and bought by Norman Webb in the early 1960s; over the years, all the bikes were recreated.

1937 Vincent-HRD TTR, 499cc overhead-valve single, 84 x 90mm bore and stroke.
£9,000–11,000 / $13,000–16,000 ⚲ Bon
Ted Prestwich had sold Philip Vincent the latest state-of-the-art JAP engine for the 1934 TT, and the disastrous outcome made Vincent determined to design his own engine. The result was a short-stroke (84 x 90mm) engine with high camshaft and hairpin valve springs. On the Island in 1935, the new engine earned its colours in the Senior TT, finishing seventh, ninth and twelfth. The TT Replicas could beat the magic ton, and Williams, Irving, Croft and West rode them to good effect. They were the basis for Vincent's future V-twins.

1938 Excelsior Manxman, 350cc overhead-camshaft single-port single, 75 x 79mm bore and stroke.
£6,000–7,000 / $8,700–10,200 ⚲ Bon
Although it had proved fast enough to win the 1933 Lightweight TT in Syd Gleave's hands, Excelsior's twin-cam, radial four-valve 'Mechanical Marvel' proved something of a disappointment thereafter, and at the end of the 1934 season, the firm opted for a simpler design – the Manxman. Like the Marvel, it had a Blackburne engine, although increasing friction with the engine supplier forced Excelsior to take over production itself early in 1936. A single-overhead-camshaft, two-valve design, the Manxman was built in 250, 350 and 500cc capacities. Road and race versions were offered, although the 500 was only ever marketed as a sports roadster. Although it never won a TT, the Manxman enjoyed considerable success in international racing and the Manx Grand Prix. Notable developments included the switch to a shorter-stroke 250 engine in 1937, and adoption on the 250 and 350 of an aluminium cylinder head with right-hand exhaust port.

1938/50 Norton Manx Special, 499cc 1950 double-overhead-camshaft Manx engine, Lucas racing magneto, ES2 gearbox with Manx internals and outer cover, Newby belt-drive conversion, conical brake hubs, 1938-type plunger frame, Roadholder forks, aluminium tanks.
£10,000+ / $14,500 ⊞ MW

1938 Norton Model 40M, 348cc overhead-camshaft single, 71 x 88mm bore and stroke, racing magneto, megaphone exhaust, conical front hub, girder front forks.
£7,500–8,500 / $11,000–12,500 ⚲ Bon
This machine was one of the first production 40Ms to receive plunger rear suspension, which had appeared on the works bikes a few months before.

◄ **1948 AJS 7R,** 348cc chain-driven overhead-camshaft single, racing magneto, Burman close-ratio 4-speed gearbox, AMC 'jampot' rear shocks.
£9,500–10,000 / $14,000–14,500 ⚒ Bon
AJS announced the single-cylinder 7R as 'The Race-bred Motorcycle' in 1948. It was powered by a 348cc, overhead-camshaft engine with bore and stroke of 74 x 81mm. The 7R was marketed as the Junior, but it became affectionately known as the 'Boys Racer'. It featured strongly in the 1949 racing season, dominating the finishers' lists in the Junior TT on the Isle of Man. As a production racer, the 7R had few equals, although some say that it lacked some of the flexibility of the Manx Norton; its reliability compensated for the extra speed of the Velocette KTT.

1948 Moto Morini 125 SS, 124cc.
£2,000–3,000 / $3,000–4,400 ⚒ Bon
During 1937, Alfonso Morini split with his partner at MM, Mario Mezzetti, to set up his own company. Initially, the firm concentrated on the production of three-wheeled commercial vehicles and subsequently aero engine components during WWII. With the end of hostilities, Morini was finally able to achieve his goal of producing his own motorcycles. His first was a 123cc two-stroke single, which displayed the influence of the pre-war DKW RT125; this machine was rapidly followed by a competition variant. The over-the-counter racer featured plunger rear suspension and blade girder forks. In its first year of competition, it defeated its main rival, the two-stroke MV, in the Italian championship, ensuring its popularity with privateers. The following seasons saw a three-way fight in the World Championship between the two-strokes from Morini and MV and the four-stroke Mondial.

◄ **1949 Velocette KTT Mk VIII,** 349cc overhead-camshaft single, 74 x 81mm bore and stroke, Amal 10TT carburettor, girder forks, Dowty oleo-leg rear shocks.
£14,000–16,000 $20,000–23,000 ⊞ MW
The final version of the famous KTT, the Mk VIII ran from 1939 through to 1950 (excluding the war years).

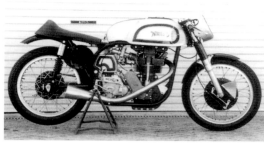

1952/55 Norton 30M Manx Special, 348cc double-overhead-camshaft single, BTH magneto, twin-leading-shoe front brake, Smiths 8,000rpm rev-counter.
£7,000–8,000 / $10,000–11,500 ⚖ **Bon**
The engine of this machine dates from 1952, although it has been fitted with a later cylinder barrel. The frame was built in 1955, the second year of the welded-on sub-frame.

1953 CZ 125, 124cc double-overhead-camshaft unit-construction single, wet-sump lubrication, 14.5bhp, telescopic front forks, swinging-arm rear suspension, alloy fuel tank, 95mph top speed.
£3,200–3,500 / $4,650–5,000 ⊞ **BB**

1953 MV Agusta 125 Competizione, 123.5cc overhead-camshaft single, 53 x 56mm bore and stroke, dry-sump lubrication, 14bhp at 10,000rpm, 4-speed close-ratio gearbox, full-width alloy brake hubs, swinging-arm rear suspension, telescopic front forks with central hydraulic damper, duplex frame.
£6,000–8,000 / $8,700–11,500 ⊞ **MW**

1953/54 Norton 40M Manx Special, 348cc double-overhead-camshaft single, Petty PGT gearbox, chain primary drive, alloy short-circuit fuel tank, unrestored.
£7,500–8,300 / $11,000–12,000 ⚖ **Bon**
This machine has a 1953 engine in a 1954 frame.

1953 NSU R22 Rennmax, 247cc double-overhead-camshaft twin-cylinder engine.
£55,000–60,000 / $80,000–87,000 ⚖ **Bon**
This machine was used by the NSU works team during the 1953 and 1954 seasons. In 1958, it was supplied to former works rider Reg Armstrong for Geoff Duke to ride in that year's North West 200, the Austrian Grand Prix and in the Isle of Man, using a new oil bearing spine frame designed by Ken Sprayson of the Reynolds Tube Company. The frame was built using Reynolds 531 tubing. Unfortunately, minor problems prevented Duke from achieving any notable successes on the machine. From 1960, Irish road-racer Dickie Carter campaigned the bike for Reg Armstrong, achieving a string of victories and notable finishes in Irish events, including wins at the Leinster 200 in 1960, 1962 and 1964, setting the fastest lap on each occasion. At the 1961 Leinster 200, Carter and the Rennmax finished second to Bob McIntyre's works Honda 250 four. It won the Skerries 100 and Mid-Antrim 150 in 1961, and the Killinchy 150 in 1962 and 1963; secured a second and a third place in the 1961 and 1962 North West 200, a third at the Carrowdore 100; and was the highest placed non-works entry in the 1961 Ulster GP, finishing eighth. It was later raced and owned by John Kidson.

◄ **1955 Ducati 98 Gran Sport,** 98cc overhead-camshaft unit-construction single, exposed valve gear with hairpin valve springs, Dell'Orto SS1 carburettor with remote float chamber, 4-speed close-ratio gearbox, external oil lines, rev-counter.
£10,000+ / $14,500+ ⊞ **MW**
Known as the Marianna, the 98GS was Fabio Taglioni's first design for Ducati after joining the company in 1954. It went on to form the basis for a whole family of bevel-driven overhead-camshaft singles, culminating with the 450 of 1969.

1950s AJS 7R, 349cc overhead-camshaft single, c1955 tank, Burman gearbox, frame, wheels and front forks, c1958 engine, c1961 rear shocks, GP2 carburettor, seat, front brake muff and flyscreen, unrestored.
£7,500–8,500 / $11,000–12,500 ⚡ Bon
This machine was imported during the 1980s from New Zealand, where it had belonged to World Champion Hugh Anderson; it was displayed for many years at the now defunct Midland Motor Museum.

1959 Norton 30M Manx, 499cc double-overhead-camshaft single, 86 x 85.62mm bore and stroke, AMC gearbox, twin-leading-shoe front brake, Isle of Man fuel tank, unrestored.
£11,000–12,000 / $16,000–17,500 ⚡ Bon

1960 AJS 7R, 349cc overhead-camshaft single, 75.5 x 78mm bore and stroke, 35.5bhp at 7,800rpm, AMC gearbox, alloy wheel rims, fork gaiters, flyscreen, 120mph top speed, largely original specification.
£9,000–11,000 / $13,000–16,000 ⚡ Bon

◀ **c1958 Norton 40M Manx Special,** 348cc double-overhead-camshaft single, Amal GP carburettor, laid-down Norton gearbox, twin-leading-shoe front brake, alloy wheel rims.
£6,500–7,300 / $9,500–10,500 ⚡ Bon
This machine dates from various years, the frame being c1958.

1960 AJS 7R, 349cc chain-driven overhead-camshaft single, Amal GP carburettor, 4-speed AMC gearbox, alloy rims, flyscreen.
£9,000–11,000 / $13,000–16,000 ⚡ BKS
From the very beginning, the name AJS was at the forefront in motorcycle competition, particularly at the Isle of Man TT. Both air-cooled and water-cooled machines were campaigned in pre-war years, and the immortal, supercharged four-cylinder Porcupine set the pace after the war. AJS introduced the 7R in February 1948, an over-the-counter racer aimed very much at the privateer, but developed so satisfactorily for the factory team. Almost all of Britain's road-race stars of the 1950s and 1960s rode a 7R at some stage of their careers.

1962 AJS 7R, 348cc overhead-camshaft single, largely standard apart from 18in rims (so modern tyres can be fitted), completely restored, concours condition.
£12,000+ / $17,500+ ⊞ MW

► **1962 Norton 30M Manx,** 499cc double-overhead-camshaft single, Featherbed frame, Roadholder forks, Works Performance rear shocks, alloy rims, double-sided front brake, short-circuit tank, one of last Manx models built.
£12,000–14,000 $17,500–20,500 ⊞ MW

1962 Itom Replica Racer, 49cc, concours condition.
£1,400–1,600 / $2,000–2,300 🚲 RFC
This machine was constructed specifically for Charlie Mates to ride in parades.

► **1962 Aermacchi Ala d'Oro,** 246.2cc overhead-valve unit-construction horizontal single, 66 x 72mm bore and stroke, 4-speed close-ratio gearbox, Oldani front and rear drum brakes, original specification.
£6,000–7,000 / $8,700–10,000 ⊞ MW
This is an early example of the famous Ala d'Oro racer with 'long-stroke' engine.

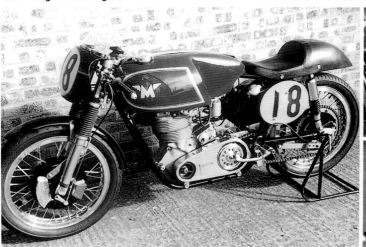

1962 Matchless G50, 496cc overhead-camshaft single, alloy head and barrel, modern magneto, belt primary drive, 18in wheels, ready to race, concours condition.
£14,000+ / $20,500+ ⊞ MW

1963 Itom Mk V, 49cc 2-stroke single, 8bhp, 4-speed foot-change gearbox, full-width alloy brake hubs, 87mph top speed.
£1,600–1,800 / $2,300–2,600 ⨴ **RFC**

1966 Ducati Mach 1/S Series 2, 248cc overhead-camshaft single, valve-spring head, Dell'Orto SS1 30A carburettor, 30bhp, large Veglia racing rev-counter, original lighting equipment, 106mph top speed, concours condition.
£8,000+ / $11,500+ ⊞ **MW**
The Series 2 model featured smaller (Oldani) brakes, and a different tank and seat than the original endurance-based machine that had been offered in 1965. Built for only a few months, these machines are now very rare.

1966 Heldun Hawk B, 49cc 2-stroke single, tuned induction and exhaust systems, 12 volt coil ignition, 5-speed close-ratio gearbox, duplex frame, teledraulic forks, swinging-arm rear suspension, alloy rims, full-width alloy brake hubs, racing tank and saddle, ball-ended controls and footrests, 80+mph top speed.
£700–800 / $1,000–1,150 ⨴ **RFC**

1967 Itom Racer, 49cc 2-stroke single, piston-port induction, alloy head, iron barrel, full-cradle duplex frame.
£1,400–1,600 / $2,000–2,300 ⨴ **RFC**

◄ **1967 Suzuki TR50,** 49cc 2-stroke single, piston-port induction, 6-speed close-ratio gearbox.
£2,000–2,500
$3,000–3,600
⊰⊱ RFC
The TR50 was a limited-production racer sold to privateers.

1968 Aermacchi Ala d'Oro, 344cc overhead-valve unit-construction horizontal single, Dell'Orto SS1 carburettor with remote float chamber, battery/coil ignition, wet-sump lubrication, 5-speed gearbox, dry clutch, 4-leading-shoe front brake, twin-leading-shoe rear brake, excellent condition.
£8,000–10,000 / $11,500–14,500 ⊞ MW

1969 Kreidler Van Veen Replica, 49cc water-cooled disc-valve single, 6-speed gearbox, front disc brake.
£2,300–2,500 / $3,350–3,600 ⊰⊱ RFC

1969 Linto Twin, 496.7cc overhead-valve horizontal twin, 72 x 67mm bore and stroke, 5-speed gearbox, Ceriani front forks, Girling rear shocks, hydraulic steering damper, Krober rev-counter.
£45,000–50,000 / $65,000–72,000 ⊰⊱ CME
Designed by Lino Tonti, the Linto was intended to be Italy's challenger in the 500cc over-the-counter production racer stakes. Based on Aermacchi components, it proved fast, but unreliable. It is now very rare. This example was raced in the Grands Prix by Australian Johnny Dodds.

1969 Ducati 450 Desmo, 436cc overhead-camshaft single, desmodromic valve gear, 86 x 75mm bore and stroke, twin-plug ignition with Lucas Rita 12 volt system feeding through twin-output Dyna coils, 5-speed gearbox, straight-cut primary gears, Scitsu electronic rev-counter, engine rebuilt with new valves, high-compression piston and V2 Australian racing camshaft.
£4,000–4,500 / $5,800–6,500 ✇ Bon

c1969 Ducati NCR 350 Desmo, 340cc overhead-camshaft single, desmodromic valve gear, 76 x 75mm bore and stroke, 4-leading-shoe front brake, Ceriani racing front forks, widecase frame, camshaft-driven rev-counter.
£3,000–3,800 / $4,400–5,500 ✇ COYS
This machine was built by the Bologna-based NCR concern.

1972 Seeley-Commando Mk IV, 749cc overhead-valve parallel twin, 77 x 80.4mm bore and stroke, high-level exhaust, front and rear disc brakes, aluminium tanks.
£5,000–7,000 / $7,250–10,250 ✇ Bon
Colin Seeley's lightweight rigid chassis proved an effective means of prolonging the competitiveness of British four-stroke singles in the late 1960s. The Mk III version (introduced in 1969) dispensed with the conventional lower duplex loop, a move that allowed privateers to fit the Norton Commando engine, for use in Formula 750 and open-class racing, as well as the more-usual Matchless G50. Several of these Commando-engined bikes were fitted with additional downtubes to support the weightier twin-cylinder engine. The Mk IV, introduced towards the end of 1970, altered the positions of the frame's main tubes: those attached to the top of the steering head ran to the seat tubes, while those attached to the bottom ran to the swinging-arm pivot, thus reversing the Mk III's arrangement.

c1969 MZ Re 250, liquid-cooled disc-valve 2-stroke twin, 54 x 54mm bore and stroke, 56bhp at 11,000rpm, high-level exhaust pipes, 6-speed gearbox, double-sided single-leading-shoe front brake.
£22,000–26,000 / $32,000–38,000 ⊞ AtMC

c1970 Staccato Gilera, 49.7cc 2-stroke single, piston-port induction, 38.4 x 43mm bore and stroke, 12bhp, 85mph top speed.
£1,500–1,800 / $2,200–2,600 ✆ RFC
This motorcycle was reworked by Pat Townsend.

1971 Moto Guzzi V7 Sport, 748cc 90-degree V-twin, 82.5 x 70m bore and stroke, 40mm Dell'Orto carburettors, open exhaust, 5-speed gearbox, shaft final drive, triple Brembo disc brakes, wire wheels, fairing, racing seat.
£4,000–5,000 / $5,800–7,250 ⊞ MW

1970 Velocette Special, 499cc overhead-valve single, Quaife 5-speed gearbox, belt primary drive, diaphragm clutch, Arter replica frame, developed over a period of 20 years.
£2,000–2,200 / $3,000–3,200 ⚹ BKS
Based on a Velocette Venom unit, this bike's engine features crankcases machined from castings to maximize bearing support, a nitrided steel crankshaft with parallel crankpin, and an ESO big end and connecting rod. Ignition is provided by a PAL generator, which, like the special camshaft, is supported by needle bearings. Extensive use of titanium fastenings and fittings helps to minimize the weight.

▶ **1972 Kreidler GP50,** 49cc liquid-cooled 2-stroke horizontal single, disc-valve induction, 18bhp, 6-speed gearbox, space-type frame, Krober electronic rev-counter, 110mph top speed.
£5,000+ / $7,250+ ⚙ RFC

1972 Minarelli WCSO, 49cc liquid-cooled 2-stroke single, Ron Ponti disc-valve conversion, 11-port Hans Hummell cylinder barrel, full duplex frame, Honda twin-leading-shoe front brake, alloy rims, alloy tank, Krober electronic rev-counter.
£1,800–2,000 / $2,600–3,000 ⚙ RFC

▶ **1972 Seeley Boyer Trident,** 740cc Triumph Trident overhead-valve triple, 67 x 70mm bore and stroke, Seeley chassis, dual-disc front brake.
£5,500–6,000
$8,000–8,700 ⚹ Bon
Developed by Boyer Racing in conjunction with Seeley Racing Developments, this machine was ridden by Peter Butler and David Nixon during the 1972 season, and in the 1973 TT by Graham Bailey.

1978 Kreidler Krauser, 49cc liquid-cooled near-horizontal 2-stroke single, disc-valve induction, Dell'Orto carburettor, 2-piston brake calipers and drilled discs, 6-spoke magnesium wheels, space frame.
£7,000+ / $10,200+ ✇ **RFC**

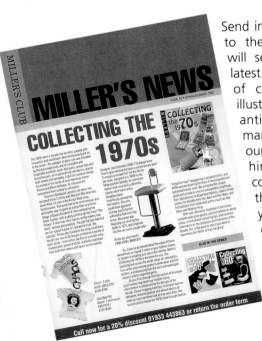

Restoration Bikes

1923 Indian Big Chief, 1200cc.
£1,800–2,000 / $2,600–3,000 🚲 **IMC**
This Big Chief was dug out of a garden in Cheshire and represents a challenging restoration project, having suffered much corrosion and being minus many parts.

c1920 Triumph Model H and Sandum Sidecar, 550cc side-valve single, Sturmey Archer 3-speed gearbox, chain/belt transmission, variety of spares including acetylene lights, Kismet pump and 2 leather-fronted tool boxes.
£3,500–4,000 / $5,000–5,800 🔨 **Bon**
The Model H arrived in 1914, and some 30,000 examples were supplied to Allied forces during WWI.

c1924 Ner-a-Car A2, 285cc, last used 1932.
£3,200–3,600 / $4,650–5,000 🔨 **Bon**
Invented by American Carl A. Neracher in 1919, the hub-centre steered Ner-a-Car was built under licence in the UK by Sheffield Simplex. The basic design remained unaltered – pressed-steel chassis, voluminous front mudguard, hub-centre steering, friction-drive transmission – but whereas US-built models were powered by a 221cc two-stroke engine, Sheffield Simplex fitted its own 285cc two-stroke single. Side-valve and (later) overhead-valve 350cc Blackburne-engined versions equipped with conventional three-speed gearboxes followed. Endowed with excellent handling and weather protection, the Ner-a-Car was a great success, production only ceasing in 1926 because of problems within other parts of the Sheffield Simplex group. This Ner-a-Car was owned by a woman who, having fallen off it once, never rode it again.

1935 AJS Model 22, 245cc overhead-valve twin-port single, 62.5 x 80mm bore and stroke, barn discovery, missing many parts including exhaust, seat and primary chaincase cover, in need of complete restoration.
£400–600 / $580–870 🔨 **Bon**

▶ **1949 Douglas Mk III,** 348cc overhead-valve flat-twin, 60.8 x 60mm bore and stroke, chain final drive, leading-link front forks, largely complete apart from exhaust system.
£800–1,300 / $1,200–2,000 🔨 **Bon**
The Mk III was only offered in 1948 and 1949, and was the revamp of the Douglas twin by Freddie Dixon, which saw the frame strengthened and the engine pepped up.

1958 Bianchi 125 2T, 124cc 2-stroke single, piston-port induction, largely complete, but badly rusted.
£250–350 / $360–500 ⊞ MAY

1960 MV Agusta 150 Turismo, 149cc overhead-valve unit-construction single, 59.5 x 54mm bore and stroke, 4-speed gearbox, 18in wheels, full-width alloy hubs, largely complete.
£500–600 / $720–870 ⊞ MAY
This is an easier restoration project than most, as it has not deteriorated too badly, with the exception of the exhaust system.

1963 BSA A50, 499cc overhead-valve unit twin, 65.5 x 74mm bore and stroke, 4-speed foot-change gearbox, virtually complete, side panels in need of fitting, good condition.
£550–650 / $800–950 ⚘ Bon
The unit-construction A50 was introduced in 1962 alongside the 654cc A65, replacing the pre-unit A7 and A10 models.

1920 Kenilworth Scooter, 125cc.
£2,500+ / $3,600+ ⚘ CGC
One of the earliest scooters, this example was discovered behind a wall in an old car dealership that was being demolished during 1998.

Scooters

My first sight of a motor-scooter during the 1950s saw me instantly smitten and yearning for the day when I could exchange my bicycle clips for freedom astride an Italian Stallion of the two-stroke and small-wheeled variety. The Italian scooter of the 1950s and 1960s was an accessory that no self-respecting 'face' could afford to be without; they were considered cool and fashionable.

Manufacturers such as Piaggio and Innocenti, with their respective Vespa and Lambretta machines, were responsible for the mobilization of a whole new European youth culture. The Mod of the 1960s, with his previously unheard of disposable income, was a far cry from the buying public at whom the scooters were targeted a decade earlier. The origin of the post-war scooter was borne out of a necessity for cheap, practical transport.

In 1919, UK motorcycle manufacturer ABC (All British Cycle) introduced the Skootamota to the roads of the British Isles. ABC was the first of many motorcycle companies in Great Britain to construct and market scooters alongside their larger-wheeled machines. Names such as BSA, Triumph, Sunbeam, Ariel, Velocette, Excelsior and Douglas all followed suit with varying degrees of success.

The list of European scooter makers was seemingly endless. Countries such as Germany, France, Austria and even Czechoslovakia had long production runs of well engineered bikes, including the famous names of Zündapp, NSU, Heinkel, Puch, Peugeot and Jawa.

In Asia, Japan still continues to turn out desirable machines sporting hosts of technological extras at little additional cost, and in the ever-growing marketplace, the Land of the Rising Sun is a serious player where the small-wheeled motorcycle industry is concerned. The way forward for the new generation of scooters points to automatic 'twist and go' transmission powered by four-stroke engines (a worldwide trend).

While not wishing to bury my head in the sand, I am, however, saddened by the demise of the traditional two-stroke multi-gear machine and console myself with the knowledge that what I once saw as a style statement on wheels is now very much an icon of the 20th century, designed and built during a chapter of history when life moved at a sedate pace and with attitude.

As I enter my fourth decade of 'hands-on' scootering, the urge is as intense as ever to celebrate my freedom through scooter riding and share the buzz with others – for scooters are a way of life.

Greg Kinge

1948 Swallow Gadabout, 122cc Villiers 9D 2-stroke single-cylinder engine, 3-speed gearbox, rigid duplex frame, unsprung front forks, 8in tyres.
£700–1,000 / $1,000–1,500 ⊞ BLM
Swallow was best known for its sidecars, but it also built the Gadabout scooter. However, the machine's performance did not compare to such foreign models as the Lambretta and Vespa. A Mk II version appeared in 1950 with a Villiers 10D engine and fan cooling; production ceased in 1951.

1949 Brockhouse Corgi, 98cc 2-stroke single, 50 x 50mm bore and stroke.
£1,200–1,500 / $1,750–2,150 ⚡ **CGC**
The Corgi was developed from the wartime Excelsior Welbike.

1955 Rumi Formichino, 124.68cc engine, monocoque chassis, 10in wheels, aluminium bodywork, leg shields, footboards.
£3,500–4,000 / $5,000–5,800 ⊞ **NLM**
Built from 1954 until 1960, the Formichino is the best known of all Rumi's two-wheeled creations.

1955 Iso Scooter, 124cc fan-cooled 2-stroke split single, 38 x 2 x 55mm bore and stroke, 7bhp at 5,200rpm, 3-speed gearbox, chain primary drive, needing restoration.
£360–400/ $500–580 🚲 **VMSC**
Iso was founded by Renzo Rivolta in Bresso during 1939, but all production plans were halted due to the outbreak of WWII. In 1948, Iso began building motorcycles and scooters. Later came the Isetta micro-car and, from 1962, luxury cars.

◀ **1955 Vespa VS1 GS150,** 148cc, completely restored to original specification, excellent condition.
£2,500–3,000
$3,600–4,400
⊞ **MAY**

1956 Progress Scooter, 200cc, automatic neutral finder, pivoting-fork front suspension, 16in wheels, full-width hubs, 12 volt electric starter, fully restored.
£1,800–2,000 / $2,600–3,000 ⊗ **VMSC**

1958 Vespa 150, 148cc fan-cooled 2-stroke single, period accessories including crash bars, front mudguard trims, spare wheel, mats and pillion pad.
£1,000–1,200 / $1,500–1,750 ⊞ **MAY**

1959 Zündapp Bella 150, fan-cooled 2-stroke single, 12 volt electrics, 3.50 x 12in tyres, dualseat, original, unrestored.
£270–300 / $400–440 ⊗ **VMSC**
From 1956, Zündapp used a swinging-arm front fork for its Bella scooter series, in place of the earlier telescopic fork.

1957 Dayton Albatross, 247cc Villiers 2T 2-stroke twin-cylinder engine, 50 x 63.5mm bore and stroke, 15bhp at 5,500rpm, Earles-type front forks, 72mph top speed.
£1,800–1,900 / $2,600–2,750 ⊗ **VMSC**

1959 Lambretta Li 150 Series 1, 148cc 2-stroke single, very original.
£2,000–2,250 / $3,000–3,300 ⊞ **PMo**

1960 Laverda Mini Scooter, 59cc fan-cooled overhead-valve 4-stroke engine, flywheel-magneto ignition, 9in wheels, unrestored, original specification.
£800–1,000 / $1,150–1,500 ⊗ **VMSC**
The Mini Scooter was built in two engine sizes: 49cc (39 x 40mm) and 59cc (39 x 47mm). It was also made under licence in Spain by Montesa.

◄ **1961 Velocette Viceroy,** 247cc 2-stroke twin, horizontal cylinders, 54 x 54mm bore and stroke, 12in wheels, 6in (15.2cm) brakes.
£1,200–1,600 / $1,750–2,300 ⊗ **VMSC**
The entire transmission of the Viceroy was formed into one unit, which acted as the rear suspension pivot. The clutch and four-speed gearbox came from the LE motorcycle, while the engine was suspended from a large single tube.

1963 Vespa 125, 124cc fan-cooled 2-stroke single, twistgrip gear-change, dualseat, standard specification, excellent condition.
£600–700 / $870–1,000 ⊞ MAY

1968 Winn City Electric Scooter, 12 volt electrics, unrestored.
£1,200–1,500 / $1,750–2,150 ♻ VMSC
This machine is powered by two 6 volt 57 amp batteries. It has two speeds worked by the twistgrip control – 6 volt slow start and 12 volt fast.

◀ **1969 Vespa Primavera 125,** 124cc fan-cooled 2-stroke single.
£450–550 / $650–800 ⊞ MAY
The Primavera came onto the market after the scooter boom had collapsed, so few were sold outside Italy.

Sidecars

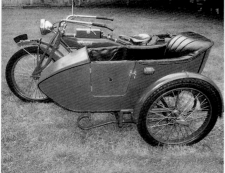

1919 Indian 1000 and Sidecar, 1000cc side-valve V-twin, hand-change gearbox, front and rear leaf-spring suspension, left-hand throttle, foot clutch, full lighting, sprung sidecar.
£14,000–16,000 / $20,000–23,000 ⊞ MW

1923 James V-twin and Sidecar, 800cc side-valve V-twin, hand-change gearbox, fully enclosed rear chain, aluminium chaincase, caliper brakes, kickstarter, concours condition.
£10,000+ / $14,500+ ⊞ MW
The single-seat sidecar was constructed by the James concern.

Auction prices

Miller's only includes motorcycles declared sold. Our guide prices take into account the buyer's premium, VAT on the premium, and the extent of any published catalogue information relating to condition and provenance. Motorcycles sold at auction are identified by the ✗ icon; full details of the auction house can be found on page 167.

◄ **1933 BSA W33-8 and BSA Sidecar,** 499cc overhead-valve single, 85 x 89mm bore and stroke, iron head and barrel, front mounted mag/dyno, sump cast into crankcase.
£3,200–3,500 / $4,650–5,000 ⮷ RRN

► **c1936 Brough Superior Petrol-Tube Sidecar,** good condition.
£2,800–3,000 / $4,000–4,400 ✗ Bon
In 1936, George Brough entered an SS80 and sidecar in the MCC's Edinburgh Trial. The sidecar was unique in that the main frame was constructed from a single 2¼in (57mm) diameter tube, shaped and butt welded to allow 2 gallons (9 litres) of petrol to be carried within it.

1938 Brough Superior SS80 and Brough Superior Petrol-Tube Sidecar, 981cc Matchless side-valve V-twin engine, 85.7 x 85mm bore and stroke.
£12,500–15,000 / $17,000–22,000 🔨 Bon

1942 Harley-Davidson ULH and Harley-Davidson Sidecar, 1206cc side-valve V-twin, export model intended for South Africa, subject of no-expense-spared restoration, over £8,000 / $11,600 spent on parts, original sidecar, concours winner.
£15,500–18,500 / $22,000–27,000 🔨 Bon
Announced in August 1929 as a replacement for the much-loved two-cam J-Type, the Model V was far from an instant success. More massively built and heavier than it's predecessor, the V lacked top-end power to such an extent that the first examples were recalled for extensive engine redesign. Revised with the frame, tank and wheels of the 61cu.in overhead-valve 'Knucklehead', plus dry-sump lubrication, the V became the Model U in 1937. Production restarted after WWII, the old side-valve 74 finally disappearing from the range at the end of 1948.

1942 Harley-Davidson ULH and Harley-Davidson Sidecar,
1206cc side-valve twin, 11,000 miles since restoration in 1998.
£10,000–11,000 / $14,500–16,000 🔨 Bon

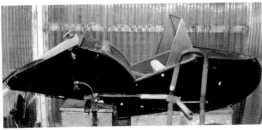

1946 Garrard S90 Mk II De Luxe Sidecar, partially restored, fitted new chassis 1980s, original duralumin body panels and interior.
£140–160 / $200–300 🔨 CGC
The Garrard sidecar is rare. It has a distinctive 'boat-prow' front, steeply raked windscreen and fluted rear deck containing a simple fold-up seat.

1954 Norton Model 18 and GP Sports Sidecar, 490cc overhead-valve single, 79 x 100mm bore and stroke, laid-down 4-speed gearbox, telescopic front forks, rigid frame, chrome fuel tank, single saddle and pillion pad, concours condition.
£4,000–5,000 / $5,800–7,250 ⊞ MW

1960 BSA C15T and Canterbury Trials Sidecar, 247cc overhead-valve unit-construction single, 67 x 70mm bore and stroke, 4-speed foot-change gearbox, in need of restoration.
£2,000–2,500 / $3,000–3,600 ⚲ Bon
This lightweight outfit was a popular combination in sidecar trials.

1960 AJS 18 and Watsonian Monza Sidecar, 497cc overhead-valve single, 82.5 x 93mm bore and stroke, coil ignition, 4-speed AMC gearbox, full-width alloy brake hubs.
£1,800–2,000 / $2,600–3,000 ⚲ Bon
The 500 version of AMC's heavyweight single, in either AJS or Matchless guise, was a popular choice for sidecar riders, who appreciated the broad spread of power delivered by the long-stroke engine.

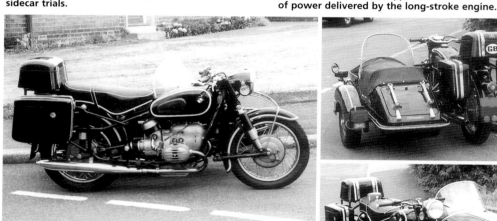

1961 BMW R60/2 and Watsonian Single-Seat Sidecar, 594cc overhead-valve flat-twin, 72 x 73mm bore and stroke, 4-speed gearbox, shaft final drive, dualseat, panniers and top box.
£4,500–5,000 / $6,500–7,250 ⊞ PM
The first of the Earles-fork BMWs appeared in early 1955, in the shape of the R50 500 and R69 600. The newcomers also sported swinging-arm rear suspension closely related to that pioneered on the factory's racing models campaigned by Walter Zeller.

◄ **1961 AJS Model 31 and Single-Seat Sidecar,** 646cc overhead-valve twin, 72 x 79.3mm bore and stroke, 4-speed AMC gearbox, telescopic front forks, swinging-arm rear suspension, full-width alloy hubs, period carrier and bar-end mirror, partly restored, new wheel rims, stainless-steel spokes, new wheel bearings, Boyer Brandsden 12 volt conversion.
£1,800–2,000 / $2,600–3,000 ⚲ Bon

Dealer prices

Miller's guide prices for dealer motorcycles take into account the value of any guarantees or warranties that may be included in the purchase. Dealers must also observe additional statutory consumer regulations, which do not apply to private sellers. This is factored into our dealer guide prices. Dealer motorcycles are identified by the ⊞ icon; full details of the dealer can be found on page 167.

1962 BMW R69S and Double-Adult Sidecar, 594cc overhead-valve flat-twin, shaft final drive, in need of some restoration.
£4,000+ / $5,800+ ⊞ MW
For sidecar use, BMW could supply alternative final-drive crown gears and revised suspension. The R69S was the top-of-the-line sports model in BMW's Earles-fork series, which ran from 1955 until 1969; the S version made its debut in 1961.

1964 Harley-Davidson Servi-car, 737cc side-valve V-twin.
£10,000–12,000 / $14,500–17,500 ⚲ **Bon**
The concept of Harley-Davidson's Servi-car dates back to the early 1930s, when the three-wheeled motorcycle was conceived to broaden sales. Many of those sales were already being made to police departments all over the United States. With a luggage compartment between the rear wheels, the big Harley trike could be used for traffic and parking duties. The Servi-car started out with a side-valve twin displacing 750cc and a three-speed-and-reverse gearbox. Usually, police Servi-cars were fitted with a left-hand throttle, supposedly to keep the officer's right hand free for his revolver. It was also used for many different civilian uses as it was easy to manoeuvre and inexpensive to operate. The Servi-car was the very first Harley-Davidson to feature an electric starter, and in 1951 it received hydraulic brakes and steel disc rear wheels.

1985 Yamaha FJ 1100 and Single-Seat Sidecar, 1100cc double-overhead-camshaft across-the-frame four, triple disc brakes, anti-dive front forks, monoshock rear suspension.
£3,000–3,200 / $4,400–4,650 ⊞ **MW**
This sidecar outfit is capable of achieving well over 100mph.

Cross Reference
See Colour Review (page 128)

Specials

Much as the captains of the established motorcycle marques might have wished to deny it, the fact is that many of the most interesting and innovative machines have been the products of small engineering workshops or single-minded privateers who have built their own specials in lock-up garages and garden sheds.

Even during the 1930s, there had been a considerable number of one-off or limited-run hand-built motorcycles, which had been constructed and ridden to gain a special place in the history books. Prime examples include George Brough's V-twin and the famous NLG (North London Garage) record breakers. Then, in the days immediately following WWII, came a large influx of specials, both for road and racing use.

Southampton enthusiast Fred Marsh built a 500 four in the 1950s, followed by a V8 in the 1960s. Then there was the Wooler four, Friedl Münch's NSU powered Mammoth and Fritz Egli's Vincent V-twin.

Even during the 1970s, many enthusiasts still built their own machines, despite the unprecedented range of exotic machinery that by then was flooding the market from mainstream. Two of the most interesting British-made creations were the Motodd-Laverda and the Quasar. The latter was truly unique – was it a motorcycle or a car? Well actually it was a combination of both. Its power came from a four-cylinder, 700cc, overhead-valve Reliant car engine; the one-off frame gave a feet-forward riding stance; and the rider was semi-enclosed.

The Motodd employed the Laverda three-cylinder engine in a special set of cycle parts, featuring a Saxon-built frame, unique front suspension (almost akin to the later BMW Telelever) and a monoshock rear end.

With the very latest breed of factory produced motorcycles at the beginning of the 21st century, much of the reason to build a special has gone – and with it, unfortunately, yet another niche motorcycling passion.

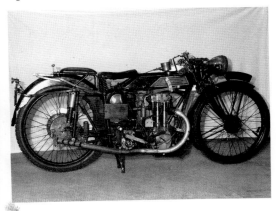

◀ **1915 New Imperial Special,** 246cc.
£2,500–3,000 / $3,600–4,400 ⚲ **Bon**
The creator of this machine, R. Rogerson, wrote a detailed report on his development of the bike in *The Motor Cycle* in February 1953, recording the fitting of a three-speed gearbox and clutch to his own design in 1922, and the successful testing of this design on trips from Newcastle to London in 1923 and 1924. Brampton forks were fitted in 1925 together with a larger fuel tank, and in 1926 the machine was converted to chain drive and a Webb drum brake front hub fitted. Electric lighting came in 1928, and in 1933 the original JAP 293cc side-valve engine was replaced with 246cc twin-port, overhead-valve New Imperial unit with dry-sump lubrication. In 1947, coil ignition was fitted, followed by pivoted-fork rear suspension. The machine remained in its creator's ownership for 57 years.

1929/32 Velocette KTT Special, 348cc overhead-camshaft single, 74 x 81mm bore and stroke, iron head and barrel, Brooklands 'can' exhaust, foot-change gearbox, unrestored, very good condition.
£8,000–10,000 / $11,500–14,500 ⊞ MW
This machine has a 1929 engine in a 1932 frame – early frames were prone to breakages. In all, 178 KTTs were built in 1929; 73 in 1932.

1950s Velocette KSS Mk II Special, 348cc overhead-camshaft single, 74 x 81mm bore and stroke, 4-speed foot-change gearbox, kickstarter, swinging-arm frame, telescopic forks, alloy rims, clip-ons, rear-set foot controls, Manx Norton flyscreen, racing tank and seat.
£6,000–7,000 / $8,700–10,000 ⊞ MW
The KSS MKII was built from 1936 until 1947.

c1954 Ariel-Excelsior Manxman Special, 399cc overhead-camshaft single, 4-speed foot-change gearbox, 1954 Ariel Huntmaster duplex frame, BSA front forks, Norton swinging arm, Norton Dominator brake hubs, alloy wheel rims, racing tank, racing-style dualseat.
£2,100–2,500 / $3,000–3,600 ⋏ Bon
This unusual special was built during the early 1970s. The c1938 Excelsior Manxman engine incorporates a BSA Gold Star cylinder head, while retaining the Excelsior's overhead-camshaft valve gear. The engine still has the 350 Manxman's standard stroke of 88mm, but the cylinder bore size has been increased to accept a 71mm Triumph Bonneville piston, giving a displacement of 399cc.

◀ c1957 Triton Roadster.
649cc Triumph Bonneville pre-unit engine, twin-carburettor head, Gold Star-pattern silencers, Triumph 4-speed gearbox, 1957 Norton wideline Featherbed frame, tank and seat, alloy rims, Grimeca 4-leading-shoe front brake, touring handlebars.
£4,500–5,000 $6,500–7,250 ⊞ BLM

◀ **c1957 Norton 88/650SS Special,** 647cc overhead-valve twin, Amal Concentric MkI carburettors, Lucas competition magneto, 4-speed AMC gearbox, twin-leading-shoe drum front brake, finished in silver and black, concours condition.
**£5,000–5,500
$7,250–8,000** ⚒ **Bon
This machine's Dominator frame dates from 1957, while the 650SS engine is from 1963.**

▶ **1960 Noriel Special,** 997cc 4-cylinder engine rebuilt at a cost of £2,600 / $3,770, Norton wideline Featherbed frame, all chrome and paintwork in very good condition.
£6,200–7,000 / $9,000–10,000 ⊞ **BB
The combination of a Norton frame and a four-pipe Ariel Square Four engine led to the name Noriel.**

1960 Triumph T100A Café Racer, 490cc overhead-valve unit twin, tuned engine, twin carb head conversion Amal 626 Concentric carburettors, high-level exhaust, alloy rims, alloy mudguards, racing seat and tank, fairing, rear-sets, clip-ons.
£1,900–2,100 / $2,750–3,000 ⊞ **MAY**

c1960 Norton Dominator Special, 647cc overhead-valve twin, 68 x 89mm bore and stroke, siamesed exhaust, alloy rims, fork gaiters, racing tank, central oil tank, dualseat, clip-ons, rear-sets, matching speedometer and rev-counter.
£2,700–3,000 / $4,000–4,400 ⊞ **MW**

c1960 Norton Dominator Special, 597cc overhead-valve twin, 68 x 82mm bore and stroke, swept-back pipes, Commando silencers, belt primary drive conversion, 12 volt electrical system with electronic ignition, hydraulic front disc brake, conical rear drum brake, well-type alloy rims, alloy tanks, Commando instruments.
£2,700–3,000 / $4,000–4,400 ⚒ **Bon**

1966 Dresda Special, 649cc Triumph T120 Bonneville pre-unit engine, belt primary drive, Norton Featherbed frame, Roadholder front forks, Oldani front brake.
£3,400–3,600 / $5,000–5,250 ⊞ MW
This machine was built by Dave Degens of Dresda Autos in South London. A similar machine was ridden to victory by Degens in the famous Barcelona 24-hour endurance event.

c1970 Norton-Matchless Mantis Special, 497cc Matchless G89CS overhead-valve single-cylinder alloy scrambles engine, 86 x 85.5mm bore and stroke, 12 volt car-type alternator, 4-speed AMC gearbox, Norton Featherbed frame and cycle parts.
£2,500–2,800 / $3,600–4,000 ➹ Bon

Components

A 1919 Sunbeam crankcase.
£80–90 / $115–130 🚲 RRN

A 1976 Laverda Jota 3C engine, 'as new' condition.
£1,350–1,500 / $2,000–2,200 🚲 ILO

A 1990 Enfield India Bullet 350 engine, good condition.
$250–300 / $360–440 ⊞ BLM

Memorabilia

An AA Motor Cycle Specialist sign, double-sided, 1930s, 26 x 36in (66 x 91.5mm).
£500–550 / $720–800 ⊞ MSMP

◀ A 1950 Sunbeam S7 cutaway engine, 489cc, display condition.
£500–600 / $720–870 🚲 SOC

A Ducati scooter dealer sign, 1960s, very rare.
£175–220 / $255–320 ⊞ MAY

◀ A Matchbox Series Triumph Tiger 110 and Sidecar, No. 4, with box, 1960.
£50–75 / $75–110 ⊞ MAY

Miller's is a price GUIDE not a price LIST

A model Lambretta SX200 with rider, 1960s, very rare.
£100–150 / $145–220 ⊞ MAY

► Moto Morini Corsarino Super Scrambler 50, colour brochure, 1972.
£12–18 / $15–20 ⊞ NLM

Moto Morini 500 Maestro, colour brochure, 1982.
£10–12 / $15–18 ⊞ NLM

Motorcycling Greats, a set of 10 cards celebrating the best of motorcycle racing over the past 40 years, including Hailwood, Agostini, Sheene, Roberts and Fogarty, 1997.
£3–4 / $4–8 ⊞ MUR

A Moto Guzzi dealer sign, double-sided, 1960s.
£175–225 / $255–325 ⊞ MAY

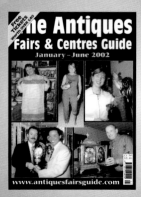

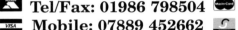

Key to Illustrations

Each illustration and descriptive caption is accompanied by a letter code.
By referring to the following list of Auctioneers (denoted by *), dealers (•), Clubs, Museums and Trusts (§), the source of any item may be immediately determined. Inclusion in this edition no way constitutes or implies a contract or binding offer on the part of any of our contributors to supply or sell the goods illustrated, or similar articles, at the prices stated. Advertisers in this year's directory are denoted by †.
If you require a valuation, it is advisable to check whether the dealer or specialist will carry out this service and if there is a charge. Please mention *Miller's* when making an enquiry. A valuation by telephone is not possible. Most dealers are willing to help you with your enquiry; however, they are very busy people and consideration of the above points would be welcomed.

AMCA§ AMCA Tel: 01543 466282

AOM § Ariel Owners Motor Cycle Club, Andy Hemingway, 80 Pasture Lane, Clayton, Bradford, Yorkshire BD14 6LN andy.hemingway@bradford.gov.uk

APM § Association of Pioneer Motorcyclists, Mrs J. MacBeath (Sec), "Heatherbank", May Close, Headley, Nr Bordon, Hampshire GU35 8LR

AtMC •† Atlantic Motorcycles, 20 Station Road, Twyford, Berkshire RG10 9NT Tel: 0118 9342266 www.classicbikesatlantic.co.uk

BB • www.britishbikes.co.uk, P O Box 1, Northwich, Cheshire CW8 2RD Tel: 01928 788500 bikes@motorcycle-classics.co.uk

BJ * Barrett-Jackson Auction Company, LLC, 3020 N Scottsdale Road, Scottsdale, Arizona, USA Tel: 480-421-6694 www.barrett-jackson.com

BLM •† Bill Little Motorcycles, Oak Farm, Braydon, Swindon, Wiltshire SN5 0AG Tel: 01666 860577 www.classicbikes.glo.cc

BKS/ Bon *† Bonhams, Montpelier Street, Knightsbridge, London SW7 1HH Tel: 020 7393 3900 www.bonhams.com

BTSC § British Two-Stroke Club, Mrs Lynda Tanner (Membership secretary), 259 Harlestone Road, Duston, Northamptonshire NN5 6DD

C * Christie, Manson & Woods Ltd, The Jack Barclay Showroom, 2–4 Ponton Road, Nine Elms, London SW8 6BA Tel: 0207 3892 217

CGC * Cheffins, 8 Hill Street, Saffron Walden, Essex CB10 1JD Tel: 01799 513131 www.cheffins.co.uk

CMAN§ Christian Motorcyclists Association, PO Box 113, Wokingham, Berkshire RG11 5UB cma-admin@bike.org.uk www.bike.org.uk/cma/

CME § Classic Motorcycle Enthusiasts Tel: 01507 490400

CotC •† Cotswold Classics, Ullenwood Court, Ullenwood, Nr Cheltenham, Gloucestershire GL53 9QS Tel: 01242 228622 tim@cotswold-classics.co.uk www.motorcyclesclassic.com

COYS * Coys of Kensington, 2–4 Queens Gate Mews, London SW7 5QJ Tel: 020 7584 7444 www.coys.co.uk

DSCM § Derbyshire and Staffordshire Classic Motorcycle Club, 51 Westwood Park, Newhall, Swadlincote, Derbyshire DE11 0R5 Tel: 01283 214542

EXM § Excelsior Manxman Tel: 01273 842433

GRA § Greeves Riders Association, Dave & Brenda McGregor, 4 Longshaw Close, North Wingfield, Chesterfield, Derbyshire S42 5QR

ILO § International Laverda Owners Club, c/o Alan Cudipp, 29 Claypath Road, Hetton-le-Hole, Houghton-le-Spring, Tyne & Wear DH5 0EL

IMC § Indian Motorcycle Owners Club, c/o John Chatterton (Membership secretary), 183 Buxton Road, Newtown, Disley, Stockport, Cheshire SK12 2RA Tel: 01663 747106

IMOC § Italian Motorcycle Owners Club (GB), John Riches, 12 Wappenham Road, Abthorpe, Towcester, Northamptonshire NN12 8QU Tel: 01327 857703 jdriches@tiscali.co.uk www.italianmotorcycles.co.uk

IVC • The Italian Vintage Company Tel: 01673 842825

JCZ § Jawa-CZ Owners Club, John Blackburn, 39 Bignor Road, Sheffield, Yorkshire S6 1JD

LDM § The London Douglas Motorcycle Club Ltd, Reg Holmes, 48 Standish Avenue, Stoke Lodge, Patchway, Bristol BS34 6AG www.douglasmotorcycles.co.uk

MAY •† Mayfair Motors, PO Box 66, Lymington, Hampshire SO41 0XE Tel: 01590 644476 mayfair@enterprise.net

MORI § Morini Riders Club, L. Skinner, 60 Watergate Lane, Leicester LE3 2XP

MSMP• Mike Smith Motoring Past, Chiltern House, Ashendon, Aylesbury, Buckinghamshire HP18 0HB Tel: 01296 651283

MUR • Murray Cards (International) Ltd, 51 Watford Way, Hendon Central, London NW4 3JH Tel: 020 8202 5688 murraycards@ukbusiness.com www.murraycards.com/

MW •† Mick Walker, 10 Barton Road, Wisbech, Cambridgeshire PE13 1LB Tel: 01945 461914

NLM •† North Leicester Motorcycles, Whitehill Road, Ellistown, Leicestershire LE67 1EL Tel: 01530 263381 stuart@motomorini.demon.co.uk www.motomorini.co.uk

NORM§ Norman Cycles Club, 8 St Francis Road, Cheriton, Folkestone, Kent CT19 4BJ www.NormanCycles.com

PBM § Ponthir British Motorcycle Club, 44 Emerald Street, Reath, Cardiff, Wales CF24 1QB

PM •† Pollard's Motorcycles, The Garage, Clarence Street, Dinnington, Sheffield, Yorkshire S25 2NA Tel: 01909 563310

PMo •† Planet Motorcycles, 44–45 Tamworth Road, Croydon, Surrey CRO 1XU
Tel: 020 8686 5650
www.planetmotorcycles.com
info@planetmotorcycles,com

PS * Palmer Snell, 65 Cheap Street, Sherbourne, Dorset DT9 3BA
Tel: 01935 812218

REOC § Royal Enfield Owners Club, Sylvia and Mick Seager, 30/32 Causeway, Burgh-Le-Marsh, Skegness, Lincolnshire PE24 5LT
Tel: 01754 810119
mickseager@mcmail.com

RFC § Racing 50 Enthusiasts Club, Chris Alty, 14a Kestrel Park, Ashhurst, Skelmersdale, Lancashire WN8 6TB

RM * RM Auctions, Inc., 9300 Wilshire Boulevard, Suite 550, Beverley Hills CA 90212, USA Tel: 310 246 9880
www.rmauctions.com

RM * RM Classic Cars, One Classic Car Drive, Ontario NOP 1AO, Canada
Tel: 00 519 352 4575
www.rmclassiccars.com

RRM • RR Motor Services Ltd, Bethersden, Ashford, Kent TN26 3DN
Tel: 01233 820219

RRN § Rolls Royce Vintage & Classic Motorcycle Club, Ken Birch, 111 Havenbaulk Lane, Littleover, Derby DE23 7AD

RSS § Raleigh Safety Seven and Early Reliant Owners Club incorporating Historic Raleigh Motorcycle Club, Mick Sleap, 17 Courtland Avenue, Chingford, London E4 6DU

SCOT § Scott Owners Club, Brian Marshall (Press Officer), Walnut Cottage, Abbey Lane, Aslockton, Nottingham NG13 9AE

SOC § Sunbeam Owners Club, Stewart Engineering, Church Terrace, Harbury, Leamington Spa, Warwickshire CV33 9HL

TCTR § Tiger Cub & Terrier Register, Mike Estall, 24 Main Road, Edingale, Tamworth, Staffordshire B79 9HY

TEN * Tennants, 34 Montpellier Parade, Harrogate, Yorkshire HG1 2TG
Tel: 01423 531661
enquiry@tennants-ltd.co.uk
www.tennants.co.uk

VER •† Verralls (Handcross) Ltd, Caffyns Row, High Street, Handcross, Haywards Heath RH17 6BJ, West Sussex
Tel: 01444 400678 www.verralls.com

VJMC § Vintage Japanese Motorcycle Club, PO Box 515, Dartford, Kent DA1 5WB
Tel: 0870 013 VJMC vjmc@vjmc.com
www.vjmc.com

VMCC §† Vintage Motor Cycle Club, Allen House, Wetmore Road, Burton-on-Trent, Staffordshire DE14 1TR
Tel: 01283 540557
hq@vmcc.net www.vmcc.net

VMSC § Vintage Motor Scooter Club, c/o Ian Harrop, 11 Ivanhoe Avenue, Lowton St Lukes, Nr Warrington, Cheshire WA3 2HX

Warr • F.H. Warr & Sons Ltd, 611 King's Road, London SW6 2EL Tel 0207 7362 934
Fax: 0207 7519 124
www.warrs.com

Index to Advertisers

Bibliography

Bacon, Roy; *British Motorcycles of the 1930s*, Osprey, 1986
Bacon, Roy; *Honda The Early Classic Motorcycles*, Osprey, 1985
Bacon, Roy; *BSA Twins & Triples*, Osprey, 1980
Rhodes, Ivan; *Velocette*, Osprey 1990
Walker, Mick; *BMW Twins The Complete Story*, Crowood, 1998
Walker, Mick; *Laverda Twins & Triples The Complete Story*, Crowood, 1999
Walker, Mick; *Moto Guzzi Twins The Complete Story*, Crowood, 1998
Walker, Mick; *MV Agusta Fours The Complete Story*, Crowood, 2000
Walker, Mick; *Gilera The Complete Story*, Crowood, 2000

Walker, Mick; *British Racing Motorcycles*, Redline, 1998
Walker, Mick; *Italian Racing Motorcycles*, Redline, 1999
Walker, Mick; *German Racing Motorcycles*, Redline, 1999
Walker, Mick; *European Racing Motorcycles*, Redline, 2000
Walker, Mick; *Hamlyn History of Motorcycling*, Hamlyn, 1997
Walker, Mick & others; *The Encyclopaedia of Motorcycles*, Silverdale 2001
Walker, Mick; *The Manx Norton*, Redline 2000
Walker, Mick; *The AJS 7R*, Redline 2001
Walker, Mick; *Japanese Grand Prix Racing Motorcycles*, Redline 2002
Webster, Mike; *Classic Scooters*, Parragon, 1997
Wherrett, Duncan; *Vincent*, Osprey 1994
Woollett, Mick; *Norton*, Osprey, 1992

Glossary

We have attempted to define some of the terms that you will come across in this book. If there are any other terms or technicalities you would like explained or you feel should be included in future editions, please let us know.

ACU – Auto Cycle Union, which controls a large part of British motorcycle sport.
Advanced ignition – Ignition timing set to cause firing before the piston reaches centre top, variation is now automatic.
Air-cooling – Most motorcycle engines rely on air-cooling, their cylinder barrels and heads being finned to dissipate heat.
Air intake – The carburettor port that admits air to mix with fuel from the float chamber.
AMCA – Amateur Motor Cycle Association, promoters of British off-road events.
APMC – The Association of Pioneer Motor Cyclists.
Auto Cycle Club – Formed in 1903, this was the original governing body of motorcycle sport. In 1907 it became the Auto Cycle Union.
Automatic inlet valve – Activated by the engine suction; forerunner of the mechanically-operated valve.
Balloon tyres – Wide-section, low-pressure tyres, fitted to tourers for comfort.
Beaded-edge tyres – Encased rubber beads in channels on wheel rim.
Belt drive – A leather or fabric belt running from the engine or gearbox to the rear wheel.
BHP – A measure of engine output; the amount of power required to lift 33,000lb to a height of 1ft in a minute equals 1bhp.
BMCRC – British Motor Cycle Racing Club, formed in 1909. Also known as Bemsee.
BMF – British Motorcycle Federation.
Bore/stroke ratio – The ratio of an engine's cylinder diameter to its piston stroke.
Caliper – A clamping device containing hydraulically-operated pistons that forms part of a disc brake.
Cam – Device for opening and closing a valve.
Camshaft – The mounting shaft for the cam; can be in low, high or overhead position.
Carburettor – Used to produce the air/fuel mixture required by the engine.
Chain drive – Primary form of drive from engine to gearbox and secondary gearbox to rear wheel.
Combustion chamber – Area where the fuel/air mixture is compressed and ignited, between the piston and cylinder head.
Compression ratio – The amount by which the fuel/air mixture is compressed by the piston in the combustion chamber.
Crankcase – The casing enclosing the crankshaft and its attachments.
Crankshaft – The shaft that converts the vertical motion of the piston into a rotary movement.
Cylinder – Contains the piston and is capped by the cylinder head. Upper portion forms the combustion chamber where the fuel/air mixture is compressed and burnt to provide power.
Cylinder head – Caps the top of the cylinder. In a four-stroke engine, it usually carries the valves and, in some cases, the camshaft(s).
Damper – Fitted to slow the movement in the suspension system, or as a crankshaft balance.
Displacement – The engine capacity or amount of volume displaced by the movement of the piston from bottom dead centre to top dead centre.
Distributor – A gear-driven contact that sends high-tension current to the spark plugs.
DOHC – Double overhead camshaft.
Dry sump – An engine lubrication system in which the oil is contained in a separate reservoir and pumped to and from the engine by a pair of pumps.
Earles forks – A front fork design incorporating long leading links connected by a rigid pivot behind the front wheel.

Featherbed – A Norton frame, designed by Rex and Crommie McCandless, of Belfast, used for racing machines from 1950; road machines from 1953.
FIM – Federation Internationale Motorcycliste, controls motorcycle sport worldwide.
Flat-twin – An engine featuring two horizontally-opposed cylinders.
Float – A plastic or brass box that floats upon the fuel in a float chamber and operates the needle valve controlling the fuel flow.
Flywheel – Attached to the crankshaft, this heavy wheel smooths intermittent firing impulses and helps slow running.
Friction drive – An early form of drive using discs in contact instead of chains and gears.
Gearbox – Cased trains of pinion wheels that can be moved to provide alternative ratios.
Gear ratios – Differential rates of speed between sets of pinions to provide faster or slower rotation of the rear wheel in relation to the engine speed.
GP – Grand Prix, an international race to a fixed formula.
High camshaft – Mounted high up in the engine to shorten the pushrods in an ohv arrangement.
IOE – Inlet over exhaust, a common arrangement with an overhead inlet valve and side exhaust valve.
Leaf spring – Metal blades clamped and bolted together, used in early suspension systems.
Magneto – A high-tension dynamo that produces current for the ignition spark; superseded by coil ignition.
Main bearings – Bearings in which the crankshaft runs.
Manifold – Collection of pipes supplying fuel/air mixture or removing exhaust gases.
MCC – The Motor Cycling Club, which runs sporting events; formed in 1902.
Moped – A light motorcycle of under 50cc with pedals attached.
OHC – See Overhead camshaft.
Overhead camshaft – An engine design in which the camshaft (or camshafts) is carried in the cylinder head.
OHV – See Overhead valve.
Overhead valve – A valve mounted in the cylinder head.
Pinking – A distinctive noise produced by an engine with over-advanced ignition or inferior fuel.
Piston – Moves up and down the cylinder, drawing in fuel/air mixture, compressing it, being driven down by combustion and forcing spent gases out.
Post-vintage – A motorcycle made after December 31, 1930, and before January 1, 1945.
Pressure plate – The plate against which the clutch springs react to load the friction plates.
Pushrods – Operating rods for overhead valves, working from cams below the cylinder.
Rotary valve – A valve driven from the camshaft for inlet or exhaust and usually of a disc or cylindrical shape; for either two- or four-stroke engines.
SACU – Scottish Auto Cycle Union, which controls motorcycle sport in Scotland.
SAE – Society of Automotive Engineers. Used in a system of classifying engine oils such as SAE30, l0W/50, etc.
Shock absorber – A damper, used to control vertical movement of suspension, or to cushion a drive train.
Silencer (muffler) – Device fitted to the exhaust system of an engine in which the pressure of the exhaust gases is reduced to lessen noise.
Swinging arm – Rear suspension by radius arms, which carry the wheel and are attached to the frame at their forward ends.
Torque – Twisting force in a shaft; can be measured to determine at what speed an engine develops most torque.

Directory of Museums

Bedfordshire

Shuttleworth Collection,
Old Warden Aerodrome, Nr Biggleswade, SG18 9EP Tel: 01767
627288
Europe's biggest collection of flying pre-1940 aircraft, also collection
of veteran and vintage vehicles including 15 motorcycles.

Stondon Museum,
Station Road, Lower Stondon, Henlow, SG16 6JN Tel: 01462 850339
Five museum halls with over 320 transport exhibits including Bentleys
and over 30 motorcycles.

Cheshire

Mouldsworth Motor Museum,
Smithy Lane, Mouldsworth, Chester, CH3 8AR Tel: 01928 731781
Collection of over 60 motorcars, motorcycles and early bicycles
housed in 1937 art deco building.

Cornwall

Automobilia Motor Museum,
The Old Mill, Terras Road, St Stephen, St Austell, PL26 7RX Tel:
01726 823092 www.3m.co.uk/automobilia
Over 50 vehicles and associated automobilia. Autojumble and
vintage and classic vehicles purchased and for sale. Open daily April,
May and October 10am-4pm, closed Sats early and late season, June
to September 10am-6pm.

Cumbria

Lakeland Motor Museum,
Holker Hall, Cark-in-Cartmel, Grange-over-Sands, LA11 7PL Tel:
015395 58328 www.visitcumbria.com/holkmus.htm
Over 150 cars, motorcycles, tractors, cycles and engines plus rare
motoring automobilia. Also the Campbell Legend Bluebird Exhibition
featuring videos, photographs and scale models of the cars and
boats used by Sir Malcolm Campbell and his son Donald Campbell.
Open daily 1st April to 31st October, 10.30am-4.45pm except
Sundays.

Western Lakes Motor Museum,
The Maltings, Brewery Lane, Cockermouth Tel: 01900 824448
Located in Jennings Castle Brewery beneath the walls of
Cockermouth Castle. Some 45 cars and 17 motorcycles from Vintage
to Formula 3.

Devon

Combe Martin Motorcycle Collection,
Cross Street, Combe Martin, Ilfracombe, EX34 0DH Tel: 01271
882346
Around 100 classic and British motorcycles plus garage memorabilia.
Souvenir shop.

Essex

Battlesbridge Motorcycle Museum,
Muggeridge Farm, Maltings Road, Battlesbridge, SS11 7RF Tel:
01268 769392
An interesting collection of classic motorcycles & scooters in a small
informal 'museum'.

Gloucestershire

Bristol Industrial Museum,
Princes Wharf, City Docks, Bristol, BS1 4RN Tel: 0117 925 1470
A small collection of Bristol-made Douglas machines, including the
only surviving V4 of 1908. There is also a 1972 Quasar.

Cotswold Motoring Museum & Toy Collection,
Sherbourne Street, Bourton-on-the-Water, Nr Cheltenham, GL54
2BY Tel: 01451 821 255
Largest collection of advertising signs in the world plus toys and
about a dozen motorcycles. This is the home of the Brough Superior
Company and of "Brum", the small open 1920's car that has a
television series.

Hampshire

Sammy Miller Museum,
Bashley Manor, Bashley Cross Roads, New Milton, BH25 6TF Tel:
01425 620777
Sammy Miller is a living legend in the world of motorcycle racing,
and what started out as a hobby 30 years ago has become a
collection of what is arguably the best selection of competition
motorcycles in the country. The museum was opened in 1983 by
John Surtees and is much more than a static collection. All bikes are

in working order and wherever possible are run in classic bike events
throughout the year. Many of the racing bikes are still fully
competitive. At present there are 200 bikes in the Museum, many of
them extremely rare. New exhibits are being sought all the time to
add to the collection, with much of the restoration work being
carried out on the premises by Sammy Miller himself. There are
interesting artefacts and items of memorabilia connected to the
motorcycling world on display, including many cups and trophies
won by Sammy over the years. A typical motorcycle workshop of
1925 has been reconstructed, showing a large display of the tools
used at that time.

National Motor Museum,
Brockenhurst, Beaulieu, SO42 7ZN Tel: 01590 612345
www.beaulieu.co.uk
Collection comprising 250 vehicles from some of the earliest
examples of motoring to legendary World Record Breakers like
Bluebird and Golden Arrow. Open every day except Christmas Day,
May to Sept 10am-6pm, Oct to April 10am-5pm.

Isle of Man

Murray's Motorcycle Museum,
Bungalow Corner, Mountain Road, Snaefell Tel: 01624 861719
Collection of 140 machines, including Hailwood's 250cc Mondial and
Honda 125cc and the amazing 500cc 4 cylinder roadster designed by
John Wooler.

Kent

Historic Vehicles Collection of C.M. Booth,
Falstaff Antiques, 63-67 High Street, Rolvenden, TN17 4LP Tel:
01580 241234
A private museum consisting mainly of Morgan three-wheelers but
also some motorbikes. A most interesting collection plus memorabilia
all to be found at the rear of the Antique shop.

Ramsgate Motor Museum,
West Cliff Hall, Ramsgate, CT11 9JX Tel: 01843 581948
Founded in 1982 and dedicated to the history of motoring, every
vehicle is set out in scenes depicting the past.

Leicestershire

Stanford Hall Motorcycle Museum,
Stanford Hall, Lutterworth, LE17 6DH Tel: 01788 860250
A collection of older machines and racers.

Lincolnshire

Geeson Bros. Motorcycle Museum and Workshop,
South Witham, Grantham Tel: 01572 767280/768195
Collection of 80 plus motorcycles restored since 1965 by the Geeson
brothers. Open days throughout the year.

Middlesex

London Motorcycle Museum,
Ravenor Farm, 29 Oldfield Lane South, Greenford, UB6 9LB Tel: 020
8579 1248/020 8575 6644 thelmm@hotmail.com www.motorcycle-
uk.com/lmm.htm
New collection of around 50 British motorcycles. Open weekends.

Whitewebbs Museum of Transport,
Whitewebbs Road, Enfield, EN2 9HW Tel: 020 8367 1898
Collection of commercial vehicles, cars and 20 to 30 motorcycles.
Ring for opening times.

Norfolk

Caister Castle Car Collection,
Caister-on-Sea, Nr Great Yarmouth Tel: 01572 787251
Private collection of cars and motorcycles dating back to 1893.
Open daily mid May to end September, closed Saturdays.

Norfolk Motorcycle Museum,
Station Yard, Norwich Road, North Walsham, NR28 0DS
Tel: 01692 406266
Over 100 motorcycles from 1920's to 1960's.

Northern Ireland

Ulster Folk & Transport Museum,
Cultra, Holywood, Co. Down, BT18 0EU
Tel: 028 90 428 428
www.nidex.com/uftm
Unique collection of wheeled vehicles, ranging from cycles and
motorcycles to trams, buses and cars. Open daily (not Christmas Day
or Boxing Day), opening times vary.

Scotland

Grampian Transport Museum,
Alford, Aberdeenshire, AB33 8AE Tel: 019755 62292
info@gtm.org.uk www.gtm.org.uk
Displays and working exhibits tracing the history of travel and
transport in the locality. Open 31st March to 31st October
10am-5pm

Moray Motor Museum,
Bridge Street, Elgin, IV30 2DE Tel: 01343 544933
Interesting collection of cars and motorcycles plus memorabilia and
diecast models.

Museum of Transport,
1 Bunhouse Road, Glasgow, G3 8DP Tel: 0141 357 2656/2720
Museum covering road, rail and sea. Replica 1938 city street and
reconstructed Glasgow Underground Station. Open daily 10am-5pm
Mon to Sat, 11am-5pm Sun

National Museum of Scotland,
The Granton Centre, 242 West Granton Road, Edinburgh, EH1 1JF
Tel: 0131 551 4106
Small display of engines and complete machines includes the world's
first 4 cylinder motorcycle, an 1895 Holden. Tours available,
book in advance.

Somerset

Haynes Sparkford Motor Museum,
Sparkford, Yeovil, BA22 7LH Tel: 01963 440804
www.haynesmotormuseum.co.uk
Haynes Publishing Company museum with collection of vintage,
veteran and classic cars and motorcycles. Some 250 cars and 50
motorcycles. Open daily Mar to Oct 9.30am-5.30pm, Nov to Feb
10am-4.30pm, closed Christmas and New Years Days.

Lambretta Scooter Museum,
77 Alfred Street, Weston-Super-Mare, BS23 1PP
Tel: 01934 822075

Surrey

A.R.E. Classic Bike Collection,
285 Worplesdon Road, Guildford, GU2 6XN Tel: 01483 232006
Around 50 mainly British bikes including memorabilia and the
workshop where restorations are carried out is open. Phone for
opening times.

Brooklands Museum,
Brooklands Road, Weybridge, KT13 0QN Tel: 01932 857381
www.brooklandsmuseum.com
Motorsport and Aviation museum including historic racing cars and
aircraft. About 20 motorcycles pre WWII. Open Tues to Sun & Bank
Holidays, Winter 10am-4pm Summer 10am-5pm.

East Sussex

Bentley Wild Fowl and Motor Museum,
Halland, Nr Lewes BN8 5AF Tel: 01825 840573 www.bentley.org.uk
Changing collection of veteran, Edwardian and vintage cars and
motorcycles. Open daily 18th March to 31st October 10.30am-5pm.

Foulkes-Halbard of Filching,
Filching Manor, Jevington Road, Wannock, Polegate, BN26 5QA
Tel: 01323 487838
About 100 cars dating from 1893 to 1993, also 30 motorcycles
including American pre 1940's bikes ex Steve McQueen.

Tyne & Wear

Newburn Hall Motor Museum,
35 Townfield Gardens, Newburn, NE15 8PY
Tel: 0191 264 2977
Private museum of about 50 cars and 10 motorcycles.

Wales

Llangollen Motor Museum,
Pentrefelin, Llangollen, LL20 8EE
Tel: 01978 860324
Cars, motorcycles, model vehicles, signs and tools and parts.

Madog Car & Motorcycle Museum,
Snowdon Street, Porthmadog, LL49 9DF Tel: 01758 713618
Cars, motorcycles plus memorabilia

Warwickshire

Museum of British Road Transport,
St. Agnes Lane, Hales Street, Coventry, CV1 1PN
Tel: 024 7683 2425
museum@mbrt.co.uk www.mbrt.co.uk
Over 230 cars and commercial vehicles, 250 cycles and 90
motorcycles. Open all year round except for Christmas Eve,
Christmas Day and Boxing Day, 10am-5pm.

West Midlands

National Motorcycle Museum,
Coventry Road, Bickenhill, Solihull, B92 0EJ Tel: 01675 443311
The largest museum of British motorcycles, 650 plus machines all
restored to original specification.

Wiltshire

Atwell-Wilson Motor Museum,
Downside, Stockley, Calne, SN11 0NF Tel: 01249 813119
www.atwell-wilson.org
Collection or cars, lorries, motorcycles, mopeds, pushbikes and a
large selection of vehicle manuals, archive material and motoring
memorabilia. Open Sunday to Thursday (except Christmas Day), also
open Good Friday. Summer opening hours 11am-5pm, Winter
11am-4pm.

Yorkshire

Bradford Industrial Museum,
Moorside Mills, Moorside Road, Bradford, BD2 3HP Tel: 01274
631756
General industrial museum including many engineering items, Jowett
cars, Panther and Scott motorcycles, a steam roller and Bradford's
last tram.

Craven's Collection of Classic Motorcycles,
Brockfield Villa, Stockton-on-the-Forest, York, YO3 9UE Tel: 01904
400493 dickcraven@supanet.com
A private collection of over 250 Vintage & Post-War Classic
Motorcycles. Also a vast collection of motoring memorabilia.
Suppliers to the TV series 'Heartbeat' and 'Emmerdale', etc.

Canada

Canadian Vintage Motorcycle Museum,
Canadian Military Heritage Museum, 347 Greenwich Street, building
#19, Brantford, Ontario museum@cvmg.ca
www.cvmg.ca/museum.htm
Collection of around 33 motorcycles along with items of
memorabilia with an emphasis on motorcycles with a Canadian
connection. Open April to Sept Tues-Sun 10.30am-4.30pm,
October to March Tues-Fri 1.00pm-4.30pm Sat and Sunday
10.30am-4.30pm.

Deeley Museum,
13500 Verdun Place, Richmond, BC Tel: (604) 273 5421
www.canadianbiker.com/deeley1.htm
Over 250 motorcycles. Open Monday to Friday 10am-4pm

U.S.A.

Otis Chandler Museum of Transportation,
1421 Emerson Ave, Oxnard, CA 93033
Tel: 805 486 5929
www.chandlerwheels.com
Over 100 motorcycles, automobiles including 1930s American cars.

Indian Motorcycle Museum,
Hall of Fame, 33 Hendee Street, PO Box 90003, Mason Sq. Station,
Springfield, MA 01139 Tel: (413) 737 2624
Fine collection of Indian motorcycles and other Indian roducts, also
toy motorcycles, photo gallery and memorabilia. Other American
made motorcycles on display. Open March to Nov Monday to
Sunday 10am-4pm, Dec to Feb Monday to Sunday 1-4pm, closed
Thanksgiving, Christmas and New Years.

Owls Head Transportation Museum,
PO Box 277, Owls Head, Maine 04854
Tel: 207 594 4418
info@ohtm.org www.ohtm.org
Antiques, classic and special interest auto, motorcycles, aircraft,
engines, bicycles and related vehicles. Open daily except for
Thanksgiving, Christmas and New Year's Day, April to October
10am-5pm, November to March 10am-4pm.

Rocky Mountain Motorcycle Museum,
308 E. Arvada, Colorado Springs, CO 80906
Tel: +1 (719) 633 6329
Over 50 motorcycles, memorabilia, Hall of Fame, photographs & art,
motorcycle restoration. Monday to Sat 10am-7pm

Solvang Motorcycle Museum,
320 Alisal Road, Solvang, CA 93463 Tel: 805 686 9522
info@motosolvang.com www.motosolvang.com
Collection of vintage and rare motorcycles as well as European race
bikes.

Sturgis Motorcycle Museum & Hall of Fame, Inc,
Sturgis, SD www.SturgisMotorcycleMuseum.org

Directory of Motorcycle Clubs

If you wish to be included in next year's directory, or if you have a change of address or telephone number, please inform us by 25th April 2003.

ABC Owners Club, D. A. Hales, The Hedgerows, Sutton St Nicholas, Hereford HR1 3BU Tel: 01432 880726

Aircooled RD Club, Membership secretary Susan Gregory, 6 Baldwin Road, Burnage, Greater Manchester M19 1LY

AJS/Matchless Owners Club of England, North American Section, PO Box 317, Yardley, Pennsylvania PA 19067, USA Tel: 215 295 4003

AMC Owners Club, c/o Terry Corley, 12 Chilworth Gardens, Sutton, Surrey SM1 3SP

American Historic Racing Motorcycle Association, Matt Benson, PO Box 882, Wassau WI 54402-0882, USA Tel: 814 778 2291 mattbenson@penn.com www.ahrma.org

Amicale du Tour du Dauphine, 82 Rue de la Chapelle, 38150 Roussillon, France

Antique Motorcycle Club of America, PO Box 3001, Sweetser IN 46987, USA www.amcausa.org

Ariel Owners Motor Cycle Club, Andy Hemingway, 80 Pasture Lane, Clayton, Bradford, Yorkshire BD14 6LN andy.hemingway@bradford.gov.uk

Association of Pioneer Motorcyclists, Secretary Mrs J. MacBeath, "Heatherbank", May Close, Headley, Nr Bordon, Hampshire GU35 8LR

Bantam Enthusiasts Club, c/o Vic Salmon, 16 Oakhurst Close, Walderslade, Chatham, Kent ME5 9AN

Benelli Motobi Club GB, Steve Peace, 43 Sherrington Road, Ipswich, Suffolk IP1 4HT Tel: 01473 461712

Best Feet Forward MCC, Membership secretary Paul Morris, 43 Finedon Road, Irthlingborough, Northamptonshire NN9 5TY

The BMW Club, Bowbury House, Kirk Langley, Derbyshire DE6 5NJ

BMW Motorcycle Owners Ltd (Vintage), Craig Vechorik, PO Box 6329, Miss State MS 39762, USA vech@ra.msstate.edu

Bristol & District Sidecar Club, 158 Fairlyn Drive, Kingswood, Bristol, Gloucestershire BS15 4PZ

British Motor Bike Owners Club, c/o Ray Peacock, Crown Inn, Shelfanger, Diss, Norfolk IP22 2DL

British Motorcycle Association, Pete Reed, AMCA, 28 Mill Park, Hawks Green Lane, Cannock, Staffordshire WS11 2XT

British Motorcycle Club of Guernsey, c/o Ron Le Cras, East View, Village De Putron, St Peter Port, Guernsey, Channel Islands

British Motorcycle Owners Club, c/o Phil Coventry, 59 Mackenzie Street, Bolton, Lancashire BL1 6QP

British Motorcycle Riders Club, Geoff Ives, PO Box 2, Eynsham, Witney, Oxfordshire OX8 1RW

British Motorcyclists Federation, Jack Wiley House, 129 Seaforth Avenue, Motspur Park, New Malden, Surrey KT3 6JU

British Two-Stroke Club, Membership secretary Mrs Lynda Tanner, 259 Harlestone Road, Duston, Northampton NN5 6DD

Brough Superior Club, Box 393, Cos Cob, Connecticut CT 06807, USA Tel: 203 661 0526

BSA Owners Club, Chris Taylor, PO Box 436, Peterborough, Cambridgeshire PE4 7WD christaylor@natsecbsaoc.screaming.net

CBX Riders Club (United Kingdom), Mel Watkins, 9 Trem Y Mynydd, Abergele, Clwyd LL22 9YY

Christian Motorcyclists Association, PO Box 113, Wokingham, Berkshire RG11 5UB cma-admin@bike.org.uk www.bike.org.uk/cma/

Classic Japanese Motorcycle Club (CJMC), Don Brown, 3139 Hawkcrest Circle, San Jose CA 95135-2224, USA Tel: 408 531 1157 doncjmc@aol.com www.netcom.com/~tickover/cjmc.html

Classic Kawasaki Club (Formerly The Kawasaki Triples Club), PO Box 235, Nottingham NG8 6DT

Classic Racing Motorcycle Club Ltd, 6 Cladgate Grove, Wombourne, Wolverhampton, West Midlands WV5 8JS

Classic Wing Club, 710 South Rush Street, South Bend IN 46601, USA Tel: 219 234 9777 classicwing@mvillage.com www.classicwingclub.org

Cossack Owners Club, Membership secretary Alan Mottram, 19 The Villas, West End, Stoke on Trent, Staffordshire ST4 5AQ

Cotton Owners Club, P. Turner, Coombehayes, Sidmouth Road, Lyme Regis, Dorset DT7 3EQ

Cushman Motor Scooter Club of America, PO Box 661, Union Springs, Alabama AL 36089, USA Tel: 205 738 3874

Derbyshire and Staffordshire Classic Motorcycle Club, 51 Westwood Park, Newhall, Swadlincote, Derbyshire DE11 0RS Tel: 01283 214542

Dot Motorcycle Club, c/o Chris Black, 115 Lincoln Avenue, Clayton, Newcastle-under-Lyne ST5 3AR

Ducati Owners Club, Membership secretary Tanya Chambers, Westview, 26 Outgate, Ealand, N. Lincolnshire DN17 4JD Tel: 01724 710175 tanya@docgb.org www.docgb.org

Excelsior Talisman Enthusiasts, Ginger Hall, Village Way, Little Chalfont, Buckinghamshire HP7 9PU Tel: 01494 762166 the.powells@virgin.net

Exeter British Motorcycle Club, c/o Bill Jones, 7 Parkens Cross Lane, Pinhoe, Exeter, Devon EX1 3TA

Exeter Classic Motorcycle Club, c/o Martin Hatcher, 11 Newcombe Street, Heavitree, Exeter, Devon EX1 2TG

Federation of Sidecars, Jeff Reynard, 5 Ethel Street, Beechcliffe, Keighley, Yorkshire BD20 6AN

Fellowship of Christian Motorcyclists, Phil Crow, 6 St Anne's Close, Formby, Liverpool, Merseyside L37 7AX

FJ Owners Club, Membership secretaries Lee & Mick Beck, 1 Glen Crescent, Stamford, Lincolnshire PE9 1SW

Forgotten Racing Club, Steve Boam, Hillside, Holt Road, Hackney, Nr Matlock, Derbyshire DE4 2QD

Francis Barnett Owners Club, Club secretary Sue Dorling, Clouds Hill, 5 Blacklands Road, Upper Bucklebury, Nr Reading, Berkshire RG7 6QP Tel: 01635 864256

Gold Star Owners Club, Maurice Evans, 211 Station Road, Mickleover, Derby DE3 5FE

Goldwing Owners Club, Gary Ingram, 60 Purley Avenue, Cricklewood, London NW2 1SB

Greeves Owners Club, c/o Dave McGregor, 4 Longshaw Close, North Wingfield, Chesterfield, Derbyshire S42 5QR

Greeves Riders Association, Dave & Brenda McGregor, 4 Longshaw Close, North Wingfield, Chesterfield, Derbyshire S42 5QR

Harley Davidson Riders Club of Great Britain, SAE to Membership Secretary, PO Box 62, Newton Abbott, Devon TQ12 2QE

Harley Davidson UK, The Bell Tower, High Street, Brackley, Northamptonshire NN13 7DT www.harley-davidson.co.uk www.harley-davidson.com

The Harley Hummer Club, Inc., 4517 Chase Avenue, Bethesda MD 20814, USA www.harleyhummerclub.org

Harley Owners Group, HOG UK, The Bell Tower, High Street, Brackley, Northamptonshire NN13 7DT

Harley Owners Group (HOG) www.hog.com

Hedingham Sidecar Owners Club, Membership secretary John Dean, Birchendale Farm, Fole Lane, Stoke-on-Trent, Staffordshire ST10 4HL

Hesketh Owners Club, Peter White, 1 Northfield Road, Soham, Cambridgeshire CB7 5UE

Historic Police Motorcycles Tel: 020 8393 4958

Honda Monkey Club, 28 Newdigate Road, off Red Lane, Coventry, Warwickshire CV6 5ES

Honda Owners Club (GB), Membership secretary, 61 Vicarage Road, Ware, Hertfordshire SG12 7BE

Indian Motorcycle Club of America, PO Box 1743, Perris CA 92572-1743, USA

Indian Motorcycle Owners Club, c/o Membership secretary John Chatterton, 183 Buxton Road, Newtown, Disley, Stockport, Cheshire SK12 2RA Tel: 01663 747106

International Laverda Owners Club, c/o Alan Cudipp, 29 Claypath Road, Hetton-le-Hole, Houghton-le-Spring, Tyne & Wear DH5 0EL

International Motorcyclists Tour Club, James Clegg, 238 Methane Road, Netherton, Huddersfield, Yorkshire HD4 7HL

Italian Motorcycle Owners Club (GB), John Riches, 12 Wappenham Road, Abthorpe, Towcester, Northamptonshire NN12 8QU Tel: 01327 857703 jdriches@tiscali.co.uk www.italianmotorcycles.co.uk

Jawa-CZ Owners Club, John Blackburn, 39 Bignor Road, Sheffield, Yorkshire S6 IJD

Jawa/CZ Register, 1548 Deerwood Drive East, Mobile AL 36618, USA Tel: 334 342 0726

Kawasaki GT Club, Club secretary D. Shucksmith, Flat K, Lichfield Court, Lichfield Road, Walsall, West Midlands WS4 2DX

Kawasaki Riders Club, Gemma, Court 1, Concord House, Kirmington, Humberside DN39 6YP

The Kettle Club, Shaun Chandler, 66 Provene Gardens, Waltham Chase, Southampton, Hampshire SO32 2LE

Kickstart Club Torbay, c/o Eddie Hine, 12 Vale Road, Kingskerswell, Newton Abbot, Devon TQ12 5AE

Laverda Owners Club, c/o Ray Sheepwash, 8 Maple Close, Swanley, Kent BR8 7YN

Leader and Arrow Club, Stan Davies, 11 Hollins Lane, Tilstock, Whitchurch SY13 3NT

Leominster Classic MCC, Ron Moore, The Yew Tree, Gorsty, Pembridge, Herefordshire HR6 9JF

LE Velo Club Ltd, Kevin Parsons, Chapel Mead, Blandford Hill, Winterborne Whitechurch, Blandford, Dorset DT11 0AB www.leveloclub.org.uk

The London Douglas Motorcycle Club Ltd, Reg Holmes, 48 Standish Avenue, Stoke Lodge, Patchway, Bristol BS34 6AG www.douglasmotorcycles.co.uk

London Sidecar Club, 107 Silverweed Road, Walderslade, Chatham, Kent ME5 0RF

Maico Owners Club, c/o Phil Hingston, "No Elms", Goosey, Faringdon, Oxfordshire SN7 8PA Tel: 01367 710408

Marston Sunbeam Register, Ray Jones, 37 Sandhurst Drive, Penn, Wolverhampton, West Midlands WV4 5RJ

Michigan Classic Muscle Bike Association, USA Tel: 616 963 2506 kens@vixa.voyager.net www.geocities.com/MotorCity/Downs/2263/main.html

Military Vehicle Trust, PO Box 6, Fleet, Hampshire GU52 6GE www.mvt.org.uk

Morini Owners Club, L. Skinner, 60 Watergate Lane, Leicester LE3 2XP

Morini Riders Club, L. Skinner, 60 Watergate Lane, Leicester LE3 2XP

Moto Guzzi Club GB, Membership Secretary Paulette Foyle, 43 Poplar Avenue, Bedworth, Nuneaton, Warwickshire CV12 9EW

MV Agusta Owners Club of GB, Chairman Mr Alan Elderton, 108 Thundersley Park Road, South Benfleet, Essex SS7 1ES

MZ Riders Club, 12 Whitehorn Avenue, Barleston ST12 9EF steve.mdx@talk21.com

National Association of Supertwins, Sue Beneke, 10A Queens Road, Evesham, Worcestershire

National Autocycle & Cyclemotor Club, Rob Harknett, 1 Parkfields, Roydon, Harlow, Essex CM19 5JA Tel: 01279 792329 harknett@loversleapdisco.fsnet.co.uk

National Sprint Association, Secretary Judith Sykes, 10 Compton Street, Clifton, York YO3 6LE

National Trailers Owners Club (NaTo), 47c Uplands Avenue, Rowley, Regis Warley, West Midlands B65 9PU

New Imperial Owners, 375 Ohio Avenue, West Springfield MA 01089, USA

New Imperial Owners Association, Mrs J. E. Jarvis, Lyndhurst House, Victoria Road, Hayling Island, Hampshire PO11 0LU

Norman Cycles Club, 8 St Francis Road, Cheriton, Folkestone, Kent CT19 4BJ www.NormanCycles.co.uk

North Devon British Motorcycle Owners Club, Hon secretary D. E. Davies, 47 Old Town, Bideford, Devon EX39 3BH

Norton Owners Club, Colin Coleman, 110 Skegby Road, Annesley Woodhouse, Nottinghamshire NG17 9FF ukmembers@noc.co.uk

Norton Owners Club, c/o Secretary Philip Hill, 11 Hammond Close, Thatcham, Newbury, Berkshire RG19 4FF Tel: 01635 864813 hillfamily1@compuserve.com www.noc.co.uk

Norton Rotary Enthusiasts Club, Alan Jones, 112 Fairfield Crescent, Newhall, Swadlingcote DE11 0TB

NSU Motorcycle Register, Val Albert, 9811 Maury Road, Fairfax VA 22032, USA Tel: 703 978 0838 NTYF35A@mailinb1.prodigy.com

Oregon Vintage Motorcyclists, PO Box 14645, Portland OR 97293-0645, USA best@efn.org www.efn.org/~best/

Panther Owners Club, Graham & Julie Dibbins, Oakdene, 22 Oak Street, Netherton, Dudley, West Midlands DY2 9LJ

Ponthir British Motorcycle Club, 44 Emerald Street, Reath, Cardiff, Wales CF24 1QB

Racing 50 Enthusiasts Club, Chris Alty, 14a Kestrel Park, Ashhurst, Skelmersdale, Lancashire WN8 6TB

Raleigh Safety Seven and Early Reliant Owners Club, incorporating Historic Raleigh Motorcycle Club, Mick Sleap, 17 Courtland Avenue, Chingford, London E4 6DU

Rolls Royce Vintage & Classic Motorcycle Club, Ken Birch, 111 Havenbaulk Lane, Littleover, Derby DE23 7AD

Rotary Owners' Club, c/o David Cameron, Dunbar, Ingatestone Road, Highwood, Chelmsford, Essex CM1 3QU rotaryoc@aol.com

Royal Automobile Club, PO Box 700, Bristol, Gloucestershire BS99 1RB

Royal Enfield Owners Club, Sylvia & Mick Seager, 30/32 Causeway, Burgh-Le-Marsh, Skegness, Lincolnshire PE24 5LT Tel:01754 810119 mickseager@mcmail.com

Rudge Enthusiasts Club Ltd, Bloomsbury, 13 Lade Fort Crescent, Lydd-on-Sea, Romney Marsh, Kent TN29 9YG www.rudge.ndirect.co.uk

Scott Owners Club, Press Officer Brian Marshall, Walnut Cottage, Abbey Lane, Aslockton, Nottingham NG13 9AE

Shrivenham Motorcycle Club, 12–14 Townsend Road, Shrivenham, Swindon, Wiltshire SN6 8AS

Sidecar Register, c/o John Proctor, 112 Briarlyn Road, Birchencliffe, Huddersfield, Yorkshire HD3 3NW

South Wales Sunbeam MCC, Kate Baxter, 17 Heol Gelynog, Beddau, Pontypridd, South Wales CF38 2SG

Spanish Motorcycle Owner's Group (SMOG), Lynn & Dorothy Mobley, 1320 Cathy Lane, Minden NV 89423, USA bultaco@nanosecond.com

Street Specials Motorcycle Club inc Rickman O/C & Harris O/C & Featherbed O/C, c/o Dominic Dawson, 12 St Mark's Close, Gosport, Hampshire PO12 2DB

Sunbeam MCC Ltd, (A club for all makes pre-1931) Ian McGill, 13 Victoria Road, Horley, Surrey RH6 9BN

Sunbeam Owners Club, Stewart Engineering, Church Terrace, Harbury, Nr Leamington Spa, Warwickshire CV33 9HL

Sunbeam Owners Fellowship, c/o Stewart Engineering, Church Terrace, Harbury, Nr Leamington Spa, Warwickshire CV33 9HL

Suzuki Owners Club, PO Box 7, Egremont, Cumbria CA22 2GE membership@suzuki-club.co.uk www.suzuki-club.co.uk

Tamworth & District Classic Motorcycle Club, Roger Steele Tel: 01827 281244 info@tanddcmcc.co.uk www.tanddcmcc.co.uk

Tiger Cub & Terrier Register, Mike Estall, 24 Main Road, Edingale, Tamworth, Staffordshire B79 9HY

Tour du Dauphine en Petrolettes, 38550 St Maurice, L'Exil, FRANCE

Trail Riders Fellowship, Tony Stuart, 'Cambrea', Trebetherick, Wadebridge, Cornwall PL27 6SG

Trident and Rocket 3 Owners Club, Club secretary John Atkins, 47 Underhill Road, Benfleet, Essex SS7 1EP

Triumph Motorcycle Club, 6 Hortham Lane, Almondsbury, Bristol, Gloucestershire BS12 4JH

Triumph Owners MCC, General secretary Mrs M. M. Mellish, 4 Douglas Avenue, Harold Wood, Romford, Essex RM3 0UT

Triumph Triples Club, H. J. Allen, 50 Sylmond Gardens, Rushden, Northamptonshire NN10 9EJ

Velocette Owners Club, Secretary Vic Blackman, 1 Mayfair, Tilehurst, Reading, Berkshire RG3 4RA

Veteran Grass Track Riders Association (VGTRA), Carl Croucher, 4 Whitmore Street, Maidstone, Kent ME16 9JU

Veteran Vespa Club, Ashley Lenton, 3 Vincent Road, Croydon, Surrey CR0 6ED

Vincent HRD Owners Club, c/o Information Officer John Wilding, Little Wildings, Fairhazel, Piltdown, Uckfield, East Sussex TN22 3XB Tel: 01825 763529

Vintage Bike Riders Group, PO Box 4287, Manuels, Newfoundland A1W 1H3, Canada Tel: 709 834 5837

Vintage Dirt Track Racers Association, 4729 S. 31W Avenue, Tulsa OK 74107, USA

Vintage Japanese Motorcycle Club, PO Box 515, Dartford, Kent DA1 5WB Tel: 0870 013 VJMC vjmc@vjmc.com www.vjmc.com

Vintage Japanese Motorcycle Club, 24 Cathy Street, Merrimack NH 03054-2840, USA Tel: 603 429 2436 ronburtn@inr.net

Vintage Motor Cycle Club, Allen House, Wetmore Road, Burton-on-Trent, Staffordshire DE14 1TR Tel: 01283 540557

Vintage Motor Scooter Club, c/o Ian Harrop, 11 Ivanhoe Avenue, Lowton St Lukes, Nr Warrington, Cheshire WA3 2HX

Vintage Motorcycle Enthusiasts, PO Box 4341, Seattle WA 98104, USA www.micapeak.com/VME/

Vintage Road Racing Association, VRRA Membership Secretary Mrs Manzi Warwick, 1870 Spruce Hill Road, Pickering, Ontario, Canada Tel: 905 839 7464 tharris@nornet.on.ca www.nornet.on.ca/~tharris/vrra/

Virago Owners Club, President John Bryning, River Green House, Great Sampford, Saffron Walden, Essex CB10 2RS

Vmax Club, H. Doyle, 87 Honiton Road, Wyken, Coventry, Warwickshire CV2 3EF

Washington Motorcycle Roadracing Association, PO Box 94323, Seattle, Washington WA 98124-5623, USA Tel: 206 972 4499

Yamaha Riders Club, Alan Cheney, 11 Lodden Road, Farnborough, Hampshire GU14 9NR

Zl Owners Club, c/o Jerry Humpage, 90 Delves Crescent, Walsall, West Midlands WS5 4LT

Zündapp Bella Club of North America, c/o Scott Kozak, 102–1966 Coquitlam Avenue, Port Coquitlam, British Columbia V38 7PB, Canada zundappbella@yahoo.com

Zundapp Bella Enthusiasts Club, Chairman Bill Dorling, 5 Blacklands Road, Upper Bucklebury, Reading, Berkshire RG7 6QP

Zündapp Bella Motor Scooter Register, 632 Crawford Street, Flint MI 48507, USA

Index

Italic Page numbers denote colour pages, **bold** numbers refer to information and pointer boxes

Whatever road you ride we have a read for you

No question, if you are serious about buying, selling or just riding vintage or classic motorcycles then you need a subscription to *Old Bike Mart*

Each issue has over 1000 classifieds and a services guide, which is quite literally the who's who of the classic world. Add the informed editorial and the best events list going and you begin to see why you can't live without it.

You could buy the odd copy at a show or specialist dealer, but to make sure you never miss a bargain you should subscribe today, you be amazed at the deal*.

Bored with the shallow? Ready for a classic read with some depth?
Then
The Classic MotorCycle
is the classic magazine for you.
More of its packed 132 pages are given over to editorial than other publication of its type.
Quality features, written by the most respected names in the hobby, are backed by the world's finest motorcycling archive.

Available from all good newsagents, but to eliminate the journey to the shops, save money*, and guarantee your copy before it goes on general sale why not subscribe.

Fancy a change of pace?
Then *Classic and Motorcycle Mechanics*
could be just what you are looking for.
Celebrating the excitement of the seventies and eighties, and delving into just what makes later classics tick this is the magazine to take you deeper. Later classics stripped bare, magnificently crafted Streetfighters, and those who made the seventies exciting are all in its packed pages.
It's available from all good newsagents, but your time will be better spent riding than searching the shops.
Get a copy mailed each month and save a quid or two*.

You wouldn't want to buy your next bike without us, now would you?
Used Motorcycle Guide
is packed to the rafters with all the info you need, to ensure you get the right deal when buying your next used bike. It's 'warts and all' buyers guide will help you avoid the dogs, and the, "by the readers for the readers," editorial eliminates the journo bull.
Available at all good newsagents, but why not avoid the shopping hassle, and save a few sovs in the bargain* by subscribing.

A magazine where legends truly live on. From racer tests of historic machinery, written by those who can actually find the limit, to tales of those who made the sport great
Classic Racer takes you so close you can actually smell the Castrol R. With the worlds finest archive, and an editorial team who live and breath the sport the only way you'll get closer will be to put on your leathers.
Available from all good newsagents, but you know you'd rather be down at the track, so why not subscribe and save*.

* Used Motorcycle Guide. By subscribing, which costs just £21 for a whole year, you save a whopping £5.40. Now just think what you can spend that on? Two and a half pints of best, a seat at the flicks or an Indian take away perhaps?

* The Classic MotorCycle. A one year subscription costs just £28 UK, £37 Europe or £48 rest of the world, saving a UK reader £9.40, but if you push the boat out and go for two years not only will you save £18.80 we'll give you a free binder worth £7.95 as well.
The free binder offer also applies to overseas readers who subscribe for 2 years, and one year subscriptions cost £37 Europe and £48 for the rest of the world.

* Classic and Motorcycle Mechanics. By subscribing for one year you can save £7.40 on the normal UK cover price, and a massive £14.80 if you go for the two year option, plus on this one we'll throw in a stainless steel multi tool worth £9.95. The multi tool deal also applies to overseas readers who subscribe for two years, and subscriptions cost, £37 Europe and £48 rest of the world for one year.

* Old Bike Mart. Why would you want to buy single copies? A one year UK costs just £9.95, saving a giant £7.45 over 12 single copies, sign up for two years and you will save £18.70, plus we will give you two extra months for free. A subscription to Europe cost just £15, and the rest of the worlds £19 for a year, and you are guaranteed to get your copy the same day as UK subscribers. Do it for two years, and we'll throw in two months free too.

* Classic Racer. Make sure you never miss a copy again, and save money too. Get yourself signed up for 12 issues (two years) at a cost of just £30, save yourself £7.20, and relieve the stress of chasing round newsagents trying to find a copy. One year subscriptions are available at £17.50 UK, £20 Europe and £25 rest of the world, with two and even four year money saving deals costing just £30 UK, £38 Europe, £45 rest of the world, and (four years) £59 UK, £75 Europe and £90 rest of the world.

 EUROS ACCEPTED – PLEASE CONTACT FOR DETAILS

For more information Tel: 01507 525771 Fax: 01507 525772
or Email: subscriptions@mortons.co.uk
or visit our website www.oldbikeshop.com
Mortons Motorcycle Media Ltd, PO Box 99, Horncastle, Lincs. LN9 6LZ